RECYCLING IN AMERICA

A Reference Handbook

RECYCLING IN AMERICA

A Reference Handbook

Debi Kimball

CONTEMPORARY WORLD ISSUES

ABC-CLIO

Santa Barbara, California
Denver, Colorado
Oxford, England

Library of Congress Cataloging-in-Publication Data

Kimball, Debi
    Recycling in America : a reference handbook / Debi Kimball.
      p. cm. — (Contemporary world issues)
    Includes bibliographical references and index.
    1. Recycling (Waste, etc.) —United States. 2. Recycling (Waste, etc.)—Law and legislation—United States. 3. Recycling (Waste, etc.)—Bibliography. I. Title II. Series.
    TD794.5.K55 1992   363.72'82'0973—dc20   92-29984

ISBN 0-87436-663-1 (alk. paper)

99 98 97 96 95 94 93   10 9 8 7 6 5 4 3 2   (hc)

ABC-CLIO, Inc.
130 Cremona Drive, P.O. Box 1911
Santa Barbara, California 93116-1911

Contents

Tables and Figures

Tables

Figures

Acknowledgments

NO BOOK, BE IT A REFERENCE WORK OR A NOVEL, is written by the author alone. For this reason, I would like to gratefully acknowledge the support and special efforts of several people and organizations. Without their assistance, the task of researching and writing this reference handbook would have been much more difficult.

My first thanks must go to my daughter, who has borne the brunt of my withdrawal into libraries, computers, and my office over the past year. She has been stalwart and mostly understanding. Thank you, Tracy.

Next, I must thank my friend and former boss, Michael Magee, who, in his clairvoyance in the field of solid waste, talked me into working for Waste Management of Denver. He always encouraged my writing and gave me the time to do it. He provided me with an opportunity, through my job, to make a bigger difference in trying to help our environment than I might have been able to make on my own. Thank you, Mike, and thank you, Waste Management of Denver.

A random luncheon discussion on possibilities in the recycling industry introduced me to Jeffrey W. Schwarz, a dedicated environmental lawyer. After that single conversation, he obtained permission from his firm of Bradley, Campbell, Carney, & Madsen to gather over a thousand pages of data on state recycling legislation through the WESTLAW database. Thank you, Jeff.

The National Solid Wastes Management Association was just another trade association to me until I began writing this book. Over months of working on the project, I had numerous telephone conversations with Allen Blakey and Brian Medley. As time passed, Allen was kind enough to grant me permission to reproduce the comprehensive graphs and tables in Chapter 5, and Brian was helpful above and beyond the call of duty when it came to locating certain publications. Thank you both for your time and efforts.

Lastly, a special thanks must go to my editor, Jeffery Serena, whose relaxed attitude kept me calm when I felt like skipping town. Thank you, Jeff.

Debi Kimball

1

Recycling: A State of Flux

THE FIELD OF RECYCLING IS ONE OF CONSTANT MOTION. Although recycling has occurred in nature for billions of years (there is, for example, approximately the same amount of water on Earth today as there was when the planet was created), we humans have only adopted recycling on a large scale in the last 25 years or so.

Recycling is, in its simplest sense, taking a used item and remaking it into a new, useful product instead of discarding it as waste. For most of human history, recycling was typically done only when people lacked the resources to manufacture a new product from virgin materials. By and large, recycling was a concept employed only by the needy.

Recycling for the environment, as opposed to recycling for sustenance or immediate necessity, is a relatively recent idea. An increased awareness of the limits of natural resources, in conjunction with the population explosion, has led to the conclusion that recycling is an idea whose time has come.

In the United States, the practice of recycling became socially accepted, instead of stigmatized, only recently, and in the past few years, it has become downright fashionable, as well as the "politically correct" thing to do.

An Overview of the Past:
Recycling for Necessity or Profit

The problem of managing solid waste dates back to the time when people began to settle in permanent communities. When the evolution from a transient life-style to a more sedentary one took place, wastes of all kinds began to accumulate.

Originally, the accumulation of garbage was treated as an aesthetic issue: Garbage looked repulsive, smelled bad, and attracted vermin. Many generations passed before people began to discover that a host of health problems were also associated with their wastes. In time, procedures for collecting and removing refuse from populated areas were established, but little thought was given to the ultimate disposal of solid wastes. It was often assumed that unlimited amounts of space were available in which to dispose of refuse and that wastes could be discarded without long-term ill effects.

Occasional efforts at recycling were made but usually only in the face of an immediate and pressing need. For example, much recycling was accomplished in the United States during World War II, but it was done out of necessity born from the scarcity of strategic materials. The nation collected and recycled scrap metals and paper for the war effort, not for the environment, and when the war ended, so did the collective effort to recycle.

In the heady economic climate of the postwar years, consumers wanted new cars, new appliances, and other products that made them feel a part of a new era. Indeed, everything had to be new, for new meant better, and industry was more than happy to oblige.

The 1950s and early 1960s saw the beginnings of the highly successful disposable industry, an industry that sold the idea that single-use, throw-away items were absolute necessities of a modern life-style. Disposables began with paper cups and napkins and ultimately evolved to include diapers, razors, cameras, and even contact lenses. "Use it once and throw it away" became the consumers' national motto, and ease and convenience became two of the most desirable qualities in consumer products.

The realization that the concept of "unlimited" might be unfounded with respect to the generation of wastes and the inherent abilities of nature began to dawn on U.S. citizens in the late 1960s. This sudden insight might be traced, in part, to the photographs of Earth from outer space provided by burgeoning space exploration programs. The pictures showed our planet sitting alone in space, an undeniably closed and finite system, and they afforded a new perspective on planetary limits for scientists and laymen alike.

During this period, we were also discovering that toxins in the land, air, and water were having deleterious effects on the environment. With the 1962 publication of Rachel Carson's *Silent Spring*, the idea that our species could so negatively impact life on Earth became a chilling reality. The environmental movement was born, the first Earth Day was organized, and recycling for environmental reasons was undertaken for the first time.

The Environmental Protection Agency (EPA) was created in 1970 as a governmental response to the public's environmental concerns, and its Office of Solid Waste was formed specifically to examine the problems caused by the generation and disposal of wastes. With the passage of the Resource Conservation and Recovery Act (RCRA) in 1976, Americans at last began to look at their waste disposal habits. Among other things, the act mandated that dumps be replaced with regulated and closely monitored landfill facilities, and it was expected that stringent restrictions on waste disposal would encourage recycling on a more widespread basis. State and local governments were given the primary responsibility for municipal solid waste management, but RCRA also granted the EPA regulatory and assistance powers to make the job easier. However, it still took the better part of another 20 years for recycling to become a mainstream movement instead of the fringe activity of committed environmentalists.

From the early 1970s to the mid-1980s, recycling by individuals and by the businesses that were salvaging used commodities and selling them for reprocessing was occurring on a limited but profitable basis. All parties involved were thriving economically, for there was a relatively small supply of recyclable commodities (such as newspaper, aluminum, and glass) and a steady demand for them. During this period, only select groups were participating in recycling, and most of them were doing so in hopes of making a profit. Helping the environment was a secondary consideration—a bonus point used to sell the idea.

However, a drastic change in the industry occurred in the late 1980s when it became increasingly apparent that cities on both coasts were facing significant problems with the disposal of their trash. Prices for getting rid of garbage were skyrocketing because of the limited amount of land available, and tipping fees at landfills were becoming prohibitive. These costs and the media's intense coverage of the

Mobro 4000, the infamous wandering "Garbage Barge," began to stir the nation's conscience.

When photographs of medical wastes and the corpses of marine mammals washing up on beaches began to appear in national magazines and on television, a sense of urgency was at long last created with regard to waste disposal. The idea that "there is no such place as away" finally became a reality to most Americans.

Sudden Changes in the Industry

The twentieth anniversary of Earth Day, in 1990, finally seemed to bring home the idea that in addition to finite resources and the toxic threats of pollution, there was also a limit on the space available to deposit wastes. People also became aware that problems such as deforestation, topsoil erosion, groundwater pollution, and global warming were all associated with their wastes. Soon *landfill, nontoxic,* and *biodegradable* became household words, and the concept of a "green life-style," referring to an environmentally responsible way of living, became socially and financially marketable. After using these words casually for a few months, however, Americans found out that they had a great deal more to learn about these terms.

Biodegradability has since become a controversial topic. At one time, it was generally believed that if a product was biodegradable, it could be disposed of without consumer guilt, for, in short order, nature would reclaim it; thus, one could throw away copious amounts of trash with impunity. With this in mind, advertisers made *biodegradable* a key word in many successful marketing campaigns during this period. The concept of biodegradability seemed to be valid—until it was applied to plastic bags. Ultimately, researchers found that bags labeled "biodegradable" actually degraded only to a certain point, leaving bits of plastic behind. Furthermore, because they only degraded in the presence of light, they would not decompose when buried in landfills.

Suddenly, the whole notion of biodegradability was in the spotlight, and research into what it really meant and how it applied to our solid waste situation was begun. When Dr. William Rathje, from the University of Arizona, started publicizing the results of his studies of deep core samples taken from landfills, one thing became clear: The fact that an item was technically biodegradable did not necessarily mean that it would, in fact, biodegrade in a landfill.

The sanitary landfills of today are not the dumps of the past. Because the waste materials are compacted and covered with soil repeatedly, air, light, and water do not circulate freely among them. Without such circulation, the biological breakdown process involved in biodegradation cannot take place in a normal fashion. Consequently, the decomposition that occurs in landfills is generally limited to the process of drying out, or desiccating.

In his studies, Rathje found easily recognizable chicken drumsticks and hot dogs that had been buried 10 years previously—certainly enough time to biodegrade. (He was able to date his finds by checking the newspapers and phone books that had been thrown away at the same time.) Soon, environmentalists began pointing out that even biodegradable materials would remain virtually unchanged in landfills for a very long period of time. And as the true meaning of the word *biodegradable* was exposed, it became apparent that biodegradation was not the answer to the solid waste problems of modern society.

Whether a grocery sack was plastic or paper really didn't matter, for both products used resources and neither would biodegrade in a landfill. (Today's environmental answer to this dilemma is to take reusable cloth bags to the supermarket and refuse both of the disposable varieties.)

A suddenly enlightened public began demanding accessibility to recycling programs on a widespread basis, believing that if biodegradability was not the answer, then recycling must be. This demand, coupled with the glut produced by the ensuing flood of materials into the commodities' markets, changed the face of the recycling industry almost overnight.

Prior to the late 1980s, recycling in the United States had been accomplished mainly through individual and grass-roots efforts. Small businesses had sprung up to successfully handle the limited supplies and demands of the recycling industry. Newspaper and aluminum can drives by churches and scout troops were common, and buy-back centers provided individuals and groups with places to take their recyclables and redeem them for cash. Drop-off centers where items could be left for recycling without payment also gained in popularity and were often located for the convenience of the community. But when the general population began to recycle its newspapers, aluminum cans, and glass en masse, the supply of these recyclables increased dramatically, leading to a significant drop in market prices for those products. Thus, the more people recycled, the less money they received for their efforts.

But even as the economic feasibility of recycling declined, the issue of solid waste continued to rear its ugly head. When Americans were repeatedly forced by the EPA, state and local governments, grass-roots environmental activists, and the media to examine the reality of the enormous amount of waste they were producing, recycling was still regarded as one of the primary solutions.

With the ever-increasing volume of solid waste, it was apparent that more landfills were needed. But where would they be placed? After all, no one wanted a landfill in his or her own neighborhood. Average Americans knew very little about landfills, but what they did know was bad. Landfills had a reputation for being ugly and smelly and for causing pollution, which was all people felt they needed to know. As a result, the NIMBY (not in my back yard) syndrome was born.

As the EPA published reports on the current state of solid waste in American communities, it became increasingly apparent that proper solid waste management—or the lack thereof—would become the key to whether or not the human race would smother under its own garbage. With every American producing an average of 3.5 pounds of garbage each day,[1] these wastes had to go somewhere, and there was a limit to what could be recycled. Therefore, landfills were still considered a necessary part of the overall solution.

Integrated Solid Waste Management: A Hierarchy

Although the EPA first published its model of integrated waste management in 1989, most people involved in the waste industry did not become familiar with it until 1990. The hierarchy of waste treatments, described in the EPA's *The Solid Waste Dilemma: An Agenda for Action*, encouraged the country to integrate several approaches to solid waste management.

Source reduction, the first approach for any solid waste management program, would ensure that wastes would be reduced at their sources. For example, the use of cloth napkins instead of paper ones would eliminate the need for either disposal or recycling, and a significant quantity of trash would no longer be sent to the landfill.

Recycling was considered the second step in the hierarchy, designed to remove and recover reusable resources from the waste stream. This step also included the natural recycling process of composting organic wastes such as food and yard trash.

Properly promoted, recycling and source reduction were expected to remove a large percentage of the materials that were being landfilled in the forms of yard waste (17.9 percent), food waste (7.9 percent), paper (41 percent), and other recyclables (approx. 20 percent). (See Figure 1.1)

Waste combustion, or incineration, with energy recovery was the next step. Waste-to-energy facilities could take refuse, burn it at extremely high temperatures to eliminate toxic emissions, and use the heat thus produced to generate steam to run turbines, helping to meet a city's electric needs. The relatively small amount of ash left over from the burning process could then be safely landfilled.

Some environmental groups view incineration with a jaundiced eye, for unless extremely high combustion temperatures are maintained, toxins are released into the air. The EPA, however, stands by its model and its permitting regulations. (A Japanese firm has come up with a creative solution to this problem: A large, neon temperature gauge is placed at the top of a stack, enabling the public to read the temperature from miles away and report any potential problems.)

Although landfilling is the last step in the integrated waste management plan, it *is*, nonetheless, a part of it. The EPA's view is that because landfills will always be necessary for some waste, it is important to make the process of landfilling as safe as possible.

Subtitle D

Following the introduction of the integrated waste management hierarchy, new and stricter guidelines for the siting, maintenance, monitoring, and closure of sanitary landfills were published by the EPA in the *Federal Register* in 1991; they are known as Subtitle D of the Resource Conservation and Recovery Act of 1976.

Figure 1-1
Materials Discarded into the Municipal Waste Stream in 1986
(percent of total)

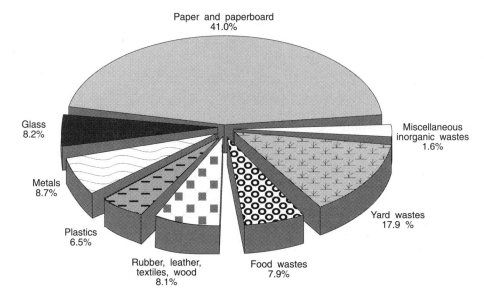

Source: Adapted from USEPA, *Decision-Maker's Guide to Solid Waste Management,* Washington, DC: USEPA 1989.

The intent of Subtitle D is not only to protect the environment and ensure the public's health by closing unsafe landfills but also to encourage the public to utilize methods other than landfilling for the disposal of solid wastes. The EPA estimates that Subtitle D will result in the closing of up to 50 percent of the nation's landfills between 1992 and 1997; it will also boost the costs for existing and new landfills built in compliance with the regulation. Higher disposal costs at the landfill are, in turn, expected to increase the success of the other three components of the integrated approach.

The Present: A Continuing State of Evolution

As public education programs are initiated to teach the importance of recycling from an environmental standpoint, people are beginning to become less concerned with the money they can earn from their trash. Consequently, environmental educators are now focusing on the idea of recycling for a cleaner, greener Earth, with more trees, cleaner water, and fresher air. The emphasis has changed from monetary incentives to environmental ones.

Today, the recycling of products traditionally deemed recyclable has climbed to record levels. And beyond that, as the concept of recycling for the environment has gained in popularity, people have begun to demand that additional products, such as plastic containers, steel cans, and office paper, be made recyclable.

However, the combination of the steady decline of market prices and the increase in services required in this new era of environmental consciousness has resulted in the demise of many recycling businesses that lacked the capital to survive such major economic changes in the industry. Increased competition from trash haulers, who are uniquely suited to run large, commercial recycling programs, sounded the death knell for many grass-roots recycling projects. In 1991, recycling in the United States reached an all-time high, but in most parts of the country, it had also moved into the global corporate arena.

The huge waste hauling industry had evolved over generations of trash production, stimulated by the need to handle society's sanitary disposal requirements in an efficient and cost-effective manner. In the past, the industry was primarily concerned with removing wastes, not recycling them. But when the demand for recycling services became as common as the demand for rubbish removal, the waste haulers took advantage of their expertise in collecting wastes and quickly learned how to give the public what it wanted: convenient recycling with the least amount of effort.

Curbside Recycling

Consumers had demanded that recycling be made easy. Sorting and collecting piles of newspapers, bottles, and cans and then transporting them to the local buy-back or drop-off center took too much time for a frenetically paced, time-conscious society. The recycling industry began to respond by offering new programs, and the concept of curbside recycling was refined.

Attempts at curbside recycling, in which recyclables were picked up from individual homes and businesses, had been started in the past by smaller recyclers, but the tremendous costs of vehicle fleet maintenance and fuel, coupled with the labor-intensive nature of the business, proved prohibitive to most.

Several different methods of curbside recycling are still being evaluated by both the public and the industry. In some programs, recyclables such as newspapers, glass, and aluminum beverage cans are sorted into three or more containers and left on the curb along with residential trash on a weekly or biweekly basis.

Variations of this program allow homeowners to comingle, or mix, certain products within the three containers. For instance, glass and plastics or aluminum and steel "tin" cans may be placed together. Drivers of the recycling trucks may sort the plastic from the glass at truckside, depositing aluminum and steel cans together to later be mechanically separated with a magnet at the processing center.

In some curbside programs, all cleaned recyclable items are comingled in a single container. Other programs allow the comingling of trash and recyclables, so that the consumer is not responsible for any sorting. However, the comingling of trash and recyclables generally results in a poor-quality product.

In a market in which they are flooded with products, buyers of recyclables can be highly selective about the quality of the materials they accept. Thus, clean glass will typically be accepted and paid for, but dirty glass will be rejected and probably end up in a landfill.

Product Contamination

The concept of contamination in recycling is becoming increasingly familiar to the consumer. Contamination refers to the presence of undesirable materials mixed in with the desired recyclable products. Glass buyers, for example, will consider plastic a contaminant in any load they look at, just as plastic buyers consider glass a contaminant in their loads.

In general, all buyers of recyclables have very specific definitions of and limits on contaminants. And entire truckloads of recyclables have often been landfilled because of extensive contamination. Therefore, the recyclables collector/hauler must either educate the public on this issue or pay higher labor costs to sort and clean materials when the consumer refuses to do so.

Most recycling companies provide lists defining acceptable and unacceptable materials in their individual programs. When consumers are unsure about the acceptability of a specific item, the general rule of the industry is, "When in doubt, leave it out!" Different programs have different specifications, depending on the markets available for the recyclable products in a given locale.

Materials Recovery Facilities: MRFs

As the recycling industry has grown, so have the places that handle the recyclables. In the past, haulers and the general public usually deposited their trash in one central location, known as a transfer station. The garbage was further compacted at this site and subsequently transported to a sanitary landfill.

From this transfer station concept came the materials recovery facility, or MRF (pronounced "murf"), where recyclable materials can be brought to be sorted, compacted, and shipped to buyers for reprocessing.

MRFs range in structure and function from simple to grandiose. The simplest are merely large warehousing areas where recyclables are brought to be hand-sorted for further transfer. More complicated versions feature mechanical separators designed to sort selected products (the magnetic separator, for example, combines a conveyor belt and a magnet to separate aluminum and steel cans). State-of-the-art MRFs include machines that can take any variety of comingled recyclables and sort them mechanically.

Most MRFs include at least one products baler. A baler is a machine that, when fed a continuous amount of a specific recyclable product such as newspaper, compacts it to create uniform bales that are generally held together by wires, much like hay bales. Balers can vary in size and in the type of bale they produce, and some are designed for specific products.

The Economics of Recycling

As the recycling business has evolved into a major industry, it has also been forced to deal with the economics of big business. Many small recyclers have failed because they could not deal with the financial realities stemming from glutted materials markets and increased consumer demand for services. But regardless of the size of a business, the current economics of recycling remain the same: The dollar cost of recycling far outweighs the dollar value of the recyclables. It may take up to five times the amount of money a recyclable product is worth to collect, process, and transport it to a buyer.

Thus, the recycling industry today is driven by consumer demand, not by profit. The profits may not exist at this time, but people are insisting that they be allowed to recycle because "it's the environmental thing to do." As a result, businesses are motivated to promote recycling in order to retain customers.

Some innovative solid waste management specialists and trash haulers have combined this recycling fervor with a lesson on source reduction by offering "pay-as-you-throw," volume-based trash fees. In such programs, a homeowner pays less money for throwing out less trash. To produce less trash, recycling, composting, and source reduction efforts are generally necessary, and in this way, economic incentives for recycling have been created.

Environmental economists also point out that in what has been termed a "sustainable" economic system (one based on the real costs to the environment resulting from the transportation and production of goods and materials), recycling would be financially cost effective. In such a system, the prices of products made from virgin materials would be prohibitive, encouraging manufacturers to use recycled materials instead. However, under such a system, the concept of curbside recycling would become even less cost effective than it is now, due to increasing transportation and energy costs.

Legislation is being considered in various parts of the country to place taxes on virgin materials and/or on the products made from them in order to stimulate the recycling economy, but no such laws have been passed at this time. However, several states, including California, Colorado, and New York, do have tax incentive laws based on promoting research and development in the recycling industry (see Chapter 5).

Completing the Cycle

In analyzing the economics of recycling, it is important to understand what recycling really means. Although the general public has typically focused on the collection of recyclables, this is, in fact, only a single part of the cycle of recycling.

The three chasing arrows of the recycling symbol (see Figure 1.2) represent the three parts of the recycling cycle:

Collection is the first part of the cycle, in which materials are gathered together by consumers, recycling centers, and curbside collection programs and taken to a MRF.

In reprocessing, the second part of the cycle, the recyclables are bought back by manufacturers and remade into new products.

Purchasing these products made from recycled materials is the final part of the cycle.

Although the collection part of the cycle is well understood by the public, the other two components are just beginning to be addressed through educational programs and the media. And here lies the fundamental cause of the economic dilemma facing the recycling industry today: Too many people have believed for too long that they are recycling if they are sorting their trash and taking items to the local recycling center or having them picked up.

Figure 1-2
Recycling Symbol

Source: American Paper Institute

In reality, these people are only participating in the very first step of the cycle. And though industrial interests handle the bulk of the second step—the reprocessing—the primary responsibility for completing the last portion of the cycle rests, again, with the consumer. For until the demand for products made from recycled materials catches up to or exceeds the supply of collected recyclables, the economic stability of the industry will remain at risk.

This failure to complete the cycle and the resulting financial hardships help to explain the growing role played by waste haulers in the field of recycling. Hauling corporations, which have other assets to carry them through the leaner times, are most likely to survive until the widespread completion of the cycle creates a healthier financial picture for recycling.

Hopes for the Future: Continuing Education, the 3Rs, and Market Development

In the meantime, industrial, governmental, educational, and environmental interests are banding together to educate the public more thoroughly about solid waste issues and the concept of integrated solid waste management. At the same time, increased efforts are being made to develop markets for recyclable materials.

On the educational front, priorities include teaching the 3Rs—reduce, reuse, and recycle—to the general populace. Successful implementation of these concepts is key to the first two approaches of the integrated waste management hierarchy (source reduction and recycling), which will, in turn, lead to the conservation of both resources and landfill space:

Reduce refers to source reduction, specifically targeting unnecessary packaging and disposable single-use products.

Reuse, a concept that fits closely with reduce, refers to using items over and over instead of just one time (e.g., using one washable ceramic coffee mug instead of many paper or polystyrene cups).

Recycle is now seen as only part of the total solution to solid waste problems, and the emphasis on completing the cycle has become a new priority.

Some states have helped the educational process along by passing legislation mandating certain types of recycling, banning the disposal of some materials, or even prohibiting the sale of certain packaging materials.

Stimulating old markets for recyclables while at the same time creating new ones is the main focus of the recycling industry today. One way to accomplish this goal is through legislation requiring taxes on virgin materials or products made from them. Much of the current recycling legislation encourages price preferences for goods made from recycled materials, but none has gone so far yet as to tax virgin materials. Although some tax incentives have been offered for efforts to research, develop, and establish recycling technologies, the main tool of the industry has been marketing—selling the idea of "green consumerism" to the public.

"If you're not recycling, you're throwing it all away" and "If you're not buying recycled, you're not really recycling" are two prevalent slogans in this campaign. More and more businesses are cropping up to cater to the new "green" consumers by offering only "environmentally friendly" products, i.e., those that are nontoxic, recyclable, made from recycled materials, and/or designed to help consumers recycle.

Additionally, new products are constantly being created for the "green" businesses: cat litter made from recycled drywall gypsum, animal bedding made from shredded newspapers, recycled plastic lumber for construction, floor tiles containing recycled glass, carpeting made from recycled plastic soda pop bottles, and carpet padding made from recycled tires. The more consumers purchase these products and others that carry a "made from recycled materials" label, the more successful the recycling industry will become.

New Technologies: Businesses Born of the Need to Recycle

An encouraging sign of the times is the new emphasis placed on inducing manufacturers to make their products in ways that facilitate recycling. Thus, automakers around the world are beginning to create programs for labeling plastic car parts with universal resin identification codes, enabling the final salvager to recycle as many pieces as possible. Similarly, large appliance makers are manufacturing their goods so that they are ultimately easier to disassemble into recyclable scrap.

Today's more environmentally educated public and sharper industries have also stimulated a new form of research called life-cycle analysis. This research is meant to show the true environmental cost of any product, from cradle to grave. In other words, the costs of energy, resources, and labor are considered from creation through disposal (or recycling), and companies are using such data to demonstrate that one product is better or more environmentally sound than another. Because the field is relatively new, it remains to be seen how carefully its standards are maintained.

Seattle: A Model City

In the search for a single locality that incorporates as many recycling projects as possible into its solid waste management program, Seattle is often considered the model city. Solid waste planners come from far and wide to study its failures as well as its successes, for recycling began early in Washington State: In 1971, it passed the first litter act in the United States, taxing litter to create a recycling fund.

In 1988, Seattle set an ambitious goal of recycling 60 percent of its garbage by 1998, and since then, the city has tried and utilized almost every recycling and source reduction program in existence in order to avoid the need for an incinerator. At the same time, a thorough public education program has been developed to ensure success.

Combined with its educational promotions, the city's curbside recycling programs, volume-based trash collection rates, and citywide composting programs have all been successful. As a result, Seattle was more than halfway to its goal by 1990.

How to Use This Book

Wherever there are recycling programs, there are changes. As this book was being written, numerous changes occurred in almost every arena of recycling, from technical procedures and community programs to political and economic developments. Thus, this book is meant, first of all, as a guide to the fundamentals of recycling and, secondly, as an extensive collection of resources where the reader can find further, up-to-the-minute information on everything that has anything to do with recycling in the United States.

This resource guide is divided into seven chapters and provides the reader with the following:

1. a chronology of recycling, beginning in ancient times and ending with a focus on the last 20 years or so of the recycling industry's history in the United States;
2. an overview of some of the prominent people in America who have affected the evolution of recycling;
3. an examination of the most commonly recycled commodities, together with interesting facts and figures on these goods, a look at how each product is manufactured from virgin materials, and a description of how each product is actually recycled, noting the additional goods that can, in turn, be made from it;
4. an overview of recycling and solid waste legislation in the 50 states;
5. an extensive directory of public and private agencies and organizations involved in this field, on both the state and national levels;
6. an annotated list of references, including various print resources on recycling (in addition to those that are specific to locales and, as such, may be listed in Chapter 5 under a state agency or organization), as well as a guide to available nonprint resources such as videotapes and

online telecommunication services that deal with recycling and solid waste issues; and

7. a comprehensive glossary of terms used in the various branches of the recycling industry.

It is my hope that any person seeking information on recycling in the United States will be able to find what is needed—or a source in which to locate it—through this book.

Notes

1. U.S. Environmental Protection Agency. *The Solid Waste Dilemma: An Agenda for Action.* Washington, DC: USEPA, 1989.

2

Chronology

THE HISTORY OF RECYCLING IS INEXTRICABLY TIED to the history of solid waste. Therefore, a partial history of garbage is presented in this chronology.

10,000 B.C.   People begin to establish permanent settlements. For the first time, garbage begins to accumulate.

400 B.C.   The first municipal dump in the Western world is established in ancient Athens. Virtually anything considered to be unwanted waste is left in the dump.

A.D. 105   Ts'ai Lun invents paper in China using reclaimed materials such as rags, worn fishnets, hemp, and China grass, solving a pressing paper shortage problem at a time when the only paper available for printing books was made from pure silk. To reward his efforts, Emperor Ho-Ti makes Ts'ai Lun a marquis.

200   The Romans create the first sanitation force: teams of two men walking along the city streets, picking up garbage, and throwing it into a wagon.

1388   The English Parliament bans waste disposal in ditches and public waterways.

1400   The waste from Paris is piled so high outside the city gates that it interferes with the city's defenses.

1415	A dump makes history as it is "captured" during a Portuguese attack on a Moroccan city. The attackers thought it was a strategic hill.
1551	The first recorded use of packaging occurs when German papermaker Andreas Bernhart begins placing his paper in wrappers that bear his name and address.
1690	Paper recycling is born in the United States when the first paper mill is established by the Rittenhouse family on the banks of the Wissahickon Creek, near Philadelphia, Pennsylvania. The paper at this mill is made from recycled rags.
1757	Benjamin Franklin starts the first street cleaning program in America.
1776	The first metal recycling in America occurs when patriots in New York City topple a statue of King George III, melt it down, and make it into 42,088 bullets.
1785	The first U.S. cardboard box is manufactured in Philadelphia by Frederick Newman.
1810	The "tin can" is patented in London, England, by Peter Durand.
1834	A law is enacted in Charleston, West Virginia, that protects vultures from hunters because of the important role they play in the city's garbage removal program.
1865	An estimated 10,000 hogs roam the streets of New York City, gorging on garbage.
1868	John Wesley Hyatt creates the first plastic from nitrocellulose and camphor; he calls it "celluloid." (By the mid-1980s, the volume of plastics used in the United States exceeded that of steel.)
1880	Private scavenging companies and municipal crews begin working together to clean up New York City, removing 15,000 horse carcasses from the city streets. (City horses have rough lives pulling streetcars; their average life expectancy is only two years.)

1885	The first garbage incinerator in the United States is built on Governor's Island in New York City's harbor.
1895	King C. Gillette, a traveling salesman, tires of sharpening his razor and creates the disposable razor blade.
1897	New York City's rubbish is now delivered to a "picking yard." Here, it is separated into five grades of paper, three grades of carpet, and four grades of metal. Burlap bags, twine, rubber, and horsehair are also "picked out" for reuse.
1904	Large-scale aluminum recycling begins in Chicago and Cleveland.
	The first junk mail is delivered when Postmaster Henry Clay Payne authorizes permit mail so that 2,000 or more pieces of third- or fourth-class mail can be posted without stamps by paying a single fee.
1908	The first paper cups are used in vending machines that dispense ice water for a penny a cup.
1912	Plastic packaging is first encouraged when the clear plastic known as "cellophane" is invented by Swiss chemist Dr. Jacques Brandenberger.
1933	New Jersey obtains a court order stopping New York City from dumping its garbage in the Atlantic Ocean. The Supreme Court upholds the decision a year later but states that the law applies to municipal waste only—commercial and industrial waste is not excluded from ocean dumping.
1935	The first beer can is produced by Kreuger's Cream Ale in Richmond, Virginia, and company sales increase 550 percent over the next six months because customers find it so convenient not to have to return bottles.
1939	Not to be outdone, the bottling industry fights back with the first "no deposit, no return" bottles, which are marketed under the "Wisconsin Select" beer label.
1943	The aerosol can is invented by two researchers at the U.S. Department of Agriculture.

1944   Dow Chemical invents polystyrene foam and dubs it "Styrofoam."[TM]

1948   Fresh Kills Landfill opens in Staten Island, New York. It is destined to become the largest city dump in the world. Indeed, the Great Wall of China and Fresh Kills are the only two man-made objects on Earth that are visible from outer space.

1961   Procter & Gamble begins test marketing the disposable diaper.

1965   The federal government realizes that garbage has become a major problem and enacts the Solid Waste Disposal Act (SWDA), which calls for the nation to find better ways of dealing with trash. Research is authorized, and state grants are provided.

1968   The U.S aluminum industry begins recycling discarded aluminum products, from beverage cans to window blinds.

1970   On April 22, the first Earth Day awakens America to the environmental crises at hand and introduces the concept of recycling to the general public.

The U.S. Environmental Protection Agency is established.

The Resource Recovery Act amends the SWDA, requiring the federal government to publish waste disposal guidelines.

1971   The state of Oregon is the first to enact legislation requiring deposits on beverage containers ($.05 per container).

1972   The first buy-back centers for purchasing recyclables from the public are opened in Washington State, accepting beer bottles, aluminum cans, and newspapers.

1974   The first municipal-wide use of curbside recycling containers occurs in University City, Missouri, where officials design and distribute containers for collecting newspapers.

1975   The disposable razor is produced and marketed by Gillette.

1976   Newspaper recycling hits its first snag when Vanderbilt University, in Nashville, Tennessee, halts its program after newsprint prices drop from $45 to $3 per ton.

Marvin L. Whisman, John W. Goetzinger, and Faye O. Cotton, all of Bartlesville, Oklahoma, file U.S. Patent 4,073,720 for a method of purifying and reclaiming used lubricating oils.

The Resource Conservation and Recovery Act is passed, mandating the replacement of all dumps with sanitary landfills, which are defined by the EPA as "land disposal facilities that will have no adverse effects on health or the environment." The enforcement of RCRA standards will increase the costs of landfill disposal, which the EPA's Office of Solid Waste believes will make resource-conserving options, such as recycling, more appealing.

1979   The EPA publishes landfill regulations that prohibit open dumping.

1986   The city of San Francisco meets its goal of recycling 25 percent of its commercial and residential waste stream.

Rhode Island becomes the nation's first state to pass a mandatory recycling law for aluminum and steel "tin" cans, glass, plastic (polyethylene terephthalate, or PET, and high-density polyethylene, or HDPE), and newspapers.

1987   The infamous "Garbage Barge," the *Mobro 4000*, sails down the East Coast, through the Bahamas, to Belize and Mexico. The barge is refused permission to dock at each port. After 6,000 miles of sailing, the ship's load of trash is incinerated and the ash buried on New York's Long Island—where the garbage originated.

1988   Several manufacturers of plastic-foam-type containers, many of them major petrochemical companies, form the National Polystyrene Recycling Corporation with the objective of recycling 25 percent of foam plastic wastes by 1995.

The Plastic Bottle Institute develops a material identification code system for plastic bottle manufacturers.

1988 *cont.*	New Jersey implements legislation requiring every community to separate at curbside and collect three categories of recyclables.
1989	Procter & Gamble starts marketing its Spic and Span cleaner in bottles made of recycled PET plastic.
	The first two polystyrene recycling plants in the United States open in Massachusetts and New York.
	Twenty-six states now have laws requiring recycling to be an integral part of waste management.
	Seven states mandate separation of recyclables at curbside.
1990	McDonald's announces plans to discontinue polystyrene packaging of its fast food due to consumer protests and the failure of its polystyrene recycling concept.
	On December 4, both the Coca-Cola Company and PepsiCo, Inc., the two largest soft drink bottlers in the world, make the same announcement within 22 minutes of each other: They will begin using a recycled PET bottle, made of about 25 percent recycled plastic resin, in 1991.

Sources

EarthWorks Group. *The Recycler's Handbook.* Berkeley, CA: EarthWorks Press, 1990.

Ecenbarger, William. "How Long Can We Keep Dumping on Ourselves?" *Philadelphia Inquirer Sunday Magazine* (1 January 1989): 8.

Glenn, Jim. "Containers at Curbside." *BioCycle* 29 (March 1988): 36.

Kane, Joseph Nathan. *Famous First Facts: A Record of First Happenings, Discoveries, and Inventions in American History.* 4th ed. New York: H. W. Wilson, 1981.

National Solid Wastes Management Association. *Garbage Then and Now.* Washington, DC: NSWMA, 1989.

Rathje, William L. "The History of Garbage." *GARBAGE* 5 (September/October 1990): 32–41.

USEPA Region VIII library, recycling file. 999 18th Street, Denver, CO.

3

Biographies

COMPILING A SECTION ON NOTEWORTHY PEOPLE in the field of recycling is not a simple task. Many women and men have labored for years to promote recycling, largely without recognition. They are the grass-roots heroes, striving to develop and implement recycling programs within their home communities.

Many individuals are nationally known in the recycling business, but few people in the industry agree on who the leaders are because they all work together in an admirable fashion to further the common cause of recycling.

The biographies that follow feature exceptional people who have truly made a difference in the national recycling arena, but be assured that they are not the only ones who deserve recognition. It is also important to remember that almost every community has its own VIP in recycling—a person who is often the most valuable resource at the local level.

Trisha L. Ferrand (1951–)

Trisha Ferrand is the solid waste program manager for the county of San Diego, California. In this position, she plans and manages materials recovery programs for wastes now entering county landfills at the rate of 3,000 tons per day. The county hopes to achieve a 25 percent reduction in waste by 1995 and 50 percent by the year 2000.

Ferrand was founder and first executive director of the Association of New Jersey Recyclers, founder of the computer bulletin board RecycleNet, and cofounder and president of the Coalition for Recyclable Waste. She is on the board of advisers for Californians Against

Waste and was a speaker on recycling at the First World Congress of Local Governments for a Sustainable Future in 1990 (sponsored by the United Nations Environmental Programme, the Union of Local Authorities, and the Center for Innovative Diplomacy).

Prior to assuming her county position, Ferrand owned and managed a waste management consulting firm, Ferrand Associates. Some of the company's more notable projects included: preparing a report on strategies for marketing recyclables for the Environmental Protection Agency; providing assistance in developing recycling programs at both DuPont Industries and Procter & Gamble; producing a training manual on composting for Waste Management of North America, Inc.; and writing the National Recycling Coalition's (NRC) "Recycling Measurement Standards and Reporting Guidelines," which was adopted by consensus of the NRC's membership in 1989. In 1988, Ferrand received the NRC's "Outstanding Environmental Group Leader" award.

She has produced a manual on implementing a curbside recycling program for Massachusetts public works officials, as well as a decision options and methodologies document for the city of Philadelphia. Ferrand has also prepared recycling publicity and education plans for Berks County, Pennsylvania; Ocean City, New Jersey; and the state of Missouri.

Ferrand's publications include "Plastics Collection and Sortation," *Resource Recycling Journal* (January/February 1989), and "Packaging Interests Begin Planning for Recycling," *Resource Recycling Journal* (July/August 1988).

Among the conference papers she has presented are: "Mandatory Recycling: Rhetoric vs. Realism," for the 18th Annual *BioCycle* National Conference on Composting and Recycling, 1988; "Measuring Success—Recommendations for Uniform Terminology and Methodology to Evaluate Curbside Collection Programs," for the 6th National Recycling Congress, 1987; and "Job Development Through Resource Recovery," for the Pennsylvania Renewable Energy Conference, 1978.

Peter L. Grogan (1949–)

Peter Grogan presently serves as the director of materials recovery and is a partner with the environmental consulting firm R. W. Beck and Associates. Prior to joining the firm, Grogan served for 11 years as the director of a community recycling program in Colorado.

Over the years, Grogan has worked for a number of state governments to develop their recycling/waste reduction programs, including

Alabama, California, Indiana, Maine, Massachusetts, and Washington. He has also worked with the Virgin Islands and all of the American flag territories in the Pacific on similar solid waste projects.

The local governments he has assisted with recycling programs include: Sitka, Alaska; San Francisco, California; Denver, Colorado; Miami and Orlando, Florida; and Honolulu, Hawaii, as well as Vancouver, British Columbia, and American Samoa.

In addition to his work with the public sector, Grogan has also provided services to develop recyclable commodity markets for private industry. He has worked with U.S. and Japanese paper mills, the plastics industry, and the international banking community and has implemented recycling systems for airports, corporations, U.S. Navy ships, and major theme parks. Currently, Grogan is assisting several municipalities with their plans to build and/or utilize materials recovery facilities.

A member of the editorial board of *BioCycle* magazine, Grogan also writes a monthly column, "Recycling View," for that publication. In addition, he is president of the National Recycling Coalition's board of directors and a member of NCR's recycling advisory council.

Richard Keller (1955–)

Richard Keller is the recycling project manager for the Northeast Maryland Waste Disposal Authority (NEA). In this position, he manages the Baltimore Regional Recycling Program, assisting both the city and county in efforts to reach a 20 percent or greater recycling goal by 1994. Prior to working for NEA, Keller spent 12 years as the state energy conservation manager for the Maryland Energy Office (MEO).

Keller has prepared documents on recycled paper purchasing, waste reduction in offices, and office paper recycling. He also provided an analysis of state procurement programs for buying recycled products for the Governors' Advisory Council on Recycling.

Keller's specialty is promoting the completion of the recycling cycle through market development. In this arena, he has served as moderator for markets sessions and has given presentations on buying recycled products at state recycling conferences since 1990. Additionally, he drafted Maryland's 1977 law on buying recycled products, which has been used as a model for over 100 other state and local governments that have established similar programs.

He served for ten years (1981 to 1991) on the National Recycling Coalition's board of directors, concentrating on market development issues. He is a member of both the Official Recycled Products Guide Advisory Board and the Maryland Department of General Services Task Force to Plan and Implement the Purchase of Materials Made from Recycled Solid Waste. He is also a technical adviser to the Californians Against Waste Foundation's Buy Recycled Campaign.

Keller has given an average of 10 to 15 major presentations a year on recycling issues, focusing on the purchasing, marketing, and economic development of products manufactured from recycled materials. His audiences have included the National Association of Educational Buyers, the Metropolitan Washington Council of Governments, the New Mexico Governor's Symposium, the U.S. Congress Environmental and Energy Study Conference, and the First United States Conference on Municipal Solid Waste Management, "Solutions for the 90s."

He received the U.S. Department of Energy Award for Energy Innovation for his 1985 "buying recycled" and auto/truck recycling programs in Maryland and the President's Award from the Maryland Auto and Truck Recyclers Association (1982 and 1985). In 1987, he also received the Outstanding Government Leader Award from the National Recycling Coalition.

Don Kneass (1945–)

Don Kneass is presently the recycling programs coordinator for Waste Management of Seattle. Kneass began his career in recycling in 1971 with the Portland Recycling Team, a nonprofit drop-site recycling business. After moving to Seattle, he established the Washington State Recycling Information Office and its recycling hotline in 1973.

In 1974, Kneass opened Seattle Recycling, Inc., a multimaterial buy-back recycling business. Ten years later, he sold this business to take a position with the City of Seattle Solid Waste Utility as a senior planner responsible for recycling program development.

In February 1988, Kneass began working for Waste Management, Inc., planning and implementing recycling programs in Alaska, western Canada, the Northwest, and the Rocky Mountain states. His responsibilities have encompassed residential curbside collection, commercial collection, recycling processing facilities and equipment, yard waste collection and composting, tire collection and shredding, and material marketing.

Kneass has served as president of the Washington State Recycling Association and as a board member of the National Recycling Coalition, and is currently president of the Committee for Litter Control and Recycling. He was chair of the Washington State Department of Trade and Economic Development's Committee for Recycling Markets and is a member of the King County Commission for Marketing Recyclable Materials.

David Gray Loveland (1954–)

David Loveland has served as the executive director of the National Recycling Coalition since 1989. In this position, he has watched the organization grow to over 3,600 members and 28 state chapters, all of which provide education, technical assistance, and policy guidance throughout the country to promote the development of recycling.

From 1985 to 1989, Loveland was the director of natural resources for the League of Women Voters Education Fund. From 1983 to 1985, he served as chief of the Division of Water Quality Planning and Public Participation for the government of the District of Columbia.

James P. McMahon (1951–)

James McMahon, a consulting ecologist in Denver, Colorado, established and served as chief executive officer for the Environmental Enhancement Group in Seattle, Washington, and Los Angeles, California, from 1985 to 1988. This consulting firm provided planning and project management services to government agencies, corporations, nonprofit organizations, and small businesses.

McMahon was the regional manager for 20-20 Recycle Centers in Los Angeles from 1987 to 1988. In this position, he initiated and managed the start-up operations for a region containing over 200 recycling centers, serving a potential client base of over 10 million people.

From 1980 until 1985, he was the aluminum division manager for Fibres International, Inc., in Bellevue, Washington. The aluminum processing/brokerage business that he developed became a highly successful operation, experiencing substantial increases in business volume and profit.

During his term as Seattle's recycling program planner from 1979 to 1980, he developed a recycling strategy that made waste reduction a priority for city government. Prior to that, he was vice-president and owner of a successful recycling business, Seattle Recycling, Inc.

Chaz Miller (1947–)

Chaz Miller is the manager of recycling programs for the National Solid Wastes Management Association (NSWMA) in Washington, D.C. He also manages the Waste Recyclers Council, which represents recycling companies that are active in promoting recycling as a proven waste reduction alternative. The council is also responsible for developing markets for recycled materials and emphasizing the role of the private sector in making recycling work.

A nationally known expert on recycling issues, Miller has been a member of the board of directors of the National Recycling Coalition since 1985 and served as chairman in 1989. In 1990, he was chairman of the NRC's Markets Development Committee, and from 1988 until 1991, he was also director of recycling for the Glass Packaging Institute (GPI).

With GPI, Miller was responsible for promoting glass recycling activities throughout the United States and also advised members on assisting recycling programs within the frameworks of different states' regulations. He coordinated the actions of state lobbyists and participated in federal legislative sessions, industry conferences, and standards-setting activities.

Before joining GPI, Miller spent 11 years with the EPA's Office of Solid Waste, working on source separation, resource recovery, hazardous wastes, and information management. He was responsible for several recycling publications and grants, as well as one of the EPA's computerized data-reporting systems.

Gary Michael Petersen (1947–)

Gary Michael Petersen is the founder of five environment-related firms, including Ecolo-Haul Recycling Services, a Los Angeles-based recycling services/environmental education firm established in 1972. He is also the founder of the California Resource Recovery Association and serves on the advisory board for the University of California Hazardous and Toxic Waste Certification Program.

Since 1972, Petersen has worked on numerous recycling and environmental education programs designed to educate both consumers and key opinion leaders about the immediacy of solid waste problems in industrialized countries. In the United States, he has been a consultant for the EPA and the National Science Foundation's Committee for National Recycling Policy, as well as a board member and adviser to the National Recycling Coalition.

Internationally, Petersen has been a consultant to the governments of Great Britain, the provincial governments of Canada, the People's Republic of China, the Republic of Palau and islands of the Korae State, Micronesia, and private industries in various countries.

In 1973, Petersen founded the magazine *Resource News* and served as editor and publisher for a time. He has also produced educational programs on recycling for primary and secondary schools in the Los Angeles area.

Politically active, Petersen lobbied for the California legislation known as SB 650 (1978), which provided grant funds for communities to establish recycling and recycling education programs. In addition, he was responsible for the initial design of AB 2020 (1987), which provided for redemption of glass, aluminum, and plastic containers.

Over the years, Petersen has received numerous awards and letters of recognition for his contributions to the fields of recycling and environmental education. Some of these have come from former President Ronald Reagan, the California Waste Management Board, California Governor Edmund G. Brown, Jr., the Cousteau Society, and the California Resource Recovery Association. He is also listed in the *International Biographical Reference* (Cambridge, England), *Who's Who in the World,* and *Who's Who in America.*

Since 1988, Petersen has served on the board of the Hazardous Materials Management Program at the University of California and is currently the director of public policy development for Waste Management of North America's western region. He also designed the curriculum and is presently an instructor for the municipal solid waste management certificate program at the University of California, Los Angeles (UCLA) extension. Additionally, he was invited to serve on the governing board of the World Conservation Corps, sponsored by the United Nations, in 1988.

Bob Rubin (1933–)

Bob Rubin is the owner of RUBICON, Ltd., a Denver-based environmental consulting company specializing in alternative solid waste issues.

Prior to forming RUBICON in July 1990, Rubin spent nearly four years as the executive director of Recycle Now!, a nonprofit educational organization promoting recycling in Colorado (see Chapter 6, Colorado Recycles, p. 144).

Since 1986, Rubin has been an active member of the National Recycling Coalition, serving on its board of directors from 1988 to

1990. He has served on the Governor's Integrated Solid Waste Management Task Force in Colorado, as well as the Denver Regional Council of Goverments' Solid Waste Task Force, the Denver-Aurora Waste-to-Energy Feasibility Study, and the Public Service Company-Denver Waste-to-Energy Feasibility Study.

Nancy VandenBerg (1946–)

Nancy VandenBerg is the principal of Markets for Recycled Products, a consulting practice she established in 1985 to focus on the importance of purchasing decisions in solid waste issues. VandenBerg pioneered formal recycled product procurement plans and introduced the corporate and nonprofit communities to buy-recycled strategies.

Over the years, she has provided critical research on products manufactured from recycled materials. Her feasibility studies on recycled construction products for the EPA resulted in an insulation guideline published in 1989, as well as four of the five new guidelines developed by the EPA in 1991 and 1992.

VandenBerg has conducted working seminars, sponsored by the Council for Solid Waste Solutions, that have led to increased acceptance of recycled plastic products by public officials in the Midwest and Northeast regions of the United States. The buy-recycled programs established by a number of major corporations are based on concepts covered by VandenBerg in her seminars.

She has served on the boards of *The Recycled Products Guide* and the *Recycled Paper News* and holds founding memberships with the Paper Definitions Working Group and the Manhattan Solid Waste Advisory Board. She is currently serving on the recycled paper and recycled plastic subcommittees of the American Society of Testing and Materials.

VandenBerg drafted and successfully defended critical sections of the 1988 *Standard Guide for the Development of Standards Relating to the Proper Use of Recycled Plastic,* which has led to specification revisions throughout the plastics industry.

Her publications include: "Recycled Materials Procurement II," *Resource Recycling* (November/December 1986); "Working Together to Buy Recycled," *Waste Age* (January 1989); "Plastic Film Recycling," *BioCycle* (December 1991); and "Recycling Policy: What Will It Be?" *PIMA Magazine* (January 1992).

Jeanne Lynn Wirka (1963–)

Jeanne Wirka is a nationally recognized expert on source reduction and recycling, especially as they relate to consumer packaging issues.

She is currently the director of the Recycling Economic Development Project at the Californians Against Waste Foundation (CAWF). In this position, she focuses on coordinating the development of local markets for recycled materials with the goals of community economic development in the nine counties of the San Francisco Bay area.

From 1987 until 1991, prior to taking her position with CAWF, Wirka served as the founder and coordinator of the Solid Waste Alternatives Project at the Environmental Action Foundation (EAF) in Washington, D.C. The project was a national campaign aimed at reducing solid waste by promoting changes in product manufacturing and materials use. While Wirka ran this campaign, she also coordinated a coalition of state activists working on uniform solid waste legislation; testified before Congress, the Federal Trade Commission, and state and local legislatures; conducted workshops for policymakers; organized press conferences; and conducted research on the role of materials in solid waste management.

From 1989 to 1991, Wirka served as a member of the board of directors of the National Recycling Coalition. From 1989 to 1990, she was also on both the board of directors and the steering committee of the Source Reduction Council of the Coalition of Northeast Governors (CONEG).

Currently, she sits on the advisory committees of the Environmental Protection Agency's project on life-cycle analysis methodology development and the Office of Technology Assessment's green product design project.

While directing EAF, Wirka wrote and edited its quarterly newsletter and public education materials. She is the author of a nationally acclaimed report on the environmental impacts of plastics packaging, entitled "Wrapped in Plastics: The Environmental Case for Reducing Plastics Packaging." Wirka's other publications include "Life Cycle Assessments: Science or PR?" Solid Waste Action Paper #1 (Environmental Action Foundation, 1991); "Degradable Plastics: The Wrong Answer to the Right Question," with Richard Denison, PhD (Environmental Action Foundation and Environmental Defense Fund, 1989); "The Degradable Plastics Hoax," *Environmental Action* (November/December 1989); and "Plastics Recycling: Missing the Forest for the Plastic Lumber," *Resource Recycling* (December 1989).

Among Wirka's conference papers are: "Plastics Recycling: A Tale of Three Planets" (presented at the Conference on Solid Waste Management and Materials Policy, sponsored by the New York State Legislative Commission on Solid Waste Management, in New York City, New York, 1991) and "The Rise and Fall of Integrated Solid

Waste Management" (presented at Recycling Earth's Resources, sponsored by the National Recycling Coalition, in San Diego, California,1990).

4

Facts and Data

THIS CHAPTER PROVIDES USEFUL FACTS AND FIGURES about widely recycled commodities, together with an explanation of how these commodities are made from virgin materials, collected for recycling, recycled, and remanufactured. Brief information on several less common recyclables, as well as some odder commodities, has also been included.

Aluminum Cans

Aluminum Can Facts

- Recycling 1 aluminum can saves the equivalent of enough energy to run a television set for three hours.
- Recycling 1 aluminum can saves enough energy to make 19 more.
- American consumers and industry throw away enough aluminum to rebuild our entire commercial airfleet every three months.
- Recycling aluminum scrap saves 95 percent of the energy that would have been required to make new aluminum from ore.
- In 1989, 2.9 million tons of scrap aluminum were recovered by the Institute of Scrap Recycling Industries, Inc.
- When aluminum can recycling began in 1972, approximately 15.4 percent of America's cans were recycled.

- In 1989, Americans recycled 49.5 billion all-aluminum beverage cans, bringing the national aluminum can recycling rate to 60.8 percent.
- In the 1980s, aluminum can recycling diverted 12 billion pounds of metal from the U.S. solid waste stream (more than 320 billion cans).
- Today's aluminum beverage can uses 30 percent less metal than the 1972 version.
- Today, 28 aluminum cans weigh one pound.
- Aluminum can be recycled and reused indefinitely.
- Aluminum can recycling is a closed-loop process, and used cans can be recycled and back on store shelves as new beverage containers in as little as 90 days.
- It takes 8,760 pounds of bauxite and 1,020 pounds of petroleum coke to produce 2,000 pounds of aluminum.
- When recycled aluminum is used instead of bauxite and petroleum coke, the amount of raw materials needed drops by 95 percent.
- Recycling aluminum reduces associated air pollution by 95 percent.
- Of all the countries in the world, the Netherlands has the highest recycling rate for aluminum.
- Approximately 40 percent of the aluminum used in the United States goes into packaging.

Making and Recycling Aluminum Cans

Although aluminum is an element, it is always found in combination with other elements in its natural state. To make virgin aluminum, bauxite, a reddish, claylike ore rich in aluminum compounds, must be surface mined; to extract the aluminum, the bauxite is refined to eliminate impurities such as iron oxide. Leading suppliers of bauxite include Brazil, Australia, Africa, Guinea, and the Caribbean.

A fine white powder called alumina, a form of aluminum oxide, is produced by the refining process. The alumina is sent to a reduction plant, or smelter, where it is deposited into cells known as pots, which are about 20 feet long, 6 feet wide, and 3 feet deep. A strong, continuous electrical current is passed through the pots, separating the alumina and producing molten aluminum metal, which settles to the bottom. All of these steps, which together involve enormous time and energy, are eliminated by aluminum recycling.

Most aluminum recycled by consumers is in the form of aluminum cans. To prepare an aluminum can for collection, the consumer merely needs to rinse it in order to remove food or beverage remnants. Crushing the can is generally optional; the main advantage is that crushed cans take up less room and can therefore be stored and transported more easily.

Aluminum cans are typically collected from consumers at recycling centers, grocery stores, and through reverse vending machines that give money back for cans deposited. There are also some direct consumer-to-processor sales programs. For example, Reynolds Aluminum, ALCOA, and Anheuser-Busch all buy cans directly from consumers as well as from recycling collection companies.

After the cans are collected, they are physically or mechanically inspected for contaminants, such as glass and cigarette butts. After the contaminants have been removed, the cans are usually crushed and packed into bales by a baling machine. These tightly packed bales are then sent to the processing plant to be melted down for reuse.

At most processing plants, the baled cans are shredded to rid them of excess moisture that could cause an explosion in the furnace. The shredded metal is then poured into a huge "pot-line" furnace and heated (the melting point of aluminum is approximately 1,280 degrees Fahrenheit). After the cans have become molten metal, the paint from the outside of the cans rises to the surface and is skimmed off.

The molten aluminum is transferred to another furnace where small amounts of other metals may be mixed with the aluminum to produce the desired characteristics in the finished product (for example, magnesium adds corrosion resistance, and copper adds strength). This newly alloyed molten metal is generally cast into ingots, or large bricks, that can weigh as much as 60,000 pounds and provide enough metal to make more than 1.5 billion beverage cans.

If the aluminum is to be made back into beverage cans, the ingots are shipped to a sheet plant, where they are reheated and rolled into thin sheets of aluminum. These sheets are sent on to a can plant, which transforms the sheet aluminum back into food or beverage cans.

Steel "Tin" Cans

Steel Can Facts

- In 1989, steel and bimetal cans (that is, cans made with steel bodies and aluminum lids) were being recycled at a rate of 21.6 percent nationwide.

- The average person in the United States throws away six pounds of steel cans each month.
- Each minute of the day, more than 9,000 steel cans are recovered for recycling.
- Recycling steel cans saves 74 percent of the energy that would be used to produce them from virgin materials.
- Every day, Americans use 100 million steel cans.

Making and Recycling Steel Cans

Steel is a form of commercial iron characterized by its malleability and by the fact that it has a lower carbon content than cast iron, which is relatively brittle. The easiest way for a consumer to distinguish a steel can from an aluminum one is to apply a magnet. Aluminum is nonferrous (without iron) and therefore nonmagnetic. Steel, on the other hand, is a ferrous metal (containing iron) and will attract a magnet.

Many people are more familiar with steel cans than they are with aluminum ones. The steel can is often called the "tin" can, a misnomer. Actually, there is very little tin in these cans; the base metal is steel, and what little tin is used forms a thin coating on the inside of the can to stabilize the flavors of its food or beverage contents. This coating also enables the manufacturer to sterilize the food by cooking it right in the can.

According to the Steel Can Recycling Institute (SCRI), more than 90 percent of food containers, including the large #10 cans used by food service operations, are made of steel. And steel is America's most recycled material.

Steel cans are prepared and collected for recycling in a number of ways. Some collectors merely request that the cans be rinsed free of food particles; others insist that they be delabeled and crushed with both ends removed.

Some recycling programs collect the steel cans separately from other materials, but other programs allow them to be mixed with a variety of recyclables. In fact, they are among the easiest items to remove from a mixture of recyclables: A large magnet is used, often in conveyor form, to separate the steel cans from other materials.

Once collected, the steel cans are taken to a processor to be prepared for recycling. The cans may be baled, flattened, or shredded depending on the requirements of the end market user. Many prepared cans are then shipped to a detinning company, where they are shredded to facilitate the removal of food and paper contamination and then melted down. Various processes are used to remove the tin from the steel, and the detinned steel is sent to a steel mill to be made into a new product.

Some steel mills will purchase steel cans directly, in addition to what they purchase from detinners, to incorporate a certain percentage of tin into their scrap mix. Bimetal cans can be processed in the same manner, and steel aerosol and paint cans can also be recycled. It is best to consult local recycling organizations for their specific preparation guidelines for these containers.

New products made from recycled steel include automobiles, major appliances, and new food and beverage cans.

Glass

Glass Facts

- Glass is 100 percent recyclable in a true closed-loop system.
- Each person in the United States uses about 85 pounds of glass each year.
- Every glass bottle that is recycled can save enough energy to light a 100-watt bulb for four hours.
- By recycling one ton of glass, we save the energy equivalent of nine gallons of fuel oil.
- In 1989, glass bottles were being recycled at the rate of 25 percent nationwide.
- Germany recycles almost 40 percent of its glass.
- About 30 percent of today's average glass soft drink container is made of recycled glass.
- About 5 billion glass food and beverage containers are recycled each year.
- Americans still throw away enough bottles and jars to fill the twin towers of New York's World Trade Center every two weeks.
- Some 75 percent of the glass used in the United States goes into packaging.
- Of all the packaging available for food and beverage products, consumers prefer glass packaging.
- The average person in the United States can save at least seven pounds of glass each month.

- Each day, Americans recycle approximately 13 million glass bottles and jars.

Making and Recycling Glass

There are many different kinds of glass, which vary widely in their basic chemical composition and physical characteristics. There are two major types of commercial glass: "soda-lime-silica" and "special."

Most general recycling programs handle only soda-lime-silica glass, which includes beverage and food containers exclusively. Special glass, which is not widely recycled, includes glass cookware, mirrors, windowpanes, windshields, optical glass, ceramics, and lead crystal.

Soda-lime-silica glass is, as the name suggests, made from soda (sodium carbonate), limestone (calcium carbonate), and sand (silicon dioxide). The optimum combination of these ingredients—15 percent soda, 10 percent lime, and 75 percent silica—produces a strong, resilient product with a moderately low melting point. The variable qualities of special glass make it incompatible with soda-lime-silica glass for recycling purposes, and for this reason, most recycling programs do not accept special glass and actually consider it to be a contaminant.

Colored glass is produced by adding different metallic oxides to the mixture. For example, iron oxides create the common green color, and brown or amber glass is created when several colors are mixed together. Because glass manufacturers often want a specific color or no color at all, many recyclers require that the glass they purchase from consumers and processors be sorted according to color (clear or "flint," green, and amber). Some processors will not accept green glass at all.

To simplify glass recycling in the future, methods of dipping clear bottles in colored inks and acrylics are being investigated. These dipped bottles would not need to be color separated before being recycled because the glass itself would be clear and the dyes could be removed.

Glass is one of the easiest commodities to recycle. The consumer merely needs to rinse out any remnants of food products and remove the plastic or metal top. Labels may be left on the containers as they burn off at the high temperatures in the furnace. A local recycler should be consulted for any color-sorting requirements for a specific area.

After being collected, glass must be made "furnace ready"; it is color sorted, if necessary, and made contaminant free. Contaminants include metal caps and lids, plastic caps, dirt, stones, and special glass. Glass that does not meet a buyer's strict specifications is rejected and taken to a landfill.

A glass plant will often designate the number of times that a specific supplier's glass can be rejected before the plant will stop buying from that supplier. The Coors Brewing Company in Colorado, for example, will cease buying from a supplier after three separate loads have been rejected. Thus, it is very important for the consumer to make sure that the products put into the glass collection bin are clean and uncontaminated. The success of a glass recycling program rests directly with the consumer.

After collection and inspection, the glass is crushed into small pieces called cullet. The cullet is cleaned and then may be mixed directly with whatever additional raw materials are needed to make new glass. This mixture is melted at temperatures of up to 2,800 degrees Fahrenheit. Although the raw materials of glass are still in abundant supply, a great amount of energy is saved by utilizing cullet instead.

The melted glass is dropped into a forming machine, where it is either blown or pressed into shape. Newly formed glass containers are then cooled slowly in an annealing lehr, which keeps the glass from becoming brittle.

Most recycled glass is reprocessed back into food and beverage containers, but some goes to other markets. For example, companies that sell stained glass for artistic purposes may use recycled glass, as do some fiberglass companies. Recycled glass is also used by producers of a road composite called glassphalt, which is made of crushed glass and asphalt.

Plastic

Plastic Facts

- Americans throw away 2.5 million plastic bottles every hour.
- 26 plastic soft drink bottles can make one polyester suit.
- 5 recycled soft drink bottles will make enough fiberfill for a man's ski jacket.
- 35 recycled plastic soft drink bottles will make enough fiberfill for a sleeping bag.

- 1,050 recycled milk jugs can be made into a six-foot park bench.
- Plastics comprise approximately 19.9 percent of the volume in U.S. landfills.
- Plastics comprise approximately 8 percent of the weight in U.S. landfills.
- Of the 14.4 million tons of all types of plastics generated in 1988, only .2 million tons (or 1.1 percent) were recovered for recycling.
- Whenever Americans buy food, they spend one out of every eleven dollars on packaging.
- Approximately 30 percent of all plastics produced go into packaging.
- More than half of the plastics Americans throw away each year, about 6 million tons, are used in packaging.
- The United States makes enough plastic film each year to shrink-wrap the state of Texas.
- Americans use about 5 million tons of plastic wrap each year, very little of which is recycled.
- 40 percent of the plastic trash in the United States consists of plastic bags and film wrappings.
- If only 10 percent of Americans bought products with less plastic packaging only 10 percent of the time, approximately 144 million pounds of plastic could be eliminated from our landfills.
- Each person in the United States uses about 190 pounds of plastic each year.
- Over 190 million pounds of plastic soft drink containers are made each year.
- About 28 percent of all plastic soft drink containers are being recycled.
- Although recycling keeps about 175 million pounds of polyethelene terephthalate (PET) out of the landfills annually, 535 million pounds of PET are still being thrown away.
- Each year, Americans use over 25 billion polystyrene foam cups—enough to encircle our planet 436 times.
- Plastics products have the highest energy values for waste-to-energy incineration facilities (because of their petroleum hydrocarbon content).
- Plastic is virtually immortal: If the Pilgrims had had six-packs, the six-pack rings would still be around today.
- About 100,000 five-gallon HDPE containers are recycled each year by Ben & Jerry's Ice Cream Company.
- Each year, Americans throw away 6 billion plastic-encased disposable pens.
- The average person in the United States throws away two pounds of plastic containers every month.

- Americans throw away over 500 million disposable plastic cigarette lighters each year.
- Every year, the U.S. plastics industry manufactures the equivalent of about ten pounds of plastic for every person on Earth.
- In 1988, 2 billion pounds of HDPE—approximately equivalent to the weight of 900,000 Honda Civics—were used in the United States to make bottles for household products.
- A discarded plastic beverage container has a longer life expectancy than the person who threw it away.

Making and Recycling Plastic

All plastics are made from a basic mixture called resin, which is derived from petroleum oil or natural gas. The resin is sold by chemical companies to manufacturers who remelt the resin, mix in additional chemical additives, and then use pressure molding or extruding processes to make the finished product.

There are over 50 types of plastic resins currently bought and sold in the United States. Fewer than 10 of these are commonly used for packaging, 6 of which were assigned codes by the Society of the Plastics Industry, Inc., in 1988, to facilitate their recycling by consumers.

The industry code, placed on the bottom of the plastic container, consists of a triangle formed by three arrows, with a number in its center and a corresponding letter abbreviation beneath the triangle. The codes range from approximately .5 inch to 1 inch in size and can be applied either by molding or imprinting. The codes and their accompanying letters refer to different types of resins. (See Figure 4.1)

In general, the basic requirements for recycling a plastic container are the same as those for other containers: The consumer should rinse it thoroughly and remove its top or lid because these are usually made of a different resin that cannot be widely recycled at this time. Recyclers also request that consumers flatten or crush the container as much as possible. This helps the collection program by eliminating a good deal of the dead air space that composes most of the volume in plastic containers. The less space it fills up, the more economical it is for the recycler to store the plastic for later sale.

In some recycling programs, the public is asked to separate two or three resin types. In other programs, certain resin types may be mixed together. However, the majority of plastics recycling programs in this country still accept only the two most commonly recycled resins: PET and HDPE. This is generally believed to be because the process of recycling plastics is still evolving and because these two resin types are the most prevalent in our packaging industry.

CODE	MATERIAL
1 PET	Polyethylene Terephthalate (PET)*
2 HDPE	High-Density Polyethylene
3 V	Vinyl/Polyvinyl Chloride (PVC)*
4 LDPE	Low-Density Polyethylene
5 PP	Polypropylene
6 PS	Polystyrene
7 OTHER	All Other Resins and Layered Multimaterial

* Stand alone bottle code is different from standard industry identification to avoid confusion with registered trademarks.

Figure 4-1
Plastic Container Code System

Source: Society of the Plastics Industry, Inc.

After being collected and sorted, each type of resin is treated in a similar manner. As with glass and aluminum recycling, industry specifications for scrap plastic are set within strict limits. Very little contamination from other commodities, including other resins, is allowed. Consequently, inspection for cleanliness is the first step in any processing plant. The plastics are then compressed into bales that weigh over 1,000 pounds each. The recycling facility subsequently sends these bales on to its buyer/processor.

At this new location, the plastic is washed to remove residues from former uses. Paper labels, metal rings or caps, and other contaminants are also removed at this time. Next, the plastic is shredded, dried, and then processed further into pellets or flakes, which form the new raw materials for the next plastic product.

Plastics recycling is usually not a closed-loop process for soft drink bottles are typically not reprocessed back into bottles (because they may have held a product such as motor oil). However, bottling companies are working with the plastics industry to produce new soft drink bottles containing at least 25 percent recycled resin.

In general, the recycling of plastics is not nearly as straightforward as that of glass or aluminum due to the variety of resins and the light weight of the products. These two factors make plastics recycling neither cost effective nor energy efficient. For these reasons, some people in the field would like to see the entire plastics industry evolve out of existence.

Others, such as J. Winston Porter, former assistant administrator for solid waste and emergency response for the EPA, believe that plastics should be handled in three ways: (1) recycled in some cases, if it is relatively simple to do so (as with PET and HDPE); (2) landfilled in other instances because the inert properties of most plastics keep them from polluting the air or water while they sit underground indefinitely; and (3) burned in waste-to-energy plants where their high energy content can be used as a resource to produce electricity. (Plastics have about twice the heat energy of coal.)

There is another factor that could come into play in the near future and may greatly simplify the plastics recycling process. This is a new technology, currently being investigated by Eastman Chemical Company, to make the sorting of plastic recyclables easier. In this new sorting process, an organic molecular marker would be built into all plastics in low concentrations. Sorting machines would utilize sophisticated electronic sensors to identify the different plastic types and separate them quickly and efficiently, at a lower cost to recyclers.

A basic problem with plastics production and recycling in general, according to environmentalists, is that the plastics industry uses five of the top six chemicals that the EPA lists as "most hazardous waste" during the initial production of virgin plastics. However, both industry and environmental factions agree that by recycling plastics, the initial production toxicity can be reduced because less virgin resin would be needed in the long run.

Recycling the Most Common Plastic Packaging Types

Polyethylene Terephthalate (PET)

PET comprises 7 percent of plastic packaging. This is the type of plastic most often used to make transparent soft drink and liquor bottles, as well as peanut butter jars. It is not only the most recycled plastic in the United States but also the only plastic that can retain carbonation.

The largest use for recycled PET is in fiber applications. About 35 percent of all polyester carpeting produced each year includes recycled content. Some companies even manufacture carpeting made of 100 percent recycled PET soft drink bottles. Other fiber uses include fiberfill for jackets, gloves, sleeping bags, pillows, and cushions. Polyester upholstery and clothing, as well as geotextiles used in roadbeds and landfills, may also contain recycled fibers. In addition, recycled PET can be found in auto parts, paint bristles, and industrial strapping.

Procter & Gamble began incorporating recycled PET into non-food containers in 1989, and Coca-Cola and Pepsi began using it in their beverage bottles in 1991.

When recycling PET, always double-check for the code number 1

because another resin type, vinyl, looks very similar but is coded with the number 3.

Even a small amount of vinyl in a PET batch can ruin the entire mixture as well as the machinery.

High-Density Polyethylene (HDPE)

HDPE comprises 31 percent of plastic packaging. This type of plastic is typically used to make the common one-gallon milk and water jugs. The HDPE in these products is transparent but thicker and less clear than PET. Detergent, bleach, motor oil, and some margarine and yogurt containers are made of HDPE in its colored and more rigid, opaque form. Some plastic grocery sacks are also made of this resin.

Processors of HDPE are generally more selective about the types of containers they buy. Clear containers are almost always accepted by plastics recycling programs, as are colored bleach and detergent bottles. But the smaller, more variable containers that hold products such as shampoo, suntan lotion, yogurt, margarine, or hair spray, as well as HDPE plastic bags, are often excluded. It is important to check with local recycling facilities for requirements in any specific area.

Most HDPE is recycled back into bottles or similar containers. Unfortunately, because the color of recycled HDPE cannot be controlled, the bottles containing some percentage of it are still covered with a layer of virgin plastic.

Other end products from recycled HDPE include many of the nesting recycling containers used in curbside recycling programs, as well as flowerpots and traffic cones.

Vinyl

Vinyl comprises 5 percent of plastic packaging. Vinyl bottles can look quite similar to those made of PET; they are also transparent but a bit less rigid and are often used to package cooking oil, water, and shampoo. The more specific name for this plastic is polyvinyl chloride, or PVC. Water pipes, garden hoses, credit cards, and shower curtains are among the many products made of PVC.

Vinyl is clear when molded, but unlike PET, a white crease will appear where it is folded. The difference is critical, for the inclusion of even a few vinyl bottles in a batch of PET can destroy recycling equipment. When vinyl gets too hot, it produces hydrochloric acid, which eats away any chrome that might be present. When collecting clear plastic bottles for recycling, it is important to double-check for the code numbers 1 or 3.

It is not easy to find recycling programs that will accept vinyl at this time. Some recycled vinyl can be made into mats for use in truck trailers, auto interiors, and weight rooms.

Low-Density Polyethylene (LDPE)

LDPE comprises 33 percent of plastic packaging. Products made of LDPE include shrink-wrap, dry cleaner bags, plastic sandwich bags, and some plastic grocery bags.

Technically, plastic bags can be recycled in a closed-loop system, bags-to-bags, and some recycling programs do accept them. But most LDPE is thrown away, making up 40 percent of our plastic trash.

Sticky "cling" wraps are not LDPE and are not recyclable because of the ingredient that causes them to stick.

Polypropylene (PP)

PP comprises 9 percent of plastic packaging. Although it is technically possible to recycle PP, it is difficult to find a program that will accept it. Of the 3.5 million tons used each year in the United States, only about 1 percent is being recycled.

PP is the material used to make most plastic tops and lids for containers. Other products made of PP include maple syrup bottles, automotive battery casings, and disposable diaper linings.

When it is accepted for recycling, PP is usually mixed with other resins and made into such items as squeegies and road marker reflectors.

Polystyrene (PS)

PS comprises 11 percent of plastic packaging. Polystyrene may be one of the most controversial plastics around due to its connection with chlorofluorocarbons (CFCs), chemicals notorious for their large role in the destruction of the Earth's protective ozone layer. The U.S. foam food service packaging industry voluntarily stopped using fully halogenated CFCs in 1988.

PS also received a great deal of publicity when McDonald's Corporation decided to discontinue both using and recycling it after study and consultation with the Environmental Defense Fund.

Polystyrene is manufactured in two forms: foam and rigid. The foam is often called by Dow Chemical's trade name of "Styrofoam,"™ but its correct generic name is polystyrene foam. In this form, polystyrene is injected with gases in order to puff it up. CFCs were originally used for this purpose, but today, either pentane or HCFC-22 is used, both of which still contribute to atmospheric problems.

Polystyrene foam is commonly found in packing "peanuts," coffee cups, carry-out food boxes, and insulating materials. The rigid form is found in some yogurt and sour cream tubs, as well as salad bar carry-out containers. To determine if a product is polystyrene, look for the code number 6 on the bottom of the item.

Recycled PS can be made into videocassette tape boxes, combs, reusable cafeteria trays, license plate frames, trash cans, notepad and desk calendar holders, flying discs, rulers, and yo-yos. It is not made back into cups or packaging and therefore is not recycled in a closed-loop system. This means that even if all the PS used was being recycled, production of virgin PS would not be affected in the least and the same amount of raw materials and toxic wastes would be produced.

Other Plastics ♳

Miscellaneous plastics comprise 4 percent of plastic packaging. Some of these plastics contain a mixture of the resins discussed earlier; others are made of entirely different resins.

The latest process by which mixed resins are recycled was developed around 1990 by the Center for Plastics Recycling Research at Rutgers University and is known as ET-1. The end product of the ET-1 mixed plastics recycling process is a plastic lumber that can be used structurally like wood but is immune to damage from water, chemicals, bacteria, insects, and rodents. It does not conduct electricity, does not rust, and will not splinter or split. However, this technology is not in use over a wide geographic area.

When recycling programs do accept these mixed resin products, they are usually reprocessed into items such as curb stops, traffic barriers, fencing, park benches, playground equipment, and docks and piers.

Paper

Paper Facts

- Every year, Americans use more than 75 million tons of paper and paperboard products (about 600 pounds per person).
- Currently, the United States recycles about 20 million tons of paper annually.
- Every day, U.S. businesses generate enough paper to encircle the Earth 20 times.
- Approximately 70 percent of office trash is recyclable waste paper.
- The paper industry is the single largest user of fuel oil in the United States.
- Manufacturing recycled paper uses up to 64 percent less energy than manufacturing virgin paper.
- Manufacturing recycled paper reduces water pollution by 35 percent.
- Manufacturing recycled paper reduces air pollution by 74 percent.

- Manufacturing recycled paper uses 58 percent less water.
- The collection and recycling of paper provides five times as many jobs as the harvesting of virgin timber.
- Every ton of paper that gets recycled saves approximately 17 trees.
- Every ton of paper that gets recycled keeps 60 pounds of pollutants out of the air.
- Every ton of paper that gets recycled saves 4,100 kilowatt hours (enough energy to heat the average home for six months).
- Manufacturing one ton of recycled paper uses 7,000 gallons less water than manufacturing one ton of paper from virgin pulp.
- Each year, Americans throw away enough office and writing paper to build a wall 12 feet high, stretching from New York City to Los Angeles.
- The average office worker throws away about 180 pounds of high-grade paper (white bond and computer paper) every year.
- Paper comprises about 40 percent of the volume in U.S. landfills.
- Americans make about 750,000 photocopies every minute of every day.
- The average 100-person company uses about 378,000 sheets of copier paper per year, an amount that would make a stack about seven stories high.
- By photocopying on both sides of a piece of paper, paper usage can be cut by 50 percent.
- One pulp tree can produce about 12.5 reams of paper.
- Thermographic (shiny) FAX paper is not recyclable.
- If everyone who owns a FAX machine used a half-page cover sheet instead of a full page, the United States could save about 2 million miles of unrecyclable FAX paper in one year.
- If one out of every ten FAX users switched to a plain-paper FAX machine, we could save 500,000 miles of paper each year.
- In a recycling program, white paper is worth more than colored.
- Each ton of paper that gets recycled saves 3.3 cubic yards of landfill space.
- The U.S. scrap paper industry handles enough paper and cardboard each year to make 26 million pizza boxes.

Making and Recycling Paper

The technology used to manufacture recycled paper is one of the oldest in the recycling industry. Indeed, paper produced from recycled textile fiber was the only kind of paper available in the United States from 1690 to the mid-nineteenth century.

Then the demand for paper rose so sharply that there was not enough recycled fiber to supply the industry. Paper producers therefore created a technology to use wood pulp from trees to supplement their fiber needs. Eventually, wood fiber became the material of choice for papermaking because of its strength, and it supplanted the use of recycled fibers.

All paper is made in essentially the same way, whether it is recycled or not. It is made of pulp, a mixture of pulverized plant fibers and water. In the United States, most virgin pulp (that is, pulp that does not contain recycled fibers) is made from the wood of trees harvested specifically for this purpose. Once the trees have been chopped, shredded, and mixed with water to make pulp, the paper-making process begins.

There are two basic types of commercial papermaking facilities: the paper mill and the board mill. In a paper mill, the pulp is placed in a head box that controls the amount of fiber that is distributed onto a wire screen. This screen, which can be hundreds of feet long, skims through the head box, catching and holding the fibers from the pulp while allowing the water to drain away. The wire screen travels a complicated path, taking the relatively uniform layer of fibers through a series of rollers that squeeze out the excess moisture. When most of the moisture has been removed, the fibers have become pressed into a continuous sheet of paper. This sheet is passed through more hot rollers that remove the last traces of moisture, and the paper is collected into huge rolls to be sent to buyers.

In a board mill, the process is similar, but instead of using a head box to distribute pulp fibers, a number of cylinders below the wire screen deliver the fibers to the wire. A board mill can add to or decrease the number of cylinders, depending on the thickness and color desired in the finished product. For instance, to make the type of paperboard found in a cereal box, several cylinders of unbleached, brown-gray pulp make up most of the layers, and the final cylinder holds bleached, white fibers that form the top layer, which will later contain printing.

The major difference between virgin and recycled papers is the pulp. Virgin paper is made from virgin pulp, processed directly from trees. Recycled paper is made from recycled paper pulp, which is made by mixing the collected paper with water and mechanically beating the mixture in a hydropulper (a machine similar to a giant blender) until the fibers are once again separated.

Another difference in the manufacturing of some recycled papers is the de-inking process. Newspaper that has been collected from consumers in recycling programs is covered, for the most part, with printing inks. And before the fibers from these papers can be reprocessed into new paper, the ink must be removed.

Until the relatively recent resurgence of interest in using recycled paper products, the few de-inking plants that were on line in the United States were just sufficient to handle the available supplies of recycled paper. Now that recycling has become popular and collection programs have grown so successfully, there is much more paper than these facilities can handle.

The glut of newspaper is the reason why the buy-back prices for this product dropped so precipitously in the late 1980s and have remained low: There is simply more newspaper being collected than can be de-inked and reprocessed at the moment. In addition, the current demand for recycled paper is not high enough to encourage investors to risk their capital on the expensive venture of de-inking plants.

However, with the advent of legislation in several states that requires certain percentages of recycled fibers to be used by newspapers, a number of de-inking plants are under construction and should begin operating in the near future.

By manufacturing paper from recycled fibers, the need for virgin pulp can be greatly reduced. However, this pulp is not likely to be totally eliminated from papermaking because paper fibers can only be recycled a finite number of times. Each time they are recycled, they are cut or broken down a bit more, and shorter fibers create papers with less strength and lower quality. For this reason, most recycled paper still contains either some virgin pulp fibers or fibers derived from waste paper with longer fibers.

What Is Recycled Paper?

Distinctions between grades of recycled paper are based on fiber content. Some brands are labeled "100 percent recycled paper" but contain only preconsumer waste. This is waste generated from the mill broke, or leftover scraps of a papermaking plant; the material has never been used by a consumer.

Other "100 percent recycled paper" brands contain a certain percentage of preconsumer waste fibers as well as postconsumer waste fibers, generated from paper that has been used by consumers and collected in a recycling program. Interestingly, board mills have always made paperboard from 100 percent recycled fibers, both pre- and postconsumer, and they do not de-ink. Thus, printing the "recycled" symbol on paperboard products is a marketing tool geared toward the modern "green" consumer.

At this time, the term recycled paper has no specific, legally binding definition. The National Recycling Coalition and the EPA are continuing to work on the issue, but it is a highly controversial one in the paper industry. Although there are specific EPA guidelines on recycled paper, they apply only to purchases made with federal monies.

The EPA guidelines concerning printing and writing papers recommend that a paper contain at least 50 percent wastepaper in order to be considered recycled. The definition of wastepaper, however, is quite broad, including both pre- and postconsumer wastes. In some instances, the inclusion of fiber made from sawdust qualifies as recycled content.

For anyone other than federally funded agencies, paper that is labeled as recycled can contain pre- or postconsumer waste in any imaginable quantities. For this reason, many states are creating their own guidelines for recycled paper procurement, based on specified amounts of each type of fiber. (These state guidelines are outlined in Chapter 5.) This is a confusing and debilitating problem for the paper industry because almost any paper can be called "recycled" according to one definition or another. As a result, manufacturing recycled paper to encompass every purchaser's specifications has become a difficult business.

Collecting Paper for Recycling

For all practical purposes, any paper good that can be made from virgin fibers can also be made from recycled fibers. Among the products manufactured from recycled paper and paperboard collected from consumers are corrugated boxes, newspaper, printing and writing papers, greeting cards, tissues, paper towels, cereal boxes, beer cartons, tissue boxes, insulation, acoustic ceiling tiles, gypsum wallboard, flooring, egg cartons and fruit trays, cement bags, shoe boxes, and grocery sacks. However, collecting the types of paper necessary to make these products can be confusing.

There are many different kinds and grades of scrap paper (at least 51 regular grades and 33 specialty grades, according to the Institute of Scrap Recycling Industries), but they can all be broadly categorized into two varieties depending on the type of fibers they contain: groundwood and free sheet.

Groundwood

Groundwood is the cheapest and most plentiful of the paper types. It includes paper made from fibers that have been manufactured solely by mechanical action, with no chemicals involved. Because no chemicals are used, groundwood contains a naturally occurring substance, normally found in trees, called lignin.

Lignin is the ingredient responsible for making paper turn yellow and brittle with age. It is also the easiest substance for paper recyclers to test for when they are trying to determine a particular paper's grade. By using the acid phloroglucinol, which reacts to the presence of lignin by turning purple, one can determine whether a paper contains groundwood fibers. This test is often referred to as the "acid test."

Because of its lignin content, groundwood paper is generally used for printed materials that are not meant to be stored in archives but are intended to be used briefly and then discarded.

Some groundwood paper is coated, and some is sold uncoated. Uncoated groundwood is used in the majority of newspapers in the United States. Coated groundwood, which has a shiny surface layer of clay (usually Georgia Kaolin clay) to improve its printing surface, is most often found in magazines and catalogs.

Free Sheet

Free sheet paper is made of fibers that have been chemically treated to remove all lignin. This type of paper can be further categorized as unbleached and bleached, according to how the fibers are treated.

Unbleached free sheet refers to paper that is free of lignin but has not been whitened or lightened from its natural brown color. This is the type of paper most often found in corrugated cardboard boxes and grocery sacks.

In bleached free sheet, the fibers have been chemically lightened and whitened either with chlorine or with hydrogen peroxide. It is noteworthy that more and more paper manufacturers are switching away from the chlorine-bleaching method because of the environmental and health hazards associated with the chemical dioxin, a toxic by-product of the chlorine-bleaching process. European countries no longer buy paper products that have been bleached with chlorine.

Most of the paper that is used for printing is a variety of bleached free sheet, which can be further broken down into two more categories—uncoated and coated—according to whether the paper is coated with a substance meant to improve its printing surface. Coatings make a paper smoother so that it will pick up inks more neatly. Coated, bleached free sheet is generally smooth, shiny, and more rigid than magazine paper; it is often used for printing high-quality brochures and posters.

The paper grades most commonly recycled by consumers include Sorted White Ledger #40, Computer Printout (CPO) #42, Groundwood CPO #25, Newspaper #8, and Corrugated #11. Together, they form a very large proportion of the paper recycled by the general public in curbside, buy-back, and office paper recycling programs.

As with other recyclable products, paper collected for recycling must be free of contaminants. It must also be free of other grades of paper whose fibers will contaminate the recycled paper products to be made. These contaminating grades of paper are called out-throws. Descriptions of the major paper grades, together with their commonly occurring contaminants and out-throws, follows. Local recycling centers or scrap paper buyers should be consulted for other specifications that may exist.

Sorted White Ledger #40

This is a high-grade paper that is free sheet, bleached, and uncoated. It is the type of paper usually found in offices as bond, xerographic, and 9 1/2 by 11-inch white, fanfold computer paper. It is acceptable for recycling with either impact printing (from a typewriter or ink printer) or laser printing on it, as well as pencil, xerographic carbon, and other writing inks. It may have staples or paper clips attached, but it cannot have crayon on it.

Common contaminants include glass, plastic, metals, foils, carbon paper, non-water-soluble adhesives, tape, self-sticking notes, food, candy wrappers, coffee grounds, and assorted other "trash."

Out-throws include colored paper, coated and chemically treated paper (including ream wrappers and "no carbon required," or NCR, paper), CPO, groundwood CPO, manila file folders, newspaper, and cardboard.

Computer Printout (CPO) #42

This is another high-grade paper that is free sheet, bleached, and uncoated. It is fanfold computer printing paper and generally has pastel-colored horizontal bars (most often green). This paper is typically used with larger-than-letter-size computer printers. It is acceptable for recycling when printed or written on in ink or pencil, but it cannot be printed on with a laser printer or with crayon.

Contaminants are the same as those for sorted white ledger, but for CPO, paper clips and staples are also considered to be contaminants.

Out-throws include sorted white ledger paper, colored paper, coated and chemically treated paper, groundwood CPO, manila file folders, newspaper, and cardboard.

Groundwood CPO #25

This is a low-grade paper that basically looks like CPO but contains groundwood. In better quality brands, it is virtually indistinguishable from CPO #42. For this reason, the acid test is used to determine its identity. It is acceptable if impact or laser printed, but it must not be colored with crayon.

Contaminants are the same as for CPO #42.

Out-throws include sorted white ledger paper, colored paper, coated and chemically treated paper, CPO, manila file folders, newspaper, and cardboard.

Newspaper #8

This is another low-grade, groundwood, uncoated paper that has been printed on and is used by most U.S. newspapers. For recycling, the glossy, colored inserts (Sunday magazines, coupons, and advertising pages) that are delivered inside the paper may be included. But newspaper that has become yellowed by age or sunlight should be excluded because the chemical reaction in the lignin within the paper fibers, which is responsible for the color change, degrades the paper.

Contaminants are the same as for CPO #42.

Out-throws include paper grocery sacks, plastic delivery bags, sorted white ledger paper, colored paper other than inserts, coated paper other than inserts, CPO, groundwood CPO, manila file folders, cardboard, telephone directories, mail-order catalogs, magazines, and junk mail. Some recycling programs and scrap paper buyers will accept a limited amount of groundwood CPO with newspaper, but local recycling programs should be consulted for more information.

Old Corrugated Containers (OCC) #11

This is a low-grade, free sheet, unbleached, and uncoated paper. Commonly called "corrugated cardboard," it is often used to make boxes. It is distinguished from other cardboards by its three-layered composition: two outer liner layers, with the wavy medium layer sandwiched between them.

Contaminants include plastic, glass, metals, foils, carbon paper, food, coffee grounds, and assorted other trash.

Out-throws include paper grocery sacks, sorted white ledger paper, colored paper, CPO, groundwood CPO, manila file folders, noncorrugated cardboard (such as beer cartons, shoe boxes, and cereal boxes), telephone directories, mail-order catalogs, magazines, and junk mail. Some recycling programs and scrap paper buyers will accept brown paper grocery bags with OCC, but local recycling programs should be consulted for more information.

Other Papers

Used brown kraft #15, another type of paper most consumers are likely to be familiar with, is collected for recycling in some areas. Like OCC, this paper is low grade, free sheet, unbleached, and uncoated. It is primarily found in brown paper grocery bags, which are often collected for reprocessing after being used by the consumer. As with other paper grades, very little contamination is permissible.

Another common grade of paper that most of the public would like to recycle is coated groundwood, which is most often found in magazines. However, at this time, few programs will accept magazines for recycling because when this type of paper is repulped, it produces more clay than paper fiber. But new technologies are starting to come on line that use clay in the de-inking process known as flotation de-inking. As facilities using the flotation method become more widespread, it is possible that recycling programs will find markets for magazines and similar types of paper.

A common contaminant in many paper grades is non-water-soluble adhesive. This includes hot glue, self-stick labels, pressure-sensitive labels and closures, and all self-stick tapes. These contaminants are called "stickies" by the scrap paper industry.

Stickies are one of the most costly contaminants in recyclable paper. Their presence is destructive in two ways: (1) They can clog the pulp preparation cleaning equipment because they normally do not dissolve in water, and (2) if the water is hot enough, they may dissolve, only to solidify later in the papermaking process, causing the paper to stick to the wire or to itself as it is being rolled, causing rips and tears.

Due to the fine distinctions between paper grades, it is imperative that anyone establishing a recycling program consult local markets for contamination specifications. Additionally, the people who are actually collecting the paper must be taught to distinguish between contaminating grades and acceptable ones. Without this knowledge, many paper recycling programs fail because it is too expensive for haulers and recycling processors to separate out the trash.

Metal

Scrap Metals Facts

- In 1988, approximately 9 million old cars were recycled in the United States, exceeding the number of new cars produced by U.S. automakers in that same year.
- Each year, Americans abandon 3 million cars.
- Aluminum was worth more than gold when it was first discovered.
- Americans throw out enough steel and iron to continually supply all the nation's automakers.
- Operating at full capacity, the U.S. scrap industry has the capacity to process 140 million tons of iron and steel annually.
- Domestic and foreign steel mills purchased only 60 million tons of ferrous scrap in recent years.
- Steel made from scrap is chemically and metallurgically equivalent to steel made from virgin ore.
- More than half of all steel manufactured in the United States today is made of recycled material.
- Recycling ferrous metals saves 74 percent of the energy used to make them from iron ore and coal.
- Making steel from scrap saves 90 percent of the virgin, nonrenewable materials used in making steel from ore.
- Recycling steel and iron reduces air pollution by 86 percent.
- Recycling steel and iron uses 40 percent less water.
- Recycling steel and iron produces 76 percent less water pollution.
- Recycling steel and iron reduces mining wastes by 96 percent.

- It takes four times as much energy to make steel from virgin iron ore as it does to make it from scrap.
- At current landfill tipping fee rates, recycled steel saves the United States over $2 billion per year in solid waste disposal costs.
- The amount of steel recycled each year equals about one-third of all the municipal solid waste that is landfilled.
- Products manufactured from recycled steel and iron, virgin ore, or a combination of the two will perform identically.
- The U.S. scrap industry reprocesses enough copper each year to make 360,000,000,000,000 pennies.
- Every year, the U.S. scrap industry handles enough stainless steel to make 11 billion spoons.
- The U.S. scrap industry annually recycles enough aluminum to make siding for 8 million homes.

Making and Recycling Metals

Scrap metals can be divided into two basic categories: ferrous and nonferrous. Ferrous metals contain iron ore, and magnets are attracted to them. Iron and steel are ferrous metals. Nonferrous metals contain little or no iron and thus have no magnetic properties. Copper, aluminum, silver, and gold are nonferrous metals.

When metals are manufactured from virgin materials, the process is, in broad outline, similar to the process for manufacturing aluminum. Basically, the ore is mined, refined, melted in a furnace, and cast into ingots to be bought by processors who will make new products. When scrap metals are collected for recycling, they are generally crushed, shredded, melted and re-refined, and poured into ingots.

There are three types of scrap metal that can be recycled: (1) obsolete or old scrap, composed of metals that have been used by a consumer, such as old cars and ships, can openers, and electrical wire; (2) industrial scrap (also known as new or prompt scrap), which is scrap produced by the manufacturing process, such as metal filings and leftover stampings from making appliance parts; and (3) home scrap, which consists of the leftover metals that steel mills and foundries produce while manufacturing new products. Home scrap is generally returned to the on-site furnace to be remelted, without ever leaving the plant.

Because metals can be remelted, re-refined, and reprocessed indefinitely without losing their required characteristics, most scrap metal is recycled into products similar to the ones originally made from virgin materials. Metals recycling is one of the most efficient ways to conserve nonrenewable natural resources.

Ferrous Metals

Ferrous metals include iron, which is produced from the refining of iron ore, and steel, which is produced when carbon and sometimes other elements are added to iron. Different grades of steel result from varying the amount of carbon. Steel is the most widely used metal alloy in the world.

Most ferrous scrap is bought by dealer/processors from the industry and general public and is torched, cut, baled, or shredded for further handling. Brokers then assist the dealer/processors in finding markets for their materials. They also help scrap consumers by locating sources for the metals they require. Finally, the consumers—mills or foundries—purchase the processed scrap and remelt it to produce their new products.

Nonferrous Metals

Aluminum, as discussed earlier, is produced by refining bauxite ore. It has been made in commercial quantities for less than 100 years, and yet it is consumed worldwide in amounts second only to steel. It has a high strength-to-weight ratio, weighing about one-third as much as steel or copper, and as such, it is suited to aircraft, ships, and automobiles. Primary sources of obsolete aluminum scrap include beverage cans, cars, aircraft, appliances, furniture, and electric utilities.

Copper, produced by refining copper ore, was first used around 8000 B.C. as a substitute for stone. Currently, it is widely employed for its chemical stability, its electrical and thermal conductivity, and its malleability. Many common alloys are made from copper: Brass, for example, is a copper alloy containing zinc as its principal alloying element, and bronze is copper alloyed with tin and zinc. Major sources of copper scrap include car radiators, pipes and other plumbing fixtures, telephone and electrical wire and cables, electric motors, and ammunition shell cases.

Lead is primarily produced by refining galena sulfide, or lead glance. It is widely used for its low electrical conductivity, its ability to absorb shortwave electromagnetic radiation, and its general chemical resistance. This last quality is the reason why the largest use of lead is in the manufacture of storage batteries. Today, lead is the most recycled metal, measured as a percentage of the virgin product that is reprocessed. However, because of its toxicity, not all recycling programs are equipped to handle lead safely. The major source of obsolete lead is scrapped automotive batteries.

There are many other grades and varieties of nonferrous metals, and aluminum, lead, and copper, along with the copper alloys of brass and bronze, have many subgrades.

A nonferrous scrap metals dealer must have a thorough knowledge of metals in order to properly identify what a recycler is selling as scrap and what a consumer requires for manufacturing. After identifying and sorting scrap components, the dealer/processor prepares the scrap and packs it for shipping according to the requirements of the consumer who will be using it. It may be baled, packed in boxes or drums, or even shipped loose in trucks or railroad cars.

For the average recycler, metals recycling can be either simple or complicated, according to local markets. There are many grades of recyclable metals, and, as with paper recycling, different markets have different specifications. Local recycling programs and scrap metals dealers should be consulted for appropriate requirements in any given locale.

Miscellaneous Recyclable Products

As public awareness about environmental issues increases and industries respond with advancing technologies, more and more products can be recycled. What follows are brief discussions of some materials that are being accepted for recycling in limited areas of the United States.

Used Oil

Americans dump an amount of waste oil equivalent to at least 25 *Exxon Valdez* oil spills each year. But motor oil is a lubricant that can be re-refined over and over again, and if all the motor oil now being thrown away in the United States were recycled, it could save the country 1.3 million barrels of oil per day. Besides saving oil, recycling this waste can keep groundwater supplies significantly cleaner—one pint of oil poured down a storm drain or gutter can create a one-acre oil slick when it reaches the nearest stream, pond, or harbor.

Local recycling facilities, EPA regional offices, and state solid waste offices are reliable sources of information about waste oil recycling in specific areas. Many programs that accept waste oil for recycling charge $.10 to $.25 per gallon to cover their expenses.

Household Hazardous Waste (HHW)

Products considered to be household hazardous waste include used motor oil as well as most brands of paints and thinners, antifreeze, toilet bowl cleaners, drain openers, household bug sprays and other pesticides, nail polish, mothballs, batteries, and oven cleaners.

Every U.S. family produces approximately 15 pounds of HHW each year, most of which is disposed of improperly down drains or in landfills. But as communities become increasingly aware of the problem, more programs are being developed to collect HHW for recycling, exchange, or proper handling and disposal.

Latex paints, used oil, and antifreeze are the HHWs most commonly collected for recycling. In addition, most HHW programs stress the importance of not generating the waste in the first place by using nontoxic alternative products or buying only small quantities of the toxic products so that they will be used in their entirety, with no excess left for disposal.

Reliable sources of information on local HHW collection programs include regional EPA offices, state health departments, and recycling facilities.

Batteries

There are two basic categories of batteries produced in the United States: automobile batteries and household batteries. Automobile batteries are lead-acid batteries, and there are numerous recycling programs throughout the country designed to handle this commodity, including national programs conducted by Sears and Walmart. Currently, about 80 percent of U.S. auto batteries are recycled; the remainder, containing approximately 330 million pounds of lead, end up in landfills.

When car batteries are recycled, they are cracked open and the components are removed. The lead is recycled, and the sulfuric acid may either be reprocessed or sent to a hazardous waste disposal facility.

Household batteries are not being recycled on a widespread basis at this time. This category includes the following types of batteries: alkaline, carbon-zinc, nickel-cadmium, zinc-air, mercuric oxide, silver oxide, and lithium. Some of these are standard flashlight-type, cylindrical batteries; others are the button types used in cameras, hearing aids, watches, and calculators.

Although household batteries compose only about .005 percent by weight of the U.S. waste stream, they account for over 50 percent of the mercury and cadmium (both toxic metals) found in our trash. Recycling programs that accept batteries are often limited to the button types, from which mercury and silver may be recovered.

Local sources of reliable information about battery recycling programs include EPA regional offices, state offices of solid waste, HHW programs, and recycling facilities.

Tires

About 250 million tires are thrown out every year in the United States. They are difficult to dispose of because the methane produced in landfills collects in the hollow inner area of the tires, causing them to "float" up to the surface. As a result, many landfills refuse to accept whole tires, and they end up being stockpiled in veritable mountains that create fire hazards to surrounding communities.

In 1989, about 2.5 million tires were recycled into a paving surface of combined rubber and asphalt. Currently, the most common way that tires are recycled in the United States is through retreading: About 20 percent of the tires made in the United States are now being retreaded.

Other tire recycling programs shred and grind the tires to recover the two major components: (1) rubber and (2) steel wires and threads. The rubber can then be remanufactured into products such as trailer flooring, carpet padding, and boat bumpers. Some companies shred tires to use them as fuel, for the high petroleum content makes tires a relatively cheap source of energy. A few enterprising businesspeople are even making fashion accessories and shoes out of used tires.

Food and Yard Wastes

Food and yard wastes are major components of U.S. landfills, with yard wastes composing approximately 20 percent of all solid waste. Composting, the aerobic (oxygen dependent) process by which plant and other organic wastes decompose under controlled conditions, is among the most natural recycling processes on Earth—the same basic process by which dead leaves, grasses, and animals decompose in the wild. When humans compost, however, they generally mix wastes in order to speed up the process, producing humus, a rich, crumbly type of soil.

In areas of the United States where moisture is plentiful, some municipal compost operations are thriving, but in more arid areas, there is less interest in this process. Many municipalities are encouraging homeowners to compost in their own backyards, as opposed to running a communitywide collection and composting program.

Local regional offices of the EPA as well as state extension services and recycling facilities can offer advice and expertise on how to compost. The periodical *BioCycle* concentrates many of its issues on municipal composting technologies and programs.

Polycoated Paper Packaging

Among the new products just beginning to enter the public recycling arena are polycoated paper packages, particularly milk cartons and aseptic juice boxes. Manufacturers of these products, competing with the rest of the beverage packaging industry, are starting to promote their products as recyclable. At this time, however, there is only one reprocessor, located in Washington State, that is capable of hydropulping the containers and separating the plastic and aluminum components from the paper fibers.

Manufacturers of polycoated paper packages claim that recycling their products is both a boon to source reduction efforts and an energy-efficient process. Environmentalists, on the other hand, claim that the manufacturers are simply trying to sell the containers to stay in business and that this particular recycling process is far from energy efficient.

White Goods

White goods include large appliances, such as water heaters, refrigerators, and clothes washers and dryers. In the past, these items were handled by scrap metals dealers who shredded and sold them. But when the EPA banned polychlorinated biphenyls, or PCBs, in 1979, scrap dealers were no longer so eager to collect white goods because the motors were likely to contain these deadly chemicals.

Currently, many trash hauling companies either pick up white goods for recycling for a fee (usually around $10) or offer programs at transfer stations that accept dropped-off white goods. Local recyclers, scrap metals dealers, or transfer stations should be consulted for specific information.

Laser Print Cartridges

It has been estimated that by 1993, the United States will be using approximately 34 million laser cartridges and throwing away more than 28 million of them every year. But a cartridge can be cleaned and refilled at a significant saving over the cost of a new one.

A local computer company that sells these cartridges can offer information on recycling them. Many large recycling companies, such as Recycle America, also have markets for these items.

Dry Wall

Canagro Agricultural Products, Ltd., which manufactures organic fertilizers in Elmira, Ontario, began successfully recycling drywall gypsum into fertilizer, cat litter, and livestock bedding in 1989.

Toilets

In Santa Barbara County, California, old porcelain toilets received at landfills are crushed and reused in roadway paving projects.

Telephone Directories

Until fairly recently, hot glue bindings, poor-quality ground-wood pages, and different grade of cover stock have combined to make phone books a difficult recycling proposition. However, due to pressure from consumers, many manufacturers of telephone directories are now offering recycling programs for their old books and are producing new directories from recycled paper. One program in New York composts the shredded books with sawdust and beer sludge from Anheuser-Busch. In other programs, directory manufacturers combine forces with local trash haulers to provide drop-off locations for the directories, which will be recycled into new paper after the bindings have been removed. The publishers of US WEST Direct expect to have a paper mill in Washington State recycle their old phone books into paper stock for new directories in the near future.

Compact Discs (CDs)

The largest manufacturer of CDs in the United States, Digital Audio Disk Corporation, is currently investigating a technology to recycle CDs in its plant in Terre Haute, Indiana. There, discs that have been rejected from the factory are recycled into the trays in which CDs are packaged.

Sources

Aluminum Association, The. *Aluminum Recycling: America's Environmental Success Story.* Washington, DC: The Aluminum Association, 1990.

American Paper Institute, Inc. *Paper Recycling and Its Role in Solid Waste Management.* New York: API, 1990.

———. *12 Facts about Waste Paper Recycling.* New York: API, 1990.

Apotheker, Steve. "Glass Containers: How Recyclable Will They Be in the 1990s?" *Resource Recycling* 10 (June 1991): 25–32.

———. "Office Paper Recycling: Collection Trends." *Resource Recycling* 10 (November 1991): 44–52.

Ball, Doug. "Recycled Phone Books Find Home in Brewery Sludge." *BioCycle* 31 (November 1991): 62.

Calem, Robert E. "Recycling the Proliferating Disk." *New York Times* (12 January 1992).

Council for Solid Waste Solutions, The. *The Facts about Plastics.* Washington, DC: Society of the Plastics Industry, 1990.

Davis, Alan, and Kinsella, Susan. "Recycled Paper: Exploding the Myths." *GARBAGE* 2 (May/June 1990): 48–54.

EarthWorks Group, The. *The Recycler's Handbook.* Berkeley, CA.: EarthWorks Press, 1990.

———. *50 Simple Things You Can Do to Save the Earth.* Berkeley, CA.: EarthWorks Press, 1989.

———. *50 Simple Things Your Business Can Do to Save the Earth.* Berkeley, CA: EarthWorks Press, 1991.

Environmental Action, eds. "Recycling Plastics: A Forum." *Environmental Action* (July/August 1988): 21–25.

Environmental Defense Fund. *Recycle. It's the Everyday Way to Save the World.* Washington, DC: EDF, 1990.

Environmental Protection Agency. *Yard Waste Composting: A Study of Eight Programs.* Washington, DC: EPA, 1989.

Erkenswick, Jane L. "Office Paper Recycling: A Look at the Ledger Grades." *Resource Recycling* 10 (November 1991): 64–68.

Glass Packaging Institute. *Americans Prefer Glass.* Washington, DC: GPI, 1990.

————. *Package to Package and Glass to Glass: The Perfect Closed Cycle System.* Washington, DC: GPI, 1990.

Institute of Scrap Recycling Industries. *Recycling Nonferrous Scrap Metals.* Washington, DC: ISRI, 1990.

————. *Recycling Paper.* Washington, DC: ISRI, 1990.

————. *Recycling Scrap Iron and Steel.* Washington, DC: ISRI, 1990.

————. *Scrap Specifications Circular/Guidelines for Paper Stock: PS-90, Domestic Transactions.* Washington, DC: ISRI, 1990.

Logsdon, Gene. "Agony and Ecstasy of Tire Recycling." *BioCycle* 30 (July 1990): 44–85.

Luoma, Jon R. "Trash Can Realities." *Audubon* 92 (March 1990): 86–97.

McEntee, Ken. "Office Paper Recycling: Boom or Bust?" *Resource Recycling* 10 (November 1991): 58–63.

National Association for Plastic Container Recovery. *Recycling PET: A Guidebook for Community Programs.* Charlotte, NC: NAPCOR, 1989.

National Recycling Coalition. *Recycled Paper Facts and Figures* (fact sheet). Washington, DC: NRC, 1990.

National Soft Drink Association. "Closing the Loop." *The Soft Drink Recycler* (Spring 1991): 1–2.

National Solid Wastes Management Association. *The Future of Newspaper Recycling.* Washington, DC: NSWMA, 1990.

————. *Recycling Solid Waste.* Washington, DC: NSWMA, 1990.

Porter, J. Winston. "Let's Go Easy on Recycling Plastics." *Philadelphia Inquirer* (6 August 1991).

Powell, Jerry, and McEntee, Ken. "Office Paper Recycling: Existing and Emerging Markets." *Resource Recycling* 10 (November 1991): 53–57.

Reutlinger, Nancy, and de Grassi, Dan. "Household Battery Recycling: Numerous Obstacles, Few Solutions." *Resource Recycling* 10 (April 1991): 24–29.

Steel Can Recycling Institute. *Recyclable Steel Cans: An Integral Part of Your Curbside Recycling Program.* Pittsburgh, PA: Steel Can Recycling Institute, 1990.

Thompson, Claudia G. *Recycled Papers: The Essential Guide.* Cambridge, MA: MIT Press, 1992.

U.S. Environmental Protection Agency. *Characterization of Municipal Solid Waste in the United States: 1990 Update, Executive Summary.* Washington, DC: USEPA, 1990. EPA/530-SW-90-042.

Wirka, Jeanne. "A Plastics Packaging Primer." *Environmental Action* (July/August 1988): 17–20.

5

State Laws and Regulations

THE ISSUE OF SOLID WASTE MANAGEMENT HAS GIVEN RISE to numerous state laws regarding recycling, many of which are described in this chapter. Because these laws vary widely in their force and language, the reader is advised to examine the actual statutes in their entirety for legal purposes.

Figures 5.1 through 5.3 and Tables 5.1 through 5.5 summarize current recycling legislation in the states and are provided courtesy of the National Solid Wastes Management Association. More detailed examinations of recycling legislation, in a state-by-state fashion, follow the tabled and charted information and are derived from the WESTLAW database. Federal laws are discussed in Chapter 1.

Figure 5-1
States Having Comprehensive Recycling Laws as of 31 December 1990

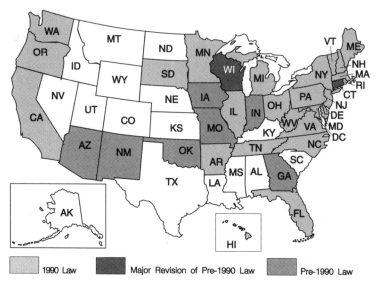

| ▨ 1990 Law | ▨ Major Revision of Pre-1990 Law | ▨ Pre-1990 Law |

Note: Comprehensive recycling laws require detailed statewide recycling plans and/or separation of recyclables and contain at least one other provision to stimulate recycling.

Source: Adapted from National Solid Wastes Management Association, *Recycling in the States 1990 Review,* Washington, DC: NSWMA, 1990.

Figure 5-2
Recycling Grants and Loans, by State

■ States that provide grants and loans for recycling

▨ States that provide grants for recycling

Source: Adapted from National Solid Wastes Management Association, *Recycling in the States 1990 Review,* Washington, DC: NSWMA, 1990.

Figure 5-3
Recycled Content Mandates, by State

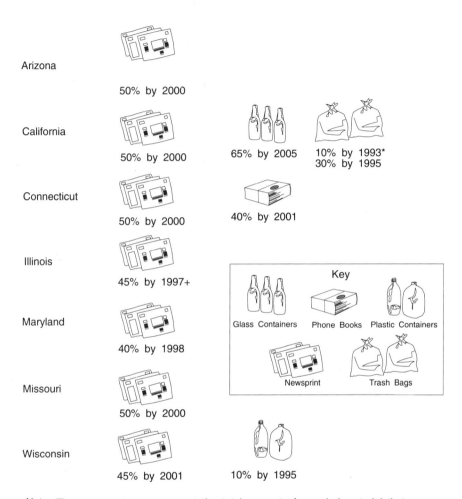

Arizona
50% by 2000

California
50% by 2000   65% by 2005   10% by 1993*
                                  30% by 1995

Connecticut
50% by 2000   40% by 2001

Illinois
45% by 1997+

Key

Glass Containers   Phone Books   Plastic Containers

Newsprint   Trash Bags

Maryland
40% by 1998

Missouri
50% by 2000

Wisconsin
45% by 2001   10% by 1995

Note: These percentages represent the total amount of recycled material that must be used. The required ratio of postconsumer to industrial scrap in recycled material varies in each state.

* The 10 percent goal applies to bags 1.0 mil thick: 30 percent goal applies to bags .75 mil thick.

+ The 45 percent goal by 1997 is a voluntary goal; the final mandatory goal is 28 percent by 1993.

Source: Adapted from National Solid Wastes Management Association, *Recycling in the States 1990 Review,* Washington, DC: NSWMA, 1990.

Table 5-1   Types of State Recycling Laws Through 1990

State	Year Enacted	Type of Plan
Arizona	1990	Opportunity to recycle only
Arkansas	1989	Recycling plans only
California	1989	Mandatory goals*
Connecticut	1990	Source separation
Delaware	1990	Opportunity to recycle only
District of Columbia	1989	Source separation
Florida	1988	Mandatory goals*; community separation
Georgia	1990	Community separation
Hawaii	1988	Opportunity to recycle only
Illinois	1988	Community separation
Indiana	1990	Recycling plans only
Iowa	1989	Recycling plans only
Maine	1989	Source separation+
Maryland	1988	Mandatory goals*; community separation
Massachusetts	1987	Recycling plans only
Michigan	1988	Recycling plans only
Minnesota	1989	Mandatory goals*; community separation
Missouri	1990	Recycling plans only
New Hampshire	1988	Recycling plans only
New Jersey	1987	Mandatory goals*; source separation
New Mexico	1990	Recycling plans only
New York	1988	Source separation
North Carolina	1989	Community separation
Ohio	1988	Mandatory goals*; community separation
Oklahoma	1990	Recycling plans only
Oregon	1983	Opportunity to recycle only
Pennsylvania	1988	Source separation
Rhode Island	1986	Mandatory goals*; source separation
Tennessee	1989	Recycling plans only
Vermont	1987	Recycling plans only
Virginia	1989	Mandatory goals*
Washington	1989	Community separation
West Virginia	1989	Recycling plans only
Wisconsin	1990	Community separation

* "Mandatory" can be subject to different interpretations.
+ For offices only.

Source: Adapted from National Solid Wastes Management Association, *Recycling in the States 1990 Review*, Washington, DC: NSWMA, 1990.

Table 5-2 States with Source Separation Requirements, 1990

State	Who Must Separate	Materials
District of Columbia	Residences, businesses	Glass containers, metal cans, newspapers, yard waste[*], paper[+]
Connecticut	All generators	Glass and metal food containers, newspaper, cardboard, office paper, used oil, car batteries, nickel-cadmium batteries, leaves, scrap metal
Maine	Businesses	Office paper, corrugated cardboard
New Jersey	Residences, businesses, institutions	Three materials[§] and leaves
New York	Residences, businesses, institutions	Paper, glass, metal cans, plastic containers, yard waste[**]
Pennsylvania	Residences	Three materials and leaves
	Businesses, institutions	High-grade office paper, corrugated cardboard, aluminum cans[++]
Rhode Island	Residences, businesses	Glass food and beverage containers, newspaper, tin and steel cans, aluminum, some plastics, large appliances
	Businesses	Cardboard, office paper
Washington	Urban areas	Materials to be determined in local plans

Note: This chart does not include separation requirements that only apply to state government agencies and institutions.

[*] Residential separation only.
[+] Separation by offices only.
[§] Municipalities choose three materials to be recycled from a state list.
[**] If "economically feasible."
[++] Municipalities may require businesses to separate additional recyclables.

Source: Adapted from National Solid Wastes Management Association, *Recycling in the States 1990 Review,* Washington, DC: NSWMA, 1990.

Table 5-3 States with Disposal Bans, 1990

State	Lead-Acid Batteries	Yard Waste	Unprocessed Tires	Used Oil	Large Appliances	Other
California	■					
Connecticut	■	*		■		A
District of Columbia				■		
Florida	■	+	■	■	■	B
Georgia	■					
Hawaii	■					
Illinois	■	■	■			
Iowa	■	■	■	■		C
Kansas	■		■			
Kentucky	■					
Louisiana	■		■	■	■	
Maine	■					
Massachusetts	■	■	■	■	■	D
Michigan	■	■		■		
Minnesota	■	■	■	■	■	E
Missouri	■	■	■	■	■	
New Hampshire	■					
New Jersey		*				
New York	■					
North Carolina	■	+	■	■	■	
Ohio	■	■	■			
Oregon	■		■			F
Pennsylvania	■	*				
Rhode Island			§			G
Tennessee	■					
Vermont	■		■	■	■	
Virginia	■					
Washington	■					
Wisconsin	■	■	**	**	■	H
Wyoming	■					

A. Nickel-cadmium batteries.

B. Construction and demolition debris.

C. Nondegradable grocery bags; beverage containers returned to wholesalers through the state's mandatory deposit law.

D. Aluminum, glass, and metal containers, single polymer plastics, and recyclable paper.

E. Dry-cell batteries that contain mercuric oxide electrodes, nickel-cadmium, or sealed lead-acid. Mixed unprocessed waste in metro area.

F. Recyclable material that has already been separated.

G. Loads of commercial waste containing more than 20 percent recyclables.

H. Nondegradable yard waste bags plus aluminum, plastic, steel and glass containers, cardboard foam polystyrene packaging, magazines, newspaper, and office paper are banned from disposal unless municipalities are certified as having an "effective" source separation program.

* Yard waste disposal bans only apply to leaves.

+ Ban applies to lined landfills only.

§ Banned only from incinerators.

** Can be incinerated with energy recovery.

Source: Adapted from National Solid Wastes Management Association, *Recycling in the States 1990 Review,* Washington, DC: NSWMA, 1990.

Table 5-4   Products Recycled in 1988

Product	Millions of Tons Recycled	Percent of Product Generated
Corrugated boxes	10.5	45.4
Newspapers	4.4	33.3
Office paper	1.6	22.5
Lead-acid batteries	1.5	90.0
Glass beer and soda bottles	1.1	20.0
Aluminum cans	0.8	55.0
Books and magazines	0.7	13.2
Junk mail	0.6	14.6
Compost	0.5	1.6
Steel food and beverage cans	0.4	13.8
Glass food containers	0.3	8.1
Folding cartons	0.3	7.7
Paper bags and sacks	0.2	7.0
Major appliances	0.2	7.0
Glass wine and spirits bottles	0.1	5.0
Plastic soft drink bottles	0.1	21.0
Rubber tires	0.1	4.8
Other	0.1	—
TOTAL	23.5	

Source: Adapted from *Characterization of Municipal Solid Waste in the United States,* prepared for the USEPA by Franklin Associates, Prairie Village, KS, 1990 (as reprinted in National Solid Wastes Management Association, *Recycling in the States 1990 Review,* Washington, DC: NSWMA, 1990).

Table 5-5 Tax Incentives for Recycling, by State

California—Banks and corporations may take 40 percent tax credit for the cost of equipment used to manufacture recycled products. Development bonds for manufacturing products with recycled materials.

Colorado—Individual and corporate income tax credits for investments in plastics recycling technology.

Florida—Sales tax exemption on recycling machinery purchased after 1 July 1988. Tax incentives to encourage affordable transportation of recycled goods from collection points to sites for processing and disposal.

Illinois—Sales tax exemptions for manufacturing equipment.

Indiana—Property tax exemptions for buildings, equipment, and land involved in converting waste into new products.

Iowa—Sales tax exemptions.

Kentucky—Property tax exemptions to encourage recycling industries.

Maine—Business tax credits equal to 30 percent of cost of recycling equipment and machinery. Subsidies to municipalities for scrap metal transportation costs. Taxpayers are also allowed a credit equal to $5 per ton of wood waste from lumber production that is incinerated for fuel or to generate energy. The total credit may not exceed 50 percent of the tax liability.

Maryland—From their state income taxes, individuals and corporations can deduct 100 percent of expenses incurred to convert a furnace to burn used oil or to buy and install equipment to recycle used freon.

New Jersey—Businesses may take a 50 percent investment credit for recycling vehicles and machinery, 6 percent sales tax exemption on purchases of recycling equipment.

North Carolina—Industrial and corporate income tax credits and exemptions for equipment and facilities.

Oregon—Individuals and corporations receive income tax credits for capital investment in recycling equipment and facilities. Special tax credits are available for equipment, property, or machinery necessary to collect, transport, or process reclaimed plastic.

Texas—Sludge recycling corporations are eligible for franchise tax exemptions.

Virginia—Individuals and corporations may take a tax credit worth 10 percent of the purchase price of any machinery and equipment for processing recyclable materials. The credit also applies to manufacturing plants that use recycled products.

Washington—Motor vehicles are exempt from rate regulation when transporting recovered materials from collection to reprocessing facilities and manufacturers. Tires and certain other hard-to-dispose materials are exempt from portions of sales and use taxes.

Wisconsin—Sales tax exemptions for waste reduction and recycling equipment and facilities; business property tax exemptions for some equipment.

Source: Adapted from National Solid Wastes Management Association, *Recycling in the States 1990 Review,* Washington, DC: NSWMA, 1990.

Alabama

- On 19 April 1990, Alabama mandated that, within 180 days, the Department of Environmental Management would "develop and implement a model program for the reduction and recycling of solid wastes within its own operations." This program was to include but was not limited to office papers, cardboard, yard waste, and "other materials produced by the state for which recycling markets exist or may be developed."
- Within one year after 19 April 1990, all state departments and agencies, as well as all public schools, were required to implement similar programs based on the model provided by the Department of Environmental Management. The Alabama Environmental Management Act states that the products to be recycled must include, at a minimum, both high-grade paper and corrugated paper. The act also authorizes state agencies and public schools to enter into contracts with private and nonprofit organizations to manage and sell or donate recyclable materials, as long as these materials are in fact "substantially recycled." Furthermore, any proceeds from the sale of recycled materials must be deposited back into the state treasury and credited to the agency that originally generated the recyclables.

SOURCE: State Code of Alabama 1975: Title 22, Subtitle 1, Chapter 22B (Recycling by State Agencies), s 22-22B-1 through s 22-22B-5.

Alaska

- When Alaska created and empowered its Department of Environmental Conservation in 1990, the department was directed to coordinate state efforts between public and private organizations with regard to recycling and litter control. Waste source reduction and the recycling of waste were established as the two top priorities when dealing with solid and hazardous waste, and a community solid waste management planning grant account was created within the state's general fund.
- In 1980, all state agencies were required to recycle at least paper, glass, and cans "to the greatest extent practicable."
- Beginning on 1 October 1981, all detachable, metal pull-tabs on nonglass beverage containers were prohibited. And on 1 January 1985, plastic six-pack rings and similar packaging devices were outlawed, unless they were demonstrably degradable and bore a distinguishing mark that designated them as such. Then, in 1990, a requirement was added stipulating that all plastic bottles or rigid plastic containers sold within the state must bear the plastics code

as designated by the Society of the Plastics Industry, Inc. (See Chapter 4 for more information on this code.)

- In 1991, the Department of Environmental Conservation was empowered to establish a waste reduction and recycling awards program in consultation with the Department of Education. The program would provide, as funds were available, award grants for public schools to recognize their efforts to reduce and recycle waste they had generated.

SOURCE: Alaska State Statutes 1962–1991: Title 46, Chapter 6 (Recycling and Reduction of Litter), s 46.06.010, s 46.06.021, s 46.11.060, s 46.06.090 (a) and (b); s 46.06.095, s 46.11.070.

Arizona

- Arizona requires that residents must be provided with "an opportunity to engage in recycling and waste reduction."
- The state mandates that all motor vehicle tires shall be recycled and requires all sellers of tires to post written notices containing the following language: "It is unlawful to throw away a motor vehicle tire. Recycle all used tires." Retailers must accept scrap tires if any new or recapped tires are sold, and when any new tire is purchased, an additional fee for environmental protection is charged.
- The disposal of automotive lead-acid batteries in landfills or incinerators is prohibited. These batteries must be collected and recycled.
- The Department of Environmental Quality is empowered by the state to administer, encourage, and oversee the state's recycling programs. These include a public education program, run in consultation with the State Board of Education, that addresses all facets of recycling, from source reduction to the promotion of buying recycled products.
- As of 1 July 1991, all consumers of newsprint within the state were required to use at least 25 percent recycled content in their papers (if the cost of the recycled newsprint is within 5 percent of the cost of virgin material newsprint). Further goals are specified with regard to recycled-content newsprint: 30 percent on 1 January 1994, 35 percent on 1 January 1996, 40 percent on 1 January 1998, and 50 percent on 1 January 2000.
- As of 1 July 1991, it was also mandated that all plastic bottles and rigid plastic containers must bear the recycling symbols defined by the Society of the Plastics Industry, Inc., to designate the resin used in their manufacture.
- A state recycling fund has been established to help finance a variety of interests revolving around recycling, including research, education, market development, and source reduction.

SOURCE: Arizona Revised Statutes: Title 9 (Cities and Towns), s 9-500.07; Title 11 (Counties), s 11-269; Title 44 (Trade and Commerce), Chapter 9, Article 8 (Waste Tire Disposal), s 44-1302, Article 9 (Lead-Acid Batteries), s 44-1322; Title 49 (Arizona Recycling Program), Article 8, Chapter 4, s 49-833, s 49-834, s 49-835, s 49-837.

Arkansas

- Arkansas mandated that all state agencies submit "a solid waste management plan which proposes the establishment of recycling programs and facilities" by 1 July 1991. Subsequently, the state created a Solid Waste Management and Recycling Fund, administered by the Department of Pollution Control and Ecology.
- State law requires that the public is assured an "opportunity to recycle." Specifically, all residents must have access to "curbside pick-up or collection centers for recyclable materials at sites that are convenient for persons to use." Further, as of 1 July 1993, "at least one (1) recyclable materials collection center shall be available in each county of a district unless the commission grants the district an exemption." Exemptions are possible if such a collection facility exists in a nearby county and is shown to serve both areas adequately.
- A State Marketing Board for Recyclables has been established to promote all aspects of recycling and stimulate markets for recyclable materials. Additionally, all state agencies and schools have been required to institute source separation recycling programs, and they are encouraged to give purchasing preference to products made from recycled materials or products that may be readily recycled or reused.
- The state purchasing agent has been directed to issue specifications for recycled paper content on all types of papers. Also, purchasing goals dealing with the percentage of recycled paper products to be used within state agencies are delineated as follows: 10 percent in fiscal year 1991, 25 percent in fiscal year 1992, 45 percent in fiscal year 1993, and 60 percent by calendar year 2000.
- When paper products are put out to bid, a 10 percent difference in price is permitted in recycled versus virgin paper goods. Also, an additional 1 percent preference is allowed for in "products containing the largest amount of post-consumer materials recovered within the State of Arkansas."
- The state grants a variable tax credit for the purchase of waste reduction, reuse, or recycling equipment that is used to process products made of at least 50 percent recovered waste materials, 10 percent of which includes postconsumer waste.

SOURCE: Arkansas Code of 1987: Title 8 (Environmental Law), Chapter 6 (Disposal of Solid Wastes and Other Refuse), Subchapter 6 (Solid Waste Management Recycling Fund Act), s 8-6-604, s 8-6-605, Subchapter 7, s 8-6-720, s 8-9-201, s 8-9-203, s 8-9-204, s 19-5-961, s 19-11-260, s 26-51-506.

California

- All state school districts and universities are encouraged to establish paper recycling programs and to cooperate with each other in setting up such programs. State educational agencies are also encouraged to purchase recycled paper "if the supplier of recycled paper offers the paper at a cost which does not exceed by more than 5 percent the lowest offer of nonrecycled paper of comparable quality." Moreover, state law requires that the recycled paper that is purchased should have the highest percentage of postconsumer waste, all other qualities being equal. Additionally, the agencies are asked to make all reasonable efforts to eliminate potential paper contaminating products from their purchasing programs.

- Purchase preference for recycled paper by universities and state agencies is encouraged, and goals are set for the purchasing of such products: By 1 January 1992, at least 35 percent of the total dollar amount of paper products purchased must be recycled; by 1 January 1994, at least 40 percent; and by 1 January 1996, at least 50 percent. The regents of the University of California are required to submit an annual report to the state legislature, the governor, and the California Integrated Waste Management Board that details the percentage of the total dollar amount spent that is devoted to recycled paper products.

- The state requires written certification of the percentage of secondary and postconsumer waste in all recycled paper products. Where public contracts are concerned, all contractors must certify in writing the minimum or exact percentages of both postconsumer and secondary waste contained in their products.

- Persons contracted by the state are required to use recycled paper products to the maximum extent deemed "economically feasible." Any company bidding on a printing project for any state or local agency must specify the percentage of recycled materials in their recycled paper products. State agencies are expected to achieve the following purchasing goals for high-grade recycled papers: 30 percent by 1 January 1994, 35 percent on and after 1 January 1997, and 40 percent on and after 1 January 2000.

- All state agencies and the legislature were required to have waste paper collection and recycling programs in operation by 1 June 1991; these must include educational programs for all personnel and must provide for the collection of office paper, corrugated cardboard, newsprint, beverage containers, waste oil, and "any other material at the discretion of the director," in consultation with the California Integrated Waste Management Board. Constant reevaluation of the program is specified, and there is a provision for discontinuing certain products if the economics of the program prove ineffective.

- Any revenues realized from these recycling programs are to be used according to the following priorities, in the order given: to offset recycling program costs, to offset the higher prices of purchasing recycled paper products, and, lastly, to augment California's general fund.

- All procuring agencies are required to establish policies to ensure that recycled oils are acceptable for purchase and are not excluded from state bids. Further, unless it costs more, is unavailable in a reasonable time, or cannot meet performance standards, the oil that is purchased must contain the greatest percentage of recycled oil available. In addition, the California Integrated Waste Management Board and state officers and employees are encouraged to use recycled oil products.

- Bidders on state contracts must specify the percentage of recycled content in products other than paper, and there is a purchasing preference for recycled over nonrecycled products. The following goals have also been set regarding the required percentages of recycled products in total state purchases: by 1 January 1991, at least 10 percent; by 1 January 1993, at least 20 percent; and by 1 January 1995, at least 40 percent.

- The California legislature has declared its intent to stimulate market development for recycled products, and it requires that a report be submitted to advise the state on the legislature's effectiveness in achieving this goal. The legislature itself is required to exhibit a purchasing preference for recycled paper products and has specific goals for buying these goods. In addition, state government departments must prepare annual reports for the legislature on the amount of recycled products purchased.

- A Beverage Container Recycling Advisory Committee was established on 1 March 1987, to advise the director of the California Integrated Waste Management Board on all matters concerning the recycling of beverage containers. The California Beverage Container Recycling Fund was established on 29 September 1986, to foster recycling of containers. All dealers who carry recyclable containers must identify, with signage, the nearest certified recycling center, its features, and its hours of operation. There must be at least one certified recycling center within every convenience zone (including reverse vending machines) with required minimum hours of operation. An "antiscavenging law" makes it illegal for anyone other than an authorized recycling agent of the city or county to remove segregated recyclables from collection locations.

- All commercial curbside recycling programs must submit survey forms as required by the state with information on general operations, actual volumes collected, and revenues received from sales of recyclables.

- Since 1990, each county in California has been required to create a task force at five-year intervals to assist in the development of community source reduction and recycling. All county and city source reduction and recycling elements "shall place primary emphasis on implementation of all feasible source reduction, recycling, and composting programs while identifying the amount of landfill and transformation capacity that will be needed for solid waste which cannot be reduced at the source, recycled, or composted."

- The state requires that on and after 1 January 1993, "every seller of trash bags of 1.0 mil or greater thickness sold in California shall ensure that at least 10 percent of the material used in these trash bags is recycled postconsumer material." On or after 1 January 1995, the bag thickness requirement is lowered to .75 mil, and the postconsumer content requirement is raised to 30 percent. Annual certification of trash bag sellers will be undertaken, as well as audits of sellers as the California Integrated Waste Management Board deems necessary. Problems encountered by sellers after 1 January 1995 with regard to obtaining required postconsumer materials must be certified to the board.

- The California Integrated Waste Management Board is required to review, identify, and report to the Department of General Services any impediments to the procurement of recycled plastic products. A procurement preference has been established for recycled plastic products over those manufactured from virgin resins.

- The Department of Transportation is required to use recycled paving materials as much as possible, and all bid specifications are to be reviewed with regard to the purchase of such materials.

- Since 1991, every newsprint consumer in California has been required to ensure that at least 25 percent of the paper it uses is made from recycled-content newsprint. Goals for the percentages of newsprint made from recycled-content paper are: 30 percent on and after 1 January 1994, 35 percent on and after 1 January 1996, 40 percent on and after 1 January 1998, and 50 percent on and after 1 January 2000. Consumers of newsprint may be prosecuted for fraud should they falsely certify recycled contents.

- A tire recycling program was implemented on 1 July 1991, in order to "promote and develop alternatives to the landfill disposal of used whole tires." The state established grants for research, development, education, and implementation of tire recycling programs. The Department of General Services has been directed to revise its procedures and procurement specifications for the state purchases of any products that could be derived from the recycling of used tires, and it establishes a 5 percent bidding preference. Contracts will be awarded to the bidders whose products include the greatest percentage of recycled tire content, all other things being equal.
- All unused ballots may be recycled after an election. The clerk must make and file a written affidavit stating the number of ballots recycled.

SOURCE: California Education Code: Title 1, Division 1 (General Education Code Provisions), Part 19, Chapter 3 (Miscellaneous), Article 8 (Recycling Paper), s 32372, s 3273 a–e. California Public Contract Code: Division 2 (General Provisions), Part 2 (Contracting by State Agencies), Chapter 1 (State Contract Act), Article 7 (Contract Requirements), s 10233, Chapter 2, Article 7.6 (Recycled Oil Markets), s. 10406, s 10407, Chapter 2.1, Article 2, s 10507.5, Chapter 2.5, Article 8.5, s 10860, Chapter 4, Article 2, s 12162 through s 12169, Chapter 4, Article 4, s 12205, s 12210, s 12213, s 12225, s 12226, Chapter 5, Article 2, s 12310, Article 3. California Public Resources Code: Division 3, Chapter 1, Article 9 (Used Oil Recycling Act), s 3469, Division 12.1 (California Beverage Container and Litter Reduction Act), Chapter 3, s 14530.1, s 14531, s 14538, s 14540, s 14542.1, Chapter 4, s 14551, s 14551.5, Chapter 6, s 14570, s 14571, Chapter 7, s 14580, Division 12.2 (Household Batteries), Division 30 (Waste Management), Part 1, Chapter 2, Part 2, Chapter 2, Article 4, Chapter 3, Article 4, Chapter 6, Article 1, Article 2, Chapter 7, Article 4, Chapter 9, Article 1, s 41953, Article 2, s 41970, Part 3, Chapter 4, s 42202, Chapter 6 (Plastic Recycling Program), Chapter 8 (Recycled Battery Programs), Chapter 10 (Office Paper Recovery Program), Chapter 14 (Paving Materials), Chapter 15 (Newsprint), Chapter 17 (California Tire Recycling Act). California Elections Code: Division 12, Chapter 12, s 17136.

Colorado

- Colorado requires that "major solid waste disposal sites shall be developed in accordance with sound conservation practices and shall emphasize, where feasible, the recycling of waste materials."

- On public projects, the state provides for a preference of up to 5 percent for bids on finished products that contain no less than 10 percent recycled plastics.
- The state legislature has made a series of declarations related to recycling, one of which stipulates that state government programs should be developed to address the use of recycled products. The legislature has also established a preference for the use of recycled paper in state government contracts.
- A bid preference of 10 percent is allowed for bidders who use recycled paper in the manufacture of commodities or supplies described in any state bid. The legislature expects that paper or paper products bought by the state will be made of recycled paper if the price is competitive and the quality adequate. The following goals for the purchase of recycled paper as a percentage of the total volume of paper and paper products purchased by the state have been established: at least 10 percent in fiscal year 1990–1991, 20 percent in 1991–1992, 30 percent in 1992–1993, 40 percent in 1993–1994, and 50 percent in 1994–1995 and for each subsequent fiscal year.
- Another legislative declaration states that "the recycling of plastic materials is a matter of statewide concern and that such recycling should be promoted." This declaration also says that recycling of plastics will decrease the amount disposed of in landfills and will spur economic development in Colorado's recycling industry. The intent of this declaration is "to encourage the development of the recycling industry and the development of markets for recycled plastic materials."
- A third legislative declaration speaks to the importance of proper disposal of solid wastes and recognizes that citizens are concerned about learning how to make maximum use of waste reduction and recycling programs: "Realistic waste reduction goals should be established and state and local solid waste management activities should strive to achieve such goals through source reduction, recycling, composting, and similar waste management strategies."
- Colorado requires that on or after 1 July 1992, all plastic bottles and rigid plastic containers distributed, sold, or offered for sale must be labeled according to the recycling code of the plastics industry. However, "no unit of local government shall require or prohibit the use or sale of specific types of plastic materials or products."
- A pilot program has been established to encourage research and development for new plastics recycling technologies by private industry. The executive director of local affairs is permitted by the state to make grants or loans to private industries for such research and development if the industries are located in or will

expand into Colorado. The executive director is also authorized to accept any grants or loans from private or public sources to apply to such plastics recycling projects.

- The state provides an income tax credit for Colorado residents investing in plastics recycling technologies: "a plastic recycling credit equal to 20 percent of net expenditures to third parties for rent, wages, supplies, consumable tools, equipment, test inventory, and utilities up to ten thousand dollars made by the taxpayer for new plastic recycling technology in Colorado, with a maximum credit of two thousand dollars." A similar tax credit is allowed for domestic and foreign corporations that invest in technologies for recycling plastics. A further tax credit is provided for qualified equipment utilizing postconsumer waste (applicable for income tax years beginning on 1 January 1991 and ending by 1 January 1996).
- Colorado also provides for the adoption of regulations that prohibit discrimination against the transportation of recycled or recyclable materials by rail.

SOURCE: Colorado Revised Statutes: Title 8 (Labor and Industry), Article 19.5 (Bid Preference—Recycled Plastic Products), s 101, Article 19.7 (Bid Preferences—Recycled Paper Products), s 101, s 102, s 103; Title 24 (Government—State), Article 65.1, Part 2, s 204.2, Article 103 (Source Selection and Contract Formation), Part 2 (Methods of Source Selection), s 207; Title 25 (Health; Environmental Control), Article 17 (Recycling of Plastics), s 101–106; Title 30 (Government—County; County Powers and Functions, General), Article 20, Part 1 (Solid Wastes Disposal Sites and Facilities), s 100.5, s 101, s 102.5; Title 39 (Taxation; Specific Taxes; Income Tax), Article 22 (Income Tax), Part 1, s 114.5, Part 3 (Corporations), s 309, Part 5 (Special Rules), s 515(f); Title 40 (Utilities; Public Utilities; General and Administrative), Article 3, s 113.

Connecticut

- A plan to increase state procurement of goods that contain recycled materials was first required on 1 October 1989 and is expected to be updated periodically. The plan was also expected to include specifications for postconsumer and secondary waste content in recycled products. Further plans are mandated to reduce the use of disposable and single-use products, as well as to separate and collect items deemed suitable for recycling. Annual progress reports from state agencies on the implementation of such plans are required.
- The state is also directed by the legislature to use two-sided copies whenever possible to reduce paper waste at its source. White

paper recycling programs were instituted within the legislature itself in 1989, and all other state agencies were required to follow suit by 1991.

- All state bids must be accompanied by statements that assess the recyclability of materials. Furthermore, the commissioner of transportation must ensure that materials specifications for state transportation projects encourage the use of recycled materials.

- Since 1989, all owners/operators of resources recovery facilities and solid waste disposal areas have been required to submit quarterly reports detailing the amounts of solid waste received. Recycling facilities are also required to submit similar reports for the following recyclable items: cardboard; leaves; glass, plastic, and metal food and beverage containers; newspapers; storage batteries; and waste oil.

- The state also mandates that plans be submitted and approved by the commissioner for environmental protection for the disposal or recycling of ash residue from any municipal solid waste incinerators or resource recovery facilities.

- Facilities that compost leaves are regulated by the state, but leaf composting and recycling facilities are exempt from the requirement of obtaining a solid waste facility permit.

- All municipal authorities must provide for the safe and sanitary disposal of nonhazardous solid waste (disposal of hazardous waste is the responsibility of the generator). Also, municipal authorities are allowed to inspect any recycling facilities that handle municipal wastes. As of 1 July 1993, each municipality is expected to provide for the recycling of nickel-cadmium batteries contained in consumer products.

- State law requires the establishment of municipal solid waste recycling programs. A trust fund has been created to provide municipalities with grants to assist their recycling program development. Any revenue collected through municipal solid waste programs must be deposited into this fund. A goal of recycling not less than 25 percent of the solid waste generated in the state after 1 January 1991 was set. Since that date, state residents have been required to source-separate recyclable items in their solid waste at home.

- The state is also required to: (1) coordinate litter control and recycling programs in state and local agencies; (2) develop public education programs about litter/recycling; (3) encourage, organize, and coordinate voluntary antilitter and recycling campaigns within communities; (4) investigate the availability of funding for such programs; and (5) study current research and developments in litter control and recycling.

- There is also a state plan for the promotion and support of industries using recycled materials. Progress reports are required at six-month intervals.
- Official symbols and the procedures to use them have been established to indicate that packaging is recyclable or made from recycled materials.
- Goals for the percentages of recycled fiber in the newsprint used by all publishers and other printers have been established as follows: 11 percent or more for the year ending 31 December 1992, 16 percent or more for the year ending 31 December 1993, 20 percent or more for the year ending 31 December 1994, 23 percent or more for the year ending 31 December 1995, 31 percent or more for the year ending 31 December 1996, 40 percent or more for the year ending 31 December 1997, 45 percent or more for the year ending 31 December 1998, and 50 percent or more for the year ending 31 December 1999 and thereafter.
- Goals have also been established for telephone directory publishers regarding the use of recycled fiber in directory stock: 10 percent or more for the year ending 31 December 1995, 15 percent or more for the year ending 31 December 1996, 20 percent or more for the year ending 31 December 1997, 25 percent or more for the year ending 31 December 1998, 30 percent or more for the year ending 31 December 1999, 35 percent or more for the year ending 31 December 2000, and 40 percent or more thereafter. All directory publishers were required to file a plan on or before 1 January 1991 that provided that at least 10 percent of their directories would be collected and recycled. This percentage must be increased by 5 percent annually until 50 percent or more of all directories are retrieved and recycled.

SOURCE: Connecticut General Statutes: Title 4A (Administrative Services), Chapter 58 (Purchases and Printing), s 67a; Title 4B (State Real Property), Chapter 59 (Department of Public Works and State Real Property), Part II, s 15; Title 13A (Highways and Bridges), Chapter 238 (Highway Construction and Maintenance), Part V, s 981; Title 22A (Environmental Protection), Chapter 446D (Solid Waste Management), s 208e, s 208g, s 208i, s 220, s 241, s 241a, s 241b, s 241g, s 241h, s 249, s 255c, s 256a, s 256n, s 256p, s 256t, s 256z, s 256ee; Title 32 (Commerce and Economic Development), Chapter 578 (Department of Economic Development), s 1e.

Delaware

- Delaware has declared that its citizens have a right to a clean and wholesome environment, that solid waste disposal practices in the past have not been conducive to this end, and that locally organized recycling programs have demonstrated that solid wastes generated within the state do contain recoverable resources.

- The General Assembly has established that: (1) "maximum resources recovery from solid waste and maximum recycling and reuse of such resources in order to protect, preserve and enhance the environment of the State shall be considered environmental goals of the State"; (2) "solid waste disposal and resource recovery facilities and projects are to be implemented either by the State or under state auspices, in furtherance of these goals"; (3) "appropriate governmental structure, processes and support are to be provided so that effective state systems and facilities for solid waste management and large-scale resources recovery may be developed, financed, planned, designed, constructed and operated for the benefit of the people, municipalities and counties of the State"; (4) private industry is to be utilized to the fullest extent to assist in goals of resource recovery, recycling, and reuse; and (5) "long-term contracts are authorized between the State and private persons or businesses to further resource recovery."

- To meet these goals, the Delaware Solid Waste Authority was created through the Waste Minimization and Recycling Acts of 1990. The authority is empowered to adopt rules and regulations governing the composition, quantity, quality, and transportation of source-separated recyclables to recycling centers and to develop a statewide recycling and waste reduction plan. The authority is also expected to establish recycling centers in each county, to provide for public education about source-separated recycling and resources recovery, to promote markets for recyclable materials, and to report annually on its activities.

- The General Assembly has also determined that beverage containers are "a major source of nondegradable litter" in the state and that litter control is a financial burden. With the intention of creating incentives to reuse or recycle beverage containers, the state has mandated the establishment of redemption centers, which have also been empowered to accept materials other than beverage containers for reuse or recycling.

- Delaware prohibits metal beverage containers with any detachable part; container holders, such as six-pack rings, that are not classified by the state as biodegradable, photodegradable, or recyclable; and glass beverage containers that are not recyclable or refillable.

- Recyclable materials are defined by Delaware to include newsprint, computer paper, white paper, corrugated and other cardboards, plastics, ferrous metals, nonferrous metals, white goods, organic yard waste, used motor oil, asphalt, batteries, and household paint, solvent, pesticide, and insecticide containers.

SOURCE: Delaware Code Annotated: Title 7 (Conservation), Part VII (Natural Resources), Chapter 60 (Environmental Control), Subchapter III (Beverage Containers), s 6051, s 6052, s 6056, s 6059, Chapter 64 (Delaware Solid Waste Authority), Subchapter I, s 6401, s 6402, s 6403, s 6404, s 6406, s 6407, Subchapter II (Recycling and Waste Reduction), s 6450–6459, Chapter 78 (Waste Minimization/Pollution Prevention Act), s 7802–7804. Title 21 (Motor Vehicles) delineates numerous laws that apply specifically to automotive recyclers and the automotive recycling industry.

District of Columbia

- The mayor of the District of Columbia was directed by statute to submit to the District's council, within one year of 25 July 1987, a comprehensive plan for a multimaterial recycling system for the purpose of "recovering energy and other resources from discarded materials and solid waste and for distributing reusable organic compounds for public use."
- A District Office of Recycling was subsequently established. Additionally, a priority for recycling was defined, and the District stated that no incineration facilities would be constructed until all the provisions of the D.C. Solid Waste Management and Multi-Material Recycling Act of 1988 (D.C. Law 7-226) were implemented or a 25 percent reduction in the solid waste stream was achieved through recycling, whichever came first. This act, which took effect on 1 October 1989, required every household to separate newspaper, yard waste, metals, and glass for recycling. A requirement regarding the collection of some plastics was added on 8 June 1991. The act also states that commercial businesses must recycle newspapers, metals, glass, and office paper.
- District goals include the recycling of at least 35 percent of the total solid waste stream by 1 October 1992 and the recycling of at least 45 percent of the total solid waste stream by 1 October 1994.
- The mayor was also required to establish at least one multimaterial buy-back center in the District on or before 1 October 1989, as well as at least one intermediate processing facility to receive recyclable materials.
- In addition, the act establishes a recycling surcharge on private waste haulers to fund recycling activities.
- Minimum recycled content percentage requirements are also defined for paper or paper products: Beginning 1 January 1994, all persons selling or distributing significant quantities of paper or paper products in the District must ensure that these goods

contain at least the minimum percentage of recycled content
designated by the EPA in the Resource Conservation and
Recovery Act of 1976, as set forth in 40 CFR 250.21. Newsprint
must be made of at least 40 percent postconsumer recovered
materials, and high-grade bleached printing and writing papers
must contain at least 50 percent waste paper.

- All corporations that file District annual reports and are sellers or
distributors of paper or paper products must include information
on the minimum recycled content of papers sold or distributed
per District requirements. As of 1 January 1994, a minimum
recycled content surcharge will be applied to any person who fails
to comply with the District's recycled paper requirements. All
revenues received from this surcharge will be applied to District
recycling activities.

SOURCE: District of Columbia Code: Part I (Government of District), Title 6, Chapter 32 (Multi-Material Recycling Systems), s 3202,
Chapter 34 (Solid Waste Management and Multi-Material Recycling), s 3401, s 3405–3410, s 3415, s 3419, s 3420, s 3422, s 3423.

Florida

- A Florida Seed Capital Fund has been established "to provide
equity financing for the research and development activities of
new and existing high technology small business in the state."
"High technology" businesses include those that provide products
or services in the area of recyclable materials.
- When the State Comprehensive Plan was adopted in 1988, one of
its goals was the initiation of programs to "develop or expand
recyclable material markets, especially those involving plastics,
metals, paper, and glass." The plan also encouraged "the research,
development, and implementation of recycling, resource
recovery, energy recovery, and other methods of using garbage,
trash, sewage, slime, sludge, hazardous waste, and other waste."
- Machinery and equipment used for processing recyclable materials
are exempt from sales tax, and no sales tax is added to recycled or
waste oils and solid waste materials if they are used as fuels.
- The state has permitted the Department of Education to contract
recycling firms to pick up, process, and recycle obsolete or
unusable materials from the schools.
- A program has been established to award contracts and grants to
independent, nonprofit colleges and universities for research
activities related to methods and processes for recycling solid (and
hazardous) waste. Florida also encourages collaboration between
private industry and state universities on high-technology research
projects, including projects to resolve problems associated with

the design and implementation of programs to "recycle materials such as plastics, rubber, metal, glass, paper, and other components of the solid waste stream."

- State agencies are directed to purchase recycled paper (when economical), and bidders on printing contracts must certify the percentages of recycled content in their papers. A bidding preference is provided for recycled papers.

- The Division of Purchasing is prohibited from discriminating against products and materials with recycled content.

- The state also encourages the Department of Transportation to increase the use of recovered materials in its construction programs.

- The legislature has stated that it will "promote the recovery of energy from wastes," including the recycling of manufactured products.

- A legislative declaration states that "maximum resource recovery from solid waste and maximum recycling and reuse of such resources must be considered goals of the state." The legislature also has been directed to promote the reduction, recycling, reuse, or other alternative treatment of solid waste in lieu of disposal. Moreover, state agencies are expected to develop, promote, and implement public education programs about solid waste issues and recycling, in addition to developing and implementing actual recycling programs.

- The powers and duties of the state's Department of Public Health are delineated by statute, and these include promoting "the planning and application of recycling and resource recovery systems" for the betterment of the environment, as well as for energy recovery. The department is also expected to "assist in and encourage, as much as possible, the development within the state of industries and commercial enterprises which are based upon resource recovery, recycling, and reuse of solid waste." The department's other duties include maintaining a state directory of recycling businesses, managing grants for recycling programs, and increasing public education and awareness about recycling, volume reduction, and proper methods of solid waste disposal.

- Recycling is an integral part of the state's solid waste management effort, and each county was directed to initiate a materials recycling program by 1 July 1989. These programs required the counties to: separate construction and demolition debris; separate from the waste stream and offer for recycling the majority of newspapers, aluminum cans, glass, and plastic bottles; encourage local governments to recycle plastics, metals, and all grades of paper; recycle and/or compost yard trash and mechanically treated solid waste; and ensure that the county's total municipal solid waste would be reduced by at least 30 percent by the end of 1994. No more than half of this goal could be met through recycling yard trash, white goods, construction/demolition debris, and tires.

- As of 1 October 1989 and on an annual basis thereafter, each county was required to submit a report to the department detailing its solid waste management program and recycling activities.
- The procurement of products or materials with recycled content is also addressed, with the state requiring that such products be used whenever possible. Preconsumer waste is specifically excluded from the state's definition of "recycled content."
- Penalties and prohibitions with respect to solid wastes and recycling are provided. For example, the following disposal bans were established: After 1 October 1988, used oil could no longer be disposed of in landfills; after 1 January 1989, lead-acid batteries could not be disposed of in landfills, and all persons who sell such batteries must also collect trade-ins for recycling; after 1 January 1990, white goods could not be accepted at landfills; and after 1 January 1992, yard trash could not be disposed of in sanitary landfills.
- By 1 September 1989, all state agencies were required to establish recycling programs for the recovery of, at a minumum, aluminum, high-grade office paper, and corrugated cardboard.
- Florida encourages the development of recycled materials markets, and, since 1 September 1989, it has been mandatory that a report assessing the recycling industry and its markets be submitted on an annual basis.
- A grant program has been developed for municipalities and counties to implement solid waste management recycling and education programs. The state has also directed the school board of each district to provide instructional programs on recycling to all students at both the elementary and secondary levels. Further, the Department of Education has been assigned the task of developing curriculum materials and resource guides for recycling awareness programs for kindergarten through twelfth grade classes.
- Another statute directed the capitol, the house, and the senate office buildings to institute recycling programs for wastepaper and aluminum cans as of 1 January 1989.
- A products waste disposal fee of $.10 per ton on all newsprint consumed by publishers within the state took effect after 1 January 1989, and a $.10 credit per ton is provided for the use of recycled newsprint. If it is determined on 1 October 1992 that newsprint sold within the state is being recycled at a rate of 50 percent or more, then the disposal fee will be rescinded. However,

if the recycling rate is less than 50 percent, the disposal fee and corresponding credits will be increased to $.50 per ton on that same date. Additionally, if the rate is less than 50 percent on 1 October 1992, "any producer or publisher using newsprint in publications shall accept from a person for recycling purposes reasonably clean newsprint previously produced, published, or offered for sale by that producer or publisher." A credit of $.25 per ton of newsprint used is allowed if a publisher can prove that such paper was recycled through its facility.

- If a sustained recycling rate of 50 percent has not been reached by 1 October 1992 for containers made of glass, plastic, plastic-coated paper, aluminum, or other metals, then an advance disposal fee of $.01 per container shall be charged by retailers. The proceeds from this advance disposal fee are to be deposited into the Container Recycling Trust Fund. Containers for which such a fee has been charged may be returned to recycling centers for a refund of that fee in addition to any payment for market value. If a recycling rate of 50 percent for such containers has not been reached by 1 October 1995, then the advance disposal fee will be increased to $.02 per container. Such fees will not apply to any containers that are being recycled at a rate of 50 percent or more, and refillable containers are excluded as well.

- Although the legislation states that "each consumer shall deposit with the dealer the refund value of each container purchased," containers sold for consumption on the premises of the dealer are exempt from this deposit. Dealers must accept from the public any empty, unbroken, and reasonably clean container of the type, size, and brand they have sold within the past 60 working days. Distributors will not be required to pay deposits to manufacturers on nonrefillable containers. The legislation also provides for the establishment of redemption centers.

- Florida has examined the issue of hazardous household wastes and has decided to require the establishment of programs to handle such materials. Thus far, however, only used oil has been addressed. According to state law, used oil may only be disposed of in a manner consistent with recycling or beneficial reuse (this specifically excludes its use for road oiling, dust control, weed abatement, or other similar applications that have the potential to release used oil into the environment). The state also requires the development and implementation of a public education program about collecting and recycling used oil, and it encourages the voluntary establishment of facilities to collect used oil for recycling. A 5 percent price preference for the purchase of recycled oils by state and local governments has been created to encourage the industry.

SOURCE: West's Florida Statutes Annotated: Title XI (County Organization and Intergovernmental Relations), Chapter 159 (Bond Financing), Part III, s 159.445; Title XIII (Planning and Development), Chapter 187 (State Comprehensive Plan), s 187.201; Title XIV (Taxation and Finance), Chapter 212 (Tax on Sales, Use, and Other Transactions), Part I, s 212.08; Title XVI (Education), Chapter 233 (Courses of Study and Instructional Aids), s 233.37; Chapter 240 (Postsecondary Education), Part V, s 240.5325 and s 240.539; Title XIX (Public Business), Chapter 283 (Public Printing), Part I (Executive Agency Printing), s 283.32, Chapter 287 (Procurement of Personal Property and Services), Part I, s 287.045; Title XXVI (Public Transportation), Chapter 336 (County Road System), s 336.044; Title XXVIII (Natural Resources; Conservation, Reclamation, and Use), Chapter 377 (Energy Resources), Part II, s 377.703; Title XXIX (Public Health), Chapter 403 (Environmental Control), Part IV (Resource Recovery and Management), s 403.702–403.7065, s 403.708, s 403.7095, s 403.714, s 403.7145, s 403.717, s 403.7195, s 403.7197, s 403.7198, s 403.7265, s 403,751, s 403.753; Title XXXIII (Regulation of Trade, Commerce, Investments, and Solicitation), Chapter 538 (Secondhand Dealers and Secondary Metals Recyclers); all parts and sections within this chapter regulate secondary metals recyclers.

Georgia

- Having recently examined its solid waste disposal efforts, Georgia has announced a policy to institute and maintain a comprehensive state solid waste management plan. Included in this policy are plans to educate and encourage solid waste handlers and generators to utilize source reduction, reuse, composting, recycling, and other alternative waste management methods to cut the amount of solid waste.

- The state has also declared its intention to promote markets for and engage in the purchase of products made from recovered materials and recyclable goods. A Recycling Market Development Council was established on 1 July 1990. At the same time, a review of purchases and purchasing specifications, practices, and procedures with respect to recycled materials was begun.

- A statewide goal has been set to reduce the amount of municipal solid waste disposed of in 1992 by 25 percent as of 1 July 1996.

- Georgia has directed each city and county to develop or be included in a comprehensive solid waste management plan. After 1 July 1992, no permits for solid waste facilities will be issued unless the applicant's host jurisdiction can, among other things, demonstrate an active involvement and strategy for meeting the statewide goal for the reduction of solid waste disposal by 1 July

1996. State authorities have also been empowered to establish recycling/resource recovery programs to help the public achieve this end. In addition, there is a statute encouraging the recovery and utilization of resources contained in solid waste and sewage sludge.

- After 1 January 1991, lead-acid batteries may not be disposed of in municipal solid waste landfills but must be delivered to some sort of materials recovery program. In addition, any person selling lead-acid batteries must also accept them for recycling and post signage with specified language about the law as it pertains to lead-acid batteries.
- All cities, counties, and solid waste management authorities were authorized to impose restrictions on the disposal of tires as of 1 July 1990. Such restrictions may include a ban on tire disposal and a requirement that tires "be recycled, shredded, chopped, or otherwise processed in an environmentally sound manner prior to disposal."
- Since 1 January 1991, the state has required that rigid plastic containers or bottles manufactured or sold in Georgia must be labeled (per the specifications of the Society of the Plastics Industry).
- Georgia grants an 8 percent price incentive for the purchase of paper products made from recovered fiber over similar products made from 100 percent virgin fibers. However, the state limits the total amount expended on such products to $1 million per year.

SOURCE: Code of Georgia: Title 12 (Conservation and Natural Resources), Chapter 8 (Waste Management), Article 2 (Solid Waste Management), Part 1 (General Provisions), s 12-8-21, s 12-8-28, s 12-8-31.1, s 12-8-33, s 12-8-34, s 12-8-35, s 12-8-40.1, Part 2 (Regional Solid Waste Management Authorities), s 12-8-51; Title 36 (Local Government), Chapter 63 (Resource Recovery Development Authorities), s 36-63-2; Title 50 (State Government), Chapter 5 (Department of Administrative Services), Article 3 (State Purchasing), Part 1 (General Authority, Duties, and Procedure), s 50-5-60.1, s 50-5-60.2.

Hawaii

- Hawaii has established pricing preferences for bidders offering goods containing recycled materials. Rules establishing percentages and preference guidelines were to be established by the comptroller by 1 January 1992.
- One of the state's legislative objectives is to "promote re-use and recycling to reduce solid and liquid wastes and employ a conservation ethic."

- Another statute establishes that the director of the Department of Public Health is responsible for the study of available research in the field of recycling, the study of methods for implementing such research, and the development of public educational programs.
- Hawaii prohibits the land disposal of lead-acid batteries and requires that they be recycled. Additionally, all sellers of such batteries must post the relevant law and accept used batteries (for recycling) from customers buying new ones.
- The state also prohibits the disposal of any new, used, or recycled oil either on the ground or in the water.
- The state environmental policy guidelines call for the promotion of "the optimal use of solid wastes through programs of waste prevention, energy resource recovery, and recycling so that all our wastes become utilized."

SOURCE: Hawaii Revised Statutes Annotated: Title 9 (Public Property, Purchasing, and Contracting), Chapter 103 (Expenditure of Public Money and Public Contracts), Part II, s 103-24.5; Title 13 (Planning and Economic Development), Chapter 226 (Hawaii State Planning Act), Part I, s 226-15; Title 19 (Health), Chapter 339 (Litter Control), Part I, s 339-1, s 339-3, Chapter 340A (Solid Waste), s 340A-1, Chapter 342I (Lead-Acid Battery Recycling), s 342I-1, s 342I-2, Chapter 342N (Used Oil Transport, Recycling, and Disposal), s 342N-3, Chapter 344 (State Environmental Policy), s 344-4.

Idaho

- Idaho's solid waste and recycling laws are presently limited to two disposal bans. One requires that all used tires be recycled and that any person who sells tires must post this law and accept used tires for recycling from anyone who purchases new or retreaded tires.
- The second ban prohibits the incineration or disposal of lead-acid batteries in landfills. Such batteries must be recycled, and all sellers of lead-acid batteries must post the relevant law. Also, all lead-acid batteries sold after 1 July 1992 must bear a universally accepted recycling symbol.

SOURCE: Idaho Code: Title 39 (Health and Safety), Chapter 65 (Waste Tire Disposal) s 39-6502, Chapter 70 (Sale and Disposal of Batteries), s 39-7002, s 39-7003.

Illinois

- Illinois permits local governments to contract with other local governments, private corporations, or nonprofit organizations for the purposes of garbage disposal or recycling.

- All counties with populations over 100,000 and the city of Chicago were required to develop comprehensive, 20-year waste management plans that focused on recycling, composting, waste reduction, and other landfill alternatives by 1 March 1991. County program goals included the recycling of 15 percent of municipal solid waste by the third year in operation and 25 percent of such waste by the fifth year (subject to viable markets).

- A total of twenty-five assistance grants are available to municipalities or combinations thereof with total populations of 20,000 or more for the purpose of implementing pilot recycling programs. At a minimum, such programs must include: curbside collection for at least three source-separated materials (the three materials could be chosen from glass, aluminum, steel and bimetallic cans, newsprint, corrugated cardboard, used motor oil, and plastics); a drop-off or buy-back center for at least glass, aluminum cans, and newsprint; provisions for recycling collected materials; and provisions for a public education program and enforced compliance.

- As of 1 September 1989, leaves were banned from landfills, and counties were required to begin composting them.

- Lead-acid batteries were banned from landfills as of 1990; tires will be similarly banned as of July 1995.

- A Vehicle Recycling Board was created by the state to oversee vehicle recycling. All monies collected in the Vehicle Recycling Fund are transferred to the Common School Fund.

- Illinois has a Waste Oil Recovery Act that promotes the recycling of used oil, encourages the purchase of recycled oils, and establishes educational programs designed to inform the public about recycling oil in order to conserve natural resources.

- The state also has a Recycled Newsprint Use Act requiring that on and after 1 January 1991, consumers of newsprint must meet the following goals for annual recycled fiber usage: 22 percent beginning 1 January 1991, 25 percent beginning 1 January 1992, and 28 percent beginning 1 January 1993. The act also states that if these goals are not met by 1993, every consumer of newsprint in Illinois during 1994 must ensure that its recycled fiber usage is at least 28 percent unless (1) the required newsprint cannot be found in sufficient quality or quantity or (2) contracts for procurement of newsprint were made before 1 January 1991. Criminal penalties are delineated for violations of this act.

- The Illinois Solid Waste Management Act includes a recycling program stipulating that all state agencies that maintain public lands must give preference to using composted materials and that waste reduction and recycling programs for office paper, corrugated cardboard, newsprint, and mixed paper must be instituted in all state buildings. The goals for these programs are a 25 percent reduction in such waste by 31 December 1995 and a 50 percent reduction by 31 December 2000. In addition, procurement procedures and specifications were to be reviewed and modified, where feasible, to encourage the maximum purchase of products made from recycled materials, especially those with the highest content of postconsumer waste. Goals for the percentage of the total amount of paper and paper products purchased by the state that contain recycled materials were: at least 10 percent by 30 June 1989, at least 25 percent by 30 June 1992, and at least 40 percent by 30 June 1996. Furthermore, all paper purchased for use by state agencies must be recyclable whenever possible, and such agencies are to review their paper requirements to allow the use of such paper whenever possible.

SOURCE: Smith-Hurd Illinois Annotated Statutes: Chapter 34 (Counties Code), Article 5, Division 5-1, s 5-1048, Chapter 85 (Local Government—Solid Waste Planning and Recycling Act), s 5956, s 5958, Chapter 95 1/2 (Motor Vehicles), Chapter 4, Article III (Vehicle Recycling Board), s 4-302, s 239.41, Chapter 96 1/2 (Natural Resources—Waste Oil Recovery Act), s 7702.3, s 7707, s 7708, s 7709, Chapter 96 1/2 (Recycled Newsprint Use Act), s 9752.25, s 9752.30, s 9752.35, s 9752.45, s 9753, s 9763, Chapter 111 1/2 (Public Health and Safety—Environmental Protection Act); Title I, s 1003.30, Chapter 111 1/2 (Solid Waste Management Act), s 7053, s 7056a, Chapter 127 (State Government—Illinois Purchasing Act), s 132.6-4.

Indiana

- Indiana has a Recycling Promotion and Assistance Fund designed "to promote and assist recycling throughout Indiana by focusing economic development efforts on businesses and projects involving recycling."
- The Department of the Environment is directed by statute to educate students, consumers, and business about the benefits of solid waste recycling and source reduction and to establish a recycled paper task force to develop voluntary guidelines concerning newsprint and other paper products.
- As of 1 January 1992, each plastic bottle and rigid plastic container must be imprinted with the recycling code that identifies its resin (per the Society of the Plastics Industry specifications).
- Universities and state colleges are directed to collect recyclable paper and procure recycled paper products when economically feasible.
- In offering economic development assistance, the Department of Commerce is directed to give priority to businesses and industries

whose primary activities are aimed at converting recyclable materials into useful products.

- State agencies are expected to collect and recycle paper and paper products, as well as procure the same, when economically feasible. The state defines recycled materials as those containing at least 10 percent postconsumer/postmanufacture waste.
- Indiana's 20-Year Solid Waste Management Plan is designed to reduce landfilled solid waste 35 percent by 1995 and 50 percent by 2000.

SOURCE: West's Annotated Indiana Code: Title 4 (State Offices and Administration), Article 13, Chapter 4.1 (Printing for State Agencies), s 4-13-4.1-5, Article 13.4 (State Procurement), Chapter 4, s 4-13.4-4-7, Article 23, Chapter 5.5 (Indiana Energy Development Board), s 4-23-5.5-14; Title 13 (Environment), Article 7 (Environmental Management), Chapter 3, s 13-7-3-6.1, s 13-7-3-15, Chapter 22, s 13-7-22-1, Article 9.5 (Solid Waste Management), Chapter 1, s 13-9.5-1-24; Title 20 (Education), Article 12, Chapter 67 (Recycled Paper Products), s 20-12-67-2, s 20-12-67-3; Title 24 (Trade Regulations; Consumer Sales and Credit), Article 5, Chapter 17 (Environmental Marketing Claims).

Iowa

- Iowa has directed its procurement agencies to purchase recycled paper products whenever possible if the price is "reasonably competitive" and the product is of "the quality intended."
- Soybean-based inks and starch-based plastics (which use two of the state's agricultural products—soybeans and corn) are promoted.
- State agencies were required to establish wastepaper recycling programs by 1 January 1990.
- A program was established to increase the recycling of food service and packaging items by 25 percent as of 1 January 1992 and by 50 percent as of 1 January 1993. If these goals are not met, the manufacturing, sale, and use of polystyrene packing products or food service items will be prohibited as of 1 January 1994. Iowa has directed its department of general services to comply with the recycling goal and schedule, as well as the ultimate termination of the use of polystyrene products for storing, packaging, or serving food for immediate consumption.
- A statewide waste reduction and recycling network has been established to promote the state's waste management policy, which encourages the reduction of waste volume, the development of recycling markets, and the education of the public to that end. A recycling demonstration project for polystyrene food packaging was to be implemented by 1 July 1991,

and a report on the results was to be submitted to the general assembly by 1 January 1992.

- As of 1 July 1990, land disposal of lead-acid batteries was prohibited. Battery retailers must post this law and accept old batteries for recycling when new ones are purchased.
- Iowa has banned the disposal and required the recycling of the following materials: beverage containers (1990), lead-acid batteries (1990), used oil (1990), tires (1991), yard waste (1991), and nondegradable grocery bags (July 1992).
- A Waste Volume Reduction and Recycling Fund has been established to award grants for the implementation of a pollution hotline and for projects dealing with waste reduction, recycling, and education about such issues.

SOURCE: Iowa Code Annotated: Title II, Chapter 18, Division 1, s 18.18, s 18.20, s 18.21; Title XVII (Natural Resource Regulation), Chapter 455D (Waste Volume Reduction and Recycling), s 455D.5, s 455D.10, s 455D.15, s 455D.16.

Kansas

- Kansas allows a bidding preference for products containing the highest percentage of recycled materials, but the bid must be competitive with others. Specific statutes establish exact percentages of total dollar amounts to be spent on recycled paper. In addition, state agencies are not permitted to discriminate against products containing recycled materials.
- In 1990, a statute established a statewide coordinator position to deal with waste reduction, recycling, and market development. That position will be abolished as of 1 July 1995.
- The Kansas Commission on Waste Reduction, Recycling, and Market Development was established on 1 July 1990 to evaluate and recommend specific actions that the governor and legislature may take to reduce the volume of generated solid waste, expand markets for recyclable materials, encourage local recycling and waste reduction programs, promote recycling, and create opportunities for recycling enterprises. After submitting a report on its findings, the commission is to be abolished on 1 July 1992.
- Kansas prohibits the land disposal of used tires. As of 1 July 1991, programs were established to enforce laws pertaining to tire disposal and to encourage the recycling of tires. Grant monies are available to fund research and development on recycling and reusing waste tires.

SOURCE: Kansas Statutes Annotated: Chapter 74, Article 50, s 74-5087, s 74-5088, Chapter 75, Article 37, s 75-3740, s 75-3740b, s 75-3740c,

Chapter 65 (Public Health), Article 34 (Solid and Hazardous Waste), s 65-3406, s 65-3418, s 65-3424, s 65-3424f, s 65-3431. Recycling of vehicles and vehicle parts is addressed in Chapter 8, Article 1, s 8-1,136, s 8-1,137, and Article 24, s 8-2401, s 8-2401a, and s 8-2406.

Kentucky

- Kentucky prohibits discrimination against the purchase of recycled materials and has required all state agencies to establish minimum recycled content purchasing regulations since 1 September 1991.
- Any bidder competing for a state contract and any projects financed by state bonds must use products containing recycled materials, per minimum content regulations, wherever possible.
- Products with minimum recycled content must be available through the state's central stores. Any state agency that purchases these goods will receive a 50 percent reduction in any administrative fees normally charged by the central purchasing agency.
- Kentucky offers a tax credit equal to 50 percent of the installed cost for recycling or composting equipment.
- A Kentucky Recycling Brokerage Authority was established on 1 July 1991 to further local governments' efforts to develop reliable markets for their recyclables.
- Twenty percent of the funds available to the state bond program must be used for projects that create or expand markets for materials recovered or diverted from the solid waste stream.
- The state prohibits the disposal of used oil and requires that it be recycled or reused.

SOURCE: Kentucky Revised Statutes Annotated: Title VI, Chapter 45A (Recycled Material Content Products), s 45A.515, s 45A.520, s 45A.525, s 45A.530, s 45A.540; Title XI (Revenue and Taxation), Chapter 141, s 141.390; Title XII, Chapter 152, s 152.045, s 152.052; Title XVIII (Public Health), Chapter 224 (Environmental Protection), s 224.217, s 224.218, s 224.866, s 224.895.

Louisiana

- In 1986, Louisiana created a Litter Control and Recycling Commission that is responsible for promoting recycling and for educating the public about litter problems and recycling.
- The Department of Environmental Quality is directed "to conserve and recycle our natural resources . . . maximum resource recovery from solid waste and maximum recycling and reuse of such resources must be considered goals of the state."

- State agencies are directed to use degradable or recyclable plastics whenever possible. The Department of Environmental Quality is responsible for providing a plan for the use of such plastics.
- In 1989, state agencies were directed to adopt policies to promote the use of products made from recycled materials. At the beginning of such programs, no less than 5 percent of the total goods ordered had to be recycled; the goal in five years was to reach a minimum of 25 percent. Further, the Department of Transportation was advised to initiate procedures to ensure that it used the maximum amount of recycled materials possible in highway maintenance and construction.
- Lead-acid batteries have been banned from land disposal since 1989 and are required to be recycled. Battery retailers must post signage to this effect.
- As of 1 July 1990, used oil was banned from disposal in landfills, and beginning on 1 January 1991, citizens were required to dispose of oil only at permitted used oil collection facilities.
- After 1 July 1990, white goods could no longer be disposed of and had to be recycled instead.

SOURCE: Louisiana Statutes Annotated: Title 25, Chapter 24 (Statewide Beautification), Part I (Louisiana Litter Control and Recycling Commission), s 1103, s 1105; Title 30, Subtitle II (Environmental Quality), Chapter 2 (Department of Environmental Quality), s 2038, Chapter 9, s 2184, Chapter 18 (Solid Waste Recycling and Reduction Law), s 2415, s 2417, s 2420, s 2421; Title 36, Chapter 22, Part III, s 918.

Maine

- Annual reports to the legislature are required, to advise that body of the state's efforts to purchase and promote supplies and materials composed in whole or in part of recycled materials.
- A Waste Reduction and Recycling Loan Fund has been established to aid projects aimed at reducing and/or recycling solid and hazardous wastes and promoting the reuse of postconsumer materials.
- Maine has required each municipality to review its procurement procedures and specifications to make sure there is no discrimination against any products containing recycled materials.
- In 1989, Maine set a goal to reduce its waste by increasing its recycling rate to 50 percent by 1994.
- The state's solid waste management plan was submitted to the legislature on 1 March 1990. The Office of Waste Reduction and Recycling was subsequently created to provide technical and financial assistance programs to municipalities across the state.

These programs had to deal with recycling, composting, source separation, marketing of materials, etc.

- By 1 July 1990, the capitol complex of state buildings was required to institute a recycling program that handled, at a minimum, office paper, corrugated cardboard, and returnable containers.
- By 1 January 1991, all other state agencies were required to have implemented source-separated recycling programs and to have established and implemented a waste reduction program.
- Similar requirements for recycling programs have been set for private businesses within the state. By 1 July 1993, all businesses employing 15 or more persons at one site must have office paper recycling programs implemented.
- Tax incentives for recycling in Maine consist of a tax credit equal to 30 percent of the cost of equipment and machinery. Subsidies are also available to municipalities for the costs of transporting scrap metal.
- Maine prohibits the disposal and requires the recycling of lead-acid batteries.

SOURCE: Maine Revised Statutes Annotated: Title 5, Part 4, Chapter 155 (Purchases), Subchapter I, s 1812-A; Title 10, Part 2, Chapter 110, Subchapter II, s 1023-G; Title 30A, Part 2, Subpart 9, Chapter 223, Subchapter I, s 5656; Title 38, Chapter 24 (Maine Waste Management Agency), Subchapter II, s 2122; Subchapter III (Office of Waste Reduction and Recycling), s 2131, s 2133, s 2137, s 2138.

Maryland

- The Maryland Recycling Act, passed in 1988, included the following requirements: (1) the creation of an Office of Waste Minimization and Recycling (OWMR); (2) the creation and implementation of a recycling plan by the OWMR to reduce waste generated by the state government by 20 percent (or at least 10 percent); (3) biannual reports to the governor and general assembly on recycling efforts, programs, and markets, beginning 1 January 1990; and (4) the creation and implementation of public education and grant programs.
- All counties, as well as the state government, were required to submit recycling plans in 1990 and to implement them by 1 January 1992.
- Minimum recycling goals to be attained by 1994 were assigned to jurisdictions based on population size: For jurisdictions under 150,000, the goal is 15 percent; for those over 150,000, the goal is 20 percent.
- Maryland has recycled-content requirements for newsprint consumers, stated by the percentage of total newsprint used

within a calendar year by a given publisher: 12 percent for 1992 and 1993, 20 percent for 1994, 25 percent for 1995, 30 percent for 1996, 35 percent for 1997, and 40 percent for 1998 and all subsequent calendar years.

- The Maryland Used Oil Recycling Act bans the disposal of used oil and requires that it be collected and recycled. Signs explaining this law and giving the locations of government-operated used oil collection facilities must be posted at all locations where motor oils and lubricants are sold.
- The Used Tire Recycling Act of 1991 requires that tires be recycled. Additionally, a Used Tire Clean-up and Recycling Fund was created in 1991and assigned to OWMR for management.
- By 1 January 1991, all state agencies were to review their purchasing and procurement specifications and to require the use of a percentage price preference for the purchase of supplies and commodities containing recycled materials.

SOURCE: Annotated Code of Maryland, 1988: Environment Division, Title 9 (Water, Ice, and Sanitary Facilities), Subtitle 17 (Office of Recycling), s 9-1702, s 9-1703, s 9-1706, s 9-1707; Natural Resources Division, Title 8 (Water and Water Resources), Subtitle 14 (Used Oil Recycling), s 8-1401, s 8-1411.1; State Finance and Procurement Division, Division II, Title 14 (Preferences), Subtitle 4, s 14-405. Title 13 deals with vehicle laws and has a number of sections regulating scrap metals recycling with regard to vehicles.

Massachusetts

- The state empowers local agencies to establish and fund recycling programs. Such programs may be declared mandatory for residences, schools, and businesses, and source separation may be required.
- The state's nonmandatory integrated waste management goals for the year 2000, intended to treat the solid waste stream, call for source reduction to handle 10 percent of such waste, recycling to handle 38 percent, composting to handle 3 percent, and incineration/landfilled ash to handle 49 percent.
- In 1981, the state passed a mandatory deposit law on all beverage containers.
- An executive order in 1987 advised the state to buy products made from recycled materials whenever possible.

SOURCES: Massachusetts General Laws Annotated: Part I, Title VII, Chapter 40, s 8H (Recycling Programs). Glenn, Jim, "The State of Garbage in America," *BioCycle* 32 (April 1990): 34–41.

Michigan

- In 1976, Michigan passed a mandatory beverage container deposit law.
- This state's recycling goal is a rate of 50 percent by the year 2005.
- State percentage requirements for the purchase of supplies and equipment containing recycled materials are as follows: 10 percent for 1989, 15 percent for 1990, and 20 percent for 1991 and subsequent years.
- Annual reports to the governor and the legislature are required, detailing the state's procurement and purchasing procedures and accomplishments with regard to recycled materials.
- Goals for the purchase of paper products made from recycled paper and the percentage of postconsumer waste contained in that paper have been set: In 1989, 30 percent of the paper purchased must be recycled and the minimum amount of postconsumer waste required is 25 percent; in 1990, 40 percent must be recycled, with a 35 percent minimum in postconsumer waste; and in 1991 and subsequent years, 50 percent must be recycled and a 50 percent mimimum in postconsumer waste must be attained.
- County commissioners may impose a $2 per month or $25 per year surcharge per household to fund waste reduction, recycling, composting, and household hazardous waste programs.
- The Clean Michigan Fund Act created a commission to study the feasibility of recycling and composting in 1986. Subsequently, a capital grant program and an operational grant program were established to fund recycling and composting projects within the state. More funding was allocated for the study and development of recycled materials markets.
- Michigan's Office Paper Recovery Act set the following goals for recycling rates in state offices: 1 January 1989—20 percent or more; 1 January 1990—25 percent or more; 1 January 1992—50 percent or more; and 1 January 2000—85 percent or more.
- In 1988, a Plastics Recycling Development Fund Consortium was established to study plastics recycling, packaging, and production, funded from state revenues. As of 1 January 1992, this group was disbanded by statute.
- State agencies are required to recycle all used motor oil.

SOURCE: Michigan Compiled Laws Annotated: Chapter 18, Article 2, s 18.1261 a and b, Chapter 124, s 124.508a, Chapter 299 (Natural Resources), Clean Michigan Fund Act, s 299.378, s 299.382, s

299.384, s 299.387, s 299.389a, Solid Waste Management Act, s 299.406, Office Paper Recovery Act, s 299.463, Plastics Recycling Development Fund Act, s 299.473, s 299.475, s 299.476, Chapter 319 Used Oil Recycling Act, s 319.314.

Minnesota

- In 1989, Minnesota established a recycling rate goal of 25 percent for counties outside the metropolitan area and 35 percent for counties within the metropolitan area by 31 December 1993.
- A 10 percent purchasing incentive is allowed for the procurement of state commodities that contain recycled materials. Additional consideration is to be given to products made from waste generated within the state.
- The Department of Natural Resources is required to provide recycling containers at all state parks.
- Technical assistance and funding are available for the development of recycling programs, facilities, and markets.
- All counties are mandated to give residents the opportunity to recycle. The following must be available in each county: at least one recycling center, convenient sites for the collection of recyclables, and public education information and promotion programs. Furthermore, cities with populations of 5,000 or more must provide curbside pick-up, centralized drop-off, or a local recycling center for at least four kinds of recyclables.
- All materials collected for recycling must be taken to markets for sale or reprocessing.
- To be designated a recycling center, a facility must be open a minimum of 12 hours each week, 12 months of the year, and it must accept at least four different materials.
- All containers, receptacles, and storage bins must be partly made from recycled materials and be recyclable themselves, if at all possible.
- State funding is available to counties for developing and implementing programs on source reduction, recycling, and recycling markets.
- Minnesota requires the collection and recycling of lead-acid batteries, and signage to this effect must be posted at all battery-selling locations. Leaves cannot be landfilled, and tires, white goods, and used oil may not be disposed of but must be recycled instead.

SOURCE: Minnesota Statutes Annotated: Chapter 16B, s 16B.121, Chapter 85 (Division of Parks and Recreation), s 85.205, Chapter 88, s 88.80, Chapter 115A (Waste Management), s 115A.48, s 115A.551–553, s 115A.555–557, s 115A.904, s 115A.915, s 115A.916, s 115A.931, s

115A.95, s 115A.9561, Chapter 325E, s 325E.115, Chapter 473, s 473.8441.

Mississippi

- This state promotes recycling and waste reduction through legislative declarations and has funding available to assist in recycling and solid waste reduction projects.
- Within 15 months after the publication of Subtitle D in the *Federal Register* (which occurred in October 1991), a nonhazardous solid waste management plan must be developed and administered. Such a plan is expected to include a 25 percent waste minimization goal and to define the strategy for attaining that goal by 1 January 1996.
- Lead-acid batteries may not be disposed of and must be recycled. All sellers of such batteries must erect signage stating this law and offer collection facilities.
- A state agency wastepaper recycling plan was to be implemented by 1 July 1987.
- In 1990, a Commission on Environmental Quality was authorized and empowered to promote minimization, recycling, reuse, and treatment of wastes in lieu of disposal.
- From 2 April 1990 until 1 July 1992, a moratorium on permits for new or expanded nonhazardous waste facilities was instituted.
- By 1 July 1991, the Department of Economic and Community Development was expected to assist and promote the recycling industry, as well as create a Recycling Market Development Council. This council was directed to issue a comprehensive report, due 1 January 1993, on the state of the recycling industry and how best to promote it and source reduction within the state.
- By 1 July 1992, all state agencies, branches, and institutions must establish recycling and source reduction programs, including both collection of recyclables and procurement of recycled materials.

SOURCE: Mississippi Code 1972 Annotated: Title 17, Chapter 17 (Solid Wastes Disposal), s 17-17-33, s 17-17-41, s 17-17-59, s 17-17-101, s 17-17-103, s 17-17-123, Nonhazardous Solid Waste Planning Act of 1991, s 17-17-221, s 17-17-227, Mississippi Regional Solid Waste Management Authority Act, s 17-17-305, s 17-17-319, s 17.17-401, s 17-17-403, s 17-17-429, s 17-17-431; Title 29, Chapter 5, s 29-5-2; Title 31, Chapter 7, s 31-7-13; Title 49 (Conservation and Ecology), Chapter 31, Mississippi Comprehensive Multimedia Waste Minimization Act of 1990, s 49-31-5, s 49-31-7, s 49-31-9, s 49-31-11, s 49-31-15, s 49-31-17.

Missouri

- Purchasing specifications must eliminate any discrimination against the procurement of supplies and goods made from recycled materials, and they are expected to reflect a policy of reducing and ultimately eliminating products manufactured in whole or in part from polystyrene foam that uses any fully halogenated chlorofluorocarbons.

- The required minimum percentages of recycled materials in state-purchased paper products are specified as follows: 40 percent for newsprint, 80 percent for paperboard, 50 percent for high-grade printing and writing paper, and 5 to 40 percent in tissue products. These goals are to be attained in percentages of total state purchases by the following dates: 10 percent in 1991 and 1992, 25 percent in 1993 and 1994, 40 percent in 1995, and 60 percent by 2000.

- Additionally, all state agencies are required to recycle, at a minimum, 25 percent of the paper and paper products used and 75 percent of all used motor oil.

- After 1 January 1990, all major counties were required to ensure that, to the greatest extent possible, all recyclable and reusable materials were removed from the waste stream prior to disposal or incineration.

- By 1 July 1990, all state agencies were expected to source-separate and recycle plastics, paper, metals, and other recyclable items.

- The Department of Natural Resources (DNR) is expected to conduct and contract for research into alternatives to the landfill disposal of solid wastes. It is also directed to prepare model solid waste management plans for rural and urban areas that emphasize waste reduction and recycling and are designed to achieve a reduction of 40 percent, by weight, in solid waste disposed of by 1 January 1998. Promotion of resource recovery through education, market development, technical assistance, and the establishment of state government recycling programs is another of the department's duties.

- After 1 January 1991, the following items are prohibited from disposal in landfills and are required to be collected for recycling: white goods, waste oil, and lead-acid batteries. Signs regarding the battery disposal and recycling law are to be posted at all points of sales for lead-acid batteries.

- After 1 January 1991, waste oil may not be burned without energy recovery.

- After 1 January 1992, yard waste is banned from landfills.

- After 1 January 1994, all major newspaper publishers must file annual statements certifying the number of tons of newsprint they have used in the past year and the average recycled content of that newsprint. (See statute for specific target percentages.)

- Missouri requires that all plastic products, bottles, and rigid containers must be labeled with identifying resin codes (per Society of the Plastics Industry specifications).
- Transfer stations with the sole function of separating materials for recycling are exempt from landfill fees.
- A total of $1 million has been appropriated from the solid waste management fund for fiscal years 1992–1997 for activities that promote the development of markets for recycled materials.
- The DNR is directed to collect and disseminate information, as well as to conduct educational and training programs that promote resource recovery and recycling.
- A Source Reduction Advisory Board was to be established for one year to research and write a report that would include information on how to reduce the amount of packaging material in the waste stream as well as maximize the recycling and reuse of packaging materials.
- The duties of the Missouri Rural Economic Development Council include assisting existing businesses and encouraging new businesses that promote resource recovery, waste minimization, and recycling.

SOURCE: Vernon's Annotated Missouri Statutes: Title IV, Chapter 34, s 34.031, s 34.032, Chapter 37, s 37.078; Title XVI (Conservation, Resources, and Development), Chapter 260 (Environmental Control), s 260.005, s 260.035, s 260.200, s 260.201, s 260.202, s 260.209, s 260.210, s 260.225, s 260.248, s 260.250, s 260.255, s 260.260, s 260.262, s 260.281, s 260.310, s 260.320, s 260.325, s 260.330, s 260.335, s 260.342, s 260.344, s 260.345; Title XL, Chapter 620, s 620.157, s 620.161, s 620.605.

Montana

- A 25 percent tax credit is available for capital investments in equipment used for collecting or processing recyclable materials or for manufacturing products from such materials. This provision terminates 31 December 1995.
- An additional 5 percent tax deduction is available for taxpayers who purchase recycled materials as business-related expenses. This provision terminates 31 December 1995.
- The Department of Motor Vehicles specifically encourages the recycling of used or outdated vehicle license plates, which are made from aluminum.
- The legislature has stipulated that "it is the continuing responsibility of the state of Montana to use all practicable means . . . to improve and coordinate state plans . . . to the end that the

state may enhance the quality of renewable resources and approach the maximum attainable recycling of depletable resources." A public policy articulated elsewhere declares that "maximum recycling from solid waste is necessary to protect the public health, welfare, and quality of the natural environment."

- As of 1 July 1993, the Department of Waste and Litter Control will be permanently assigned the duty of acting as "a clearinghouse for information on waste reduction and reuse, recycling technology and markets, composting, and household hazardous waste disposal, including chemical compatibility." The department is also expected to prepare a solid waste management and resource recovery plan for the state, including rules necessary for its implementation. Further, the department has been charged with implementing a statewide household hazardous waste public education program.

- Another state policy declares that it must plan for and implement an integrated approach to solid waste management, in the following order of priority: source reduction, reuse, recycling, composting, and, finally, landfill disposal or incineration. As part of this policy, each state agency, the legislature, and the university system were required to prepare source reduction and recycling plans by 1 January 1992; these plans had to include provisions for composting yard wastes and recycling office and computer paper, cardboard, used motor oil, and any other recyclables for which a market could be found or developed. A source reduction and recycling program was expected to be established and implemented by 1 July 1992.

- By 1 January 1992, state purchasing specifications were to be written to promote products made from recycled materials, including, at a minimum: paper, paper products, plastic, plastic products, glass, glass products, tires, and motor oil and lubricants.

- The state goal is to have 95 percent of the paper and paper products used by state agencies, universities, and the legislature made from recycled materials that maximize postconsumer material content by 1 January 1996.

- Waste oil may not be disposed of and must be recycled. All sellers of motor oil must post this information and give the location of the nearest waste oil collection center within 25 miles.

SOURCE: Montana Code Annotated: Title 15, Chapter 32, Part 6 (Recycling of Material), s 15-32-601 through 605, s 15-32-610 and 611; Title 61 (Motor Vehicles), Chapter 3, Part 3, s 61-3-336; Title 75 (Environmental Protection), Chapter 1, Part 1, s 75-1-103; Chapter 10 (Waste and Litter Control), Part 1, s 75-10-101 through 104, s 75-10-121, Part 2, s 75-10-203, s 75-10-215, Part 5 (which has extensive laws dealing with the recycling and disposal of motor vehicles, not described above), Part 8 (Integrated Waste Management), s 75-10-802, s 75-10-804 through 807, Part 11, s 75-10-1101.

Nebraska

- The legislature has declared that a comprehensive statewide litter and recycling program is necessary. A Nebraska Litter Reduction and Recycling Fund (to be funded by littering fees) and a Waste Reduction and Recycling Incentive Fund were created to assist in implementing this program. As of 1 July 1991, an annual waste reduction and recycling fee was imposed on all state retail businesses, with all such fees credited to the Waste Reduction and Recycling Incentive Fund; proceeds from fees imposed on new tire sales are also credited to this fund.

  SOURCE: Nebraska Revised Statutes of 1943: Chapter 69, Article 20, s 69-2006, Chapter 77, Article 23, s 77-2368, Chapter 81, Article 15B (Environmental Protection—Litter Reduction and Recycling), s 81-1535, s 81-1545, s 81-1546, s 81-1558, s 81-1561, Article 15L (Waste Reduction and Recycling), s 81-15,160, s 81-15,161, s 81-15,163, s 81-15,165, Article 16F (State Government Recycling Management Act), s 81-1646.

Nevada

- Nevada has no legislation at this time that deals with recycling, other than the recycling of wastewater and abandoned vehicles.

  SOURCE: Nevada Revised Statutes: Title 40, Chapter 445; Title 43, Chapter 487.

New Hampshire

- The state's general court has declared that the goal of the state for the years 1990–2000 is to reduce the weight of the solid waste stream by a minimum of 40 percent.
- Integrated waste management solutions are supported by the general court of the state in the following priorities: (1) source reduction; (2) recycling, reuse, and composting; (3) waste-to-energy technologies; (4) incineration (without resource recovery); and (5) landfilling.
- State agencies are required to use products incorporating recycled materials to the maximum extent possible, and information on the percentage of postconsumer waste must be included by all vendors of such products.

- A 5 percent price incentive is allowed for the state's purchase of recycled paper products. This incentive is to be applied to products containing the following percentages of recycled fiber: 10 percent by June 1991, 25 percent by June 1992, and 40 percent by June 1996.
- These percentage requirements are also applicable to the goals for the amounts of recycled paper to be purchased (e.g., 10 percent of the total amount of paper purchased by the state had to be recycled paper by June 1991).
- All state agencies are required to have recycling programs for postconsumer wastes that they generate and for which markets have been identified.
- The state's policies include implementing steps to encourage reduction of packaging and the maximum possible use of products made from recycled materials by state agencies. Any procurement specifications that discriminate against recycled materials are prohibited.
- As of 31 December 1990, all state agencies were to have implemented waste reduction and recycling programs.
- A Waste Management Council was established in 1990.
- The Division of Waste Management's responsibilities include promoting the implementation of recycling technologies as well as identifying and establishing recyclable materials markets. The division is also directed to develop and implement technical assistance programs and to allocate funds for solid waste management programs to include recycling.
- Each town in the state is responsible for its own solid waste management plans, which must consider environmental impact, economic impact (including resource recovery and recycling), and area impact.
- As of 1 January 1992, "no person shall dispose of refuse at any private solid waste landfill facility having a lining and leachate collection system, unless all recyclable materials have been removed from such refuse, or such refuse has been otherwise reduced in weight by at least 20 percent."
- Wet-cell batteries may not be disposed of and are required to be recycled.
- A recycled/recyclable labeling emblem or logo has been established by the Department of Environmental Services and may only be used as the department deems appropriate. Unauthorized use of the emblem can result in a fine of $2,500 per day for each day on which the violation continues.
- Used oil must be recycled, and the recycling of lead-acid batteries and used tires is encouraged.

SOURCE: New Hampshire Statutes Annotated: Title I, Chapter 6, s 6:12, Chapter 21-I, s 21-I:1-a, s 21-I:11, s 21-I:14-a, s 21-I:60 through 21-I:65, Chapter 21-O (Department of Environmental Services), s 21-O:9; Title X, Chapter 147, s 147:43, Chapter 149-M (Solid Waste Management), s 149-M:1, s 149-M:1-a, s 149-M:3, s 149-M:8, s 149-M:10, s 149-M:13-a and b, s 149-M:17 through 149-M:19, s 149-M:22, s 149-M:24, s 149-M:25, s 149-M:31, Chapter 149-N (Recycling Logo).

New Jersey

- As of 1987, this state mandated the source separation and collection of recyclables. A goal was set to recycle at least 25 percent of the solid waste stream by 1992.
- A New Jersey Office of Recycling was established within the Department of Environmental Protection in 1987, but most of the responsibility for recycling is assigned to individual counties. These counties are responsible for administering their own recycling plans, which must provide for the collection and recycling of at least three materials in addition to leaves.
- A recycling tax of $1.50 per ton of solid waste accepted for disposal is applied to all solid waste facilities, and the monies are credited to the State Recycling Fund, which is a funding source for recycling programs throughout the state. A Statewide Mandatory Source Separation and Recycling Program Fund has also been established to aid counties and municipalities in implementing their recycling programs, as well as for the study of recyclable materials markets.
- Plastic and bimetal beverage containers may not carry a recyclable emblem unless the state determines that feasible recycling systems for those products are available.
- Leaves may not be disposed of in landfills.
- State procurement guidelines prohibit discrimination against recycled materials, and a bidding preference is given for recycled paper containing the highest amount of postconsumer waste. Goals for the purchase of recycled paper or recycled paper products, as a percentage of the total amounts of such products purchased, were set as follows: 10 percent by 1 July 1987, 30 percent by 1 July 1988, and 45 percent by 1 July 1989.
- State specifications encourage the maximum usage of products such as recyclable asphalt pavement, crumb rubber, and glass aggregate paving materials. All products made from recycled materials must be given preference whenever the price is "reasonably competitive."

- A 50 percent taxpayer credit is available for purchasers of recycling equipment. Receipts from the sales of recycling equipment are exempt from the sales and use tax.

SOURCE: New Jersey Statutes Annotated: Title 13, Chapter 1D (Department of Environmental Protection), s 13:1D-18.3, Chapter 1E (Solid Waste Management), s 13:1E-95, s 13:1E-96, s 13:1E-96.1, s 13:1E-99.13 through 13:1E-99.21, s 13:1E-99.24 through 13:1E-99.28, s 13:1E-99.30, s 13:1E-99.31, s 13:1E-99.33, s 13:1E-99.34, s 13:1E-99.37, s 13:1E-99.38; Title 52, Subtitle 5, Chapter 34 (Purchase of Recycled Materials), s 52:34-21 through 52:34-24; Title 54 (Taxation), Subtitle 4, Part 1, Chapter 10A, s 54:10A-5.3, Subtitle 4A, Chapter 32B, s 54:32B-8.36.

New Mexico

- The state's Litter Control and Beautification Act declares a need for a state-coordinated plan of education, control, prevention, and recycling in order to eliminate litter. The Litter Control Council must have a member from RECYCLE New Mexico.
- The Department of Highways is required to encourage voluntary recycling programs, aid in identifying programs and available markets for recycled materials, and promote private recycling efforts for all recyclable items.
- In 1990, the state passed a Solid Waste Act. One of its purposes is to "plan for and regulate, in the most economically feasible, cost-effective and environmentally safe manner, the reduction, storage, collection, transportation, separation, processing, recycling, and disposal of solid waste." Another purpose of the act is to require that all state agencies set procurement policies to aid and promote the development of recycling as well as markets for recyclable materials.
- By 1 July 1992, each state agency and the legislature must implement both a source reduction program and a source-separated recycling program. The recycling program must include, at a minimum, high-grade paper, corrugated paper, and glass. Postsecondary educational institutions are also directed to implement similar programs by this date that must include a composting component.
- By 31 December 1992, a comprehensive and integrated solid waste management program must be submitted to the Environmental Improvement Board. The following priorities are to be indicated: (1) source reduction and recycling, (2) environmentally safe transformation, and (3) environmentally safe landfill disposal. Other specific components of the plan

include public education programs on solid waste management, recycling, source reduction, and composting. This solid waste program is to be designed by 1 December 1993 and fully implemented by 1 July 1994. At least once every three years, it is to be reexamined for management, efficiency, and compliance.

- By 1 July 1994 and annually thereafter, the director of the Department of Environmental Improvement is to prepare a report for the legislature on the status of solid waste management efforts in the state.
- A Division of Solid Waste was created by the Solid Waste Act to enforce and implement the act and its programs. Its responsibilities include providing technical assistance on solid waste issues, promoting and planning source reduction and recycling programs and facilities, developing information for education and technical assistance, and researching and developing recycling markets.
- The state purchasing agent and all procurement personnel are directed to establish specifications to promote goods and supplies containing recycled materials. A 5 percent price incentive is offered for such goods.
- Tax incentives in the form of investment credits are offered for equipment used in recycling or recycling/reprocessing facilities.

SOURCE: New Mexico Statutes 1978, Annotated: Chapter 7 (Taxation), Article 9A (Investment Credit), Chapter 67, Article 16 (Litter Control and Beautification), s 67-16-2 through 67-16-4, s 67-16-12, Chapter 74 (Environmental Improvement), Article 9 (Solid Waste Act), s 74-9-2 through 74-9-4, s 74-9-6, s 74-9-10, s 74-9-12 through 74-9-17, s 74-9-19.

New York

- This state's overall goal is to attain a solid waste reduction of 50 percent through integrated efforts by 1997.
- All beverage containers sold within the state are subject to a mandatory deposit.
- New York's Department of Energy Conservation (DEC) must serve as a clearinghouse for information pertaining to the reduction and recycling of waste generated by commercial and industrial enterprises. The DEC is expected to provide consumer education on the "economic and environmental benefits of solid waste management practices and the concomitant needs for waste reduction and for consumers to actively seek consumer products which contain secondary materials or which are easily recycled or reused." An annual report on solid waste and progressive reduction efforts is to be submitted to the governor.

- The Department of Economic Development and the DEC are directed to work together to conduct secondary materials market development programs.
- The DEC is responsible for designing and implementing a local resource reuse and development program that must promote the collection, intermediate processing, and marketing of waste materials that were formerly disposed of as municipal solid waste within the state.
- Within the DEC, a Bureau of Waste Reduction and Recycling was established to assist in the development and promotion of local waste reduction, source separation, and recycling programs. The bureau was directed to establish a recycling emblem and set the standards for its use, as well as penalties for its misuse.
- Lead-acid batteries may not be disposed of and must be collected for recycling.
- State-funded assistance is available for municipal recycling projects and innovative recycling demonstration projects.
- Municipalities are empowered by the legislature to require source separation of recyclable or reusable materials. As of 1 September 1992, this requirement is to be adopted into local laws and ordinances to cover, at a minimum, the recycling of paper, glass, metals, plastics, and garden and yard waste.
- All state and judicial agencies are required to buy recycled products, within a price incentive of 10 percent; the limit is raised to 15 percent if the product is made from at least 50 percent postconsumer waste.
- All public utilities are required to recycle industrial materials, as well as to use supplies and goods incorporating recycled materials whenever possible.

SOURCE: McKinney's Consolidated Laws of New York Annotated: Chapter 15, Article 14 (Energy Conservation Services), s 263, Article 27; Title 4 (Marketing of Recyclable Materials), s 27-0401, s 27-0403, s 27-0405; Title 7 (Solid Waste Management and Resource Recovery Facilities), s 27-0717, Chapter 24, Article 6 (Public Health and Safety), s 120-aa, Chapter 30, Article 2-A, s 40-a, Chapter 43-A, Article 5; Title 12, s 1285-g (Industrial Materials Recycling Program), Chapter 43-B, Article 27; Title 17 (Lead-Acid Battery Recycling), s 27-1701, Article 54 (Implementation of the 21st Century Environmental Quality Bond Act); Title 6 (Innovative Recycling Demonstration and Municipal Recycling Projects), s 54-0601, s 54-0603, s 54-0605, s 54-0607, s 54-0609, s 54-0611.

North Carolina

- This state's overall goal is to recycle 25 percent of its total waste stream by 1 January 1993. When the general assembly decided on this figure in 1989, it also stated that it would evaluate the process of reaching that goal and would consider increasing the goal "as appropriate." The general assembly had arrived at this decision after stating that the state's failure to economically recover resources and energy from solid waste had resulted in unnecessary waste and depletion of natural resources. For these reasons, one of the state's goals was the maximum resource recovery from solid waste and maximum recycling and reuse of such resources.

- North Carolina provides tax deductions for the purchase and installation of recycling or resource recovery equipment.

- The Pollution Prevention Pays Program is a nonregulatory program that was established by statute in 1989 to encourage voluntary waste and pollution reduction efforts through research and the provision of "information, technical assistance, and matching grants to businesses and industries interested in establishing or enhancing activities to prevent, reduce, or recycle waste."

- When the Division of Solid Waste Management was created within the state's Department of Health in 1989, it was to "promote sanitary processing, treatment, disposal, and statewide management of solid waste and the greatest possible recycling and recovery of resources." This was to be accomplished through public education, program development, and market development created to promote recycling.

- The Department of Health is also required to maintain a directory of state recycling and resource recovery systems. Comprehensive solid waste management reports must be prepared each year, and recommendations concerning all aspects of recycling and resource recovery are to be included.

- The state subscribes to the integrated solid waste management hierarchy in the following descending order of preference: (1) source reduction, (2) recycling/reuse, (3) composting, (4) waste-to-energy incineration, (5) volume-reduction incineration, and (6) landfill disposal.

- All counties, either individually or in a cooperative effort with others, must develop comprehensive solid waste management plans that include provisions to address the goal of recycling 25 percent of the total waste stream by 1 January 1993. Counties, cities, and towns may require participation in recycling programs.

- By 1 July 1991, all designated local governments were to initiate recycling programs.

- All beverage containers with detachable metal rings or tabs were prohibited as of 1 January 1990.
- All packing or packaging materials made from fully halogenated chlorofluorocarbons were prohibited after 1 October 1991.
- Plastic bags offered by retail establishments after 1 January 1991 must be recyclable and imprinted with such information. After 1 January 1993, the state must certify that at least 25 percent of these plastic bags are actually being recycled by individual retail establishments; if not, the retail establishment is prohibited from distributing them.
- Polystyrene food packaging may not be sold or distributed after 1 October 1991 unless it is recyclable. After 1 October 1993, the state must certify that at least 25 percent of such packaging is actually being recycled; if not, the packaging may no longer be sold or distributed.
- As of 1 July 1991, every plastic container had to carry a molded label identifying the resin from which it was made (per the Society of the Plastics Industry specifications).
- Products banned from landfills and required to be recycled include: used tires, 1 March 1990; used oil, 1 October 1990; lead-acid batteries, 1 January 1991; white goods, 1 January 1991; and yard trash, 1 January 1993.
- A Solid Waste Management Trust Fund is administered by the Department of Health. One of its purposes is to provide funding for activities that promote waste reduction and recycling. Another funding source in the statutes is the North Carolina Solid Waste Management Loan Program.
- By 1 January 1992, all state government agencies, the general assembly, the general court, and the state university were required to establish recycling programs to (1) collect, at a minimum, aluminum, high-grade office paper, and corrugated paper; (2) find markets for their materials; and (3) encourage source reduction.
- All state agencies are required to use composted products whenever possible.
- All school boards are required to encourage recycling and develop curriculum materials and resource guides for recycling awareness programs.
- The Department of Transportation is encouraged to use recycled materials whenever possible.

SOURCE: General Statutes of North Carolina: Chapter 105 (Taxation), Subchapter I, Article 3, Schedule C, s 105-122, Article 4, Schedule D, Division I, s 105-130.5, s 105-130.10, Subchapter II, Article 12, s 105-275, Chapter 113 (Conservation and Development),

Subchapter I, Article 1, s 113-8.01, Chapter 130A (Public Health), Article 9 (Solid Waste Management), Part 1, s 130A-290, Part 2, s 130A-291, s 130A-294, s 130A-309.01 (Solid Waste Management Act of 1989), Part 2A, s 130A-309.03 through 130A-309.10, s 130A-309.12, s 130A-309.14 through 130A-309.17, s 130A-309.19, s 130A-309.20, s 130A-309.24, s 130A-309.25, s 130A-309.28, s 130A-309.52, Chapter 136 (Roads and Highways), Article 2, s 136-28.8, Chapter 143, Article 8, s 143-129.2, Chapter 143B (Executive Organization Act of 1973), Article 7 (Department of Environment, Health, and Natural Resources), Part 4A (Governor's Waste Management Board), s 143-285.10, Chapter 153A (Counties), Article 6, s 153A-136, Article 22, s 153A-422, s 153A-427, Chapter 159I, s 159I-2, s 159I-8, s 159I-11, Chapter 160A (Cities and Towns), Article 8, s 160A-192.

North Dakota

- This state's Solid Waste Management and Land Protection Act includes goals of promoting resource recovery and both promoting and assisting in the development of recycled materials markets. The act also declares that the state goal is to "encourage by 1995 at least a 10 percent reduction in volume of municipal waste deposited in landfills, by 1997 at least a 25 percent reduction, and by 2000 at least a 40 percent reduction."
- A Solid Waste Management Fund was established to help finance resource recovery and recycling projects that emphasize market development.
- Public schools are encouraged to develop and disseminate educational materials promoting municipal waste reduction, source separation, reuse, and recycling.
- All state agencies are encouraged to specify the use of soybean-based ink when purchasing newsprint printing services.
- By 1 July 1990, at least 15 percent of the garbage can liners purchased by state agencies must be starch based. That percentage must increase by 5 percent annually until at least a 50 percent level is reached.
- Beginning 1 July 1993, at least 10 percent of the total volume of paper and paper products purchased by state agencies must contain at least 25 percent recycled materials. This percentage increases as follows: 30 percent beginning 1 January 1994, 40 percent beginning 1 January 1996, 60 percent beginning 1 January 1998, and 80 percent beginning 1 January 2000.

SOURCE: North Dakota Century Code: Title 23 (Health and Safety), Chapters 23–29 (Solid Waste Management and Land Protection Act), s 23-29-02, s 23-29-03, s 23-29-07.1, s 23-29-07.5, s 23-29-07.10; Title 54, Chapter 54-44.4 (State Purchasing Practices), s 54-44.4-07, s 54-44.4-08.

Ohio

- The state's goal is to recycle 25 percent of its solid waste by 1994.
- A Division of Litter Prevention and Recycling exists in the Department of Natural Resources. This division is required to administer grants and to establish and implement a comprehensive statewide litter prevention and recycling program to include public education, technical assistance, identification of existing and potential markets for recycled materials and of any barriers to their use, and encouragement of state agencies to purchase products made from recycled materials. Within the division, there is a Litter Prevention and Recycling Advisory Council, as well as a Keep Ohio Beautiful Commission.
- Tax credits are available for cash donations to corporations whose sole purpose is to promote and encourage recycling. Additional taxes were also established in 1981 to help fund litter prevention and recycling in the state.
- As of 1 July 1982, all metal beverage containers with detachable pieces were prohibited.
- As of December 1993, yard waste may no longer be disposed of in landfills.

SOURCE: Page's Ohio Revised Code Annotated: Title 15 (Conservation of Natural Resources), Chapter 1502 (Litter Control and Recycling), s 1502.01 through 1502.08, s 1502.99; Title 57 (Taxation), Chapter 5733, s 5733.064, s 5733.066, s 5733.122.

Oklahoma

- The Department of Health was directed by the legislature to provide, by 1 January 1991, a prioritized agenda of studies necessary to provide information that would facilitate the design and implementation of recycling initiatives.
- By 1992, the department was also directed to design and implement a statewide educational program on waste management that stressed recycling, litter reduction, waste reduction, and the management and disposal of "hard to dispose of" wastes.
- State agencies are required to participate in a recycling program, and a State Recycling Revolving Fund was created to assist in the funding of such recycling programs.
- State agencies are encouraged to purchase recycled paper.
- Waste tires must be recycled, and a tax on new tires helps to fund this state's tire recycling program.

SOURCE: Oklahoma Statutes Annotated: Title 47, Chapter 62A (which contains a comprehensive Automotive Dismantlers and

Parts Recycler Act); Title 63 (Public Health and Safety), Chapter 1, Article 24, s 1-2440 through 1-2443; Title 68 (Revenue and Taxation), Chapter 2 (Oklahoma Waste Tire Recycling Act), s 53001 through 53008.

Oregon

- On 4 August 1983, the Oregon Recycling Opportunity Act was signed. Many consider this legislation to be the first mandatory recycling law ever passed on a statewide basis. The act required that studies be conducted to assess the state's various waste streams to identify all possible recyclables. Individuals within each "wasteshed" area would then be notified as to what could be recycled. In addition, by 1 July 1986, cities and counties were mandated to provide the "opportunity to recycle" for all residents, although citizen participation was not required. Source separation of recyclable items was also mandated, and each wasteshed had to identify and explain how this opportunity was being provided and give details on its public education and promotional programs. The act also states that after an unspecified period of time, a wasteshed may require that certain items be recycled.
- A collection service may charge people who do not source-separate their recyclables higher fees than those who do.
- Oregon does have an antiscavenging law that prohibits the removal of recyclables from any container without the permission of the owner of the container or recyclables.
- It is illegal for anyone to mix source-separated recyclables with solid waste being collected for disposal.
- The highest percentage possible of all paper used by state agencies in any given year must be recycled paper. In Oregon, paper is considered recycled if not less than 50 percent of its total weight consists of secondary waste materials or not less than 25 percent of its total weight consists of postconsumer waste.
- All state agencies must ensure: (1) that their purchasing specifications do not discriminate against recycled products; (2) that they provide incentives for the maximum possible use of recycled materials and recovered resources; (3) that purchasing practices are developed to assure, as far as possible, that products bought are made of recycled materials or are recyclable themselves; (4) that management practices are established to promote source reduction; and (5) that they use recycled paper wherever possible and require the same of all persons with whom they contract for services.
- Specific guidelines have been established to encourage paper conservation within state offices, and a 5 percent purchasing preference is given to products containing recycled materials.

- A 10 percent investment tax credit is available for plastics recycling business investments made between 1 January 1986 and 1 July 1995.
- The Department of Environmental Quality is directed to establish percentages of plastic resins that must be recycled before a recycling program is deemed "effective." At least 15 percent of each plastic resin must be recycled statewide in 1992, but the required percentages may not exceed 75 percent before 31 December 1999.
- Oregon's legislature has established the following priorities for the state's integrated solid waste management system: (1) source reduction, (2) reuse, (3) recycling, (4) waste-to-energy incineration, and (5) landfill disposal or other disposal methods approved by the health department.
- The Department of Health is required to provide advisory technical and planning assistance for the development and implementation of recycling and solid waste management programs by state or local agencies or by anyone who provides solid waste collection services.
- In all statutes dealing with solid waste management, Oregon stresses the importance of waste reduction and recycling before landfill disposal. A $2 surcharge on each ton of solid waste disposed of in a landfill is collected to fund recycling programs.
- The state encourages both public education on household hazardous waste and the collection of such materials. The Department of Environmental Quality must implement statewide education programs on this subject.
- After 1 January 1990, lead-acid batteries were banned from landfills and required to be recycled. Signs with this information must be posted in all establishments that sell batteries; violators of this section are subject to a fine of $500 for each day that the sign is not posted.
- A fee may be charged on new tires, to be placed into a state-established Waste Tire Recycling Account. As of 1 July 1989, landfill disposal of whole tires was strongly discouraged but not expressly prohibited. Anyone who purchases tire chips or waste tires for an approved reuse may receive a partial reimbursement of costs incurred in the reuse program.
- Used oil recycling is mandatory; other forms of disposal are prohibited, with certain exceptions.
- State agencies may not purchase any food packaging products that are not biodegradable or recyclable through a local program. Vendors who sell food items in state agencies are subject to the same requirement.
- Violators of the state's recycling laws can incur civil penalties of $500 per violation.

- Tax credits are available for costs incurred in providing a pollution control facility, which includes locations that recycle used oil (as well as other facilities that are primarily concerned with the prevention, control, or reduction of air, water, or noise pollution or of solid or hazardous waste).
- Waste haulers can qualify for waste diversion credits according to the amount of waste they can divert from landfills.
- Funding is available for recycling and resource recovery projects through both the Habitat Conservation Trust Fund and the Waste Reduction Trust Fund.

SOURCE: 1989 Oregon Revised Statutes: Title 26, Chapter 279 (Public Contracts and Purchasing), s 279.729, s 279.731, s 279.733, s 279.735, s 279.737, s 279.739; Title 29, Chapter 316 (Personal Income Tax Credits), s 316.103, Chapter 317, s 317.106; Title 36 (Public Health and Safety), Chapter 459 (Solid Waste Control), s 459.005, s 459.015, s 459.035, s 459.055, s 459.165, s 459.170, s 459.175, s 459.180, s 459.185, s 459.188, s 459.190, s 459.195, s 459.200, s 459.250, s 459.280, s 459.292, s 459.294, s 459.295, s 459.305, s 459.345, s 459.411, s 459.417, s 459.420, s 459.426, s 459.614, s 459.710, s 459.770, s 459.775, s 459.780, s 459.995, Chapter 468 (Pollution Control), s 468.155, s 468.165, s 468.170, s 468.190, s 468.659, s 468.660, s 468.664, s 468.675, s 468.677, s 468.679, s 468.680, s 468.681, s 468.685, s 468.850, s 468.853, s 468.856, s 468.859, s 468.862, s 468.865, s 468.869, s 468.870, s 468.871, s 468.968, s 468.969, Chapter 469 (Energy Conservation), s 469.010, s 469.185, s 469.205.

Pennsylvania

- This state has a recycling goal of 25 percent by 1 January 1997.
- The Municipal Waste Planning, Recycling, and Waste Reduction Act created funding for recycling programs in 1988 by imposing a recycling fee of $2 per ton for all solid waste processed at incineration facilities and most solid wastes disposed of at landfills. All monies generated from this fee are deposited in the Recycling Fund.
- After September 1990, all communities with populations greater than 10,000 must start recycling programs. By September 1991, communities with populations between 5,000 and 10,000 must do the same. Counties are responsible for creating and implementing solid waste disposal plans.
- A Recycling Advisory Committee was established within the Department of Environmental Resources (DER) to oversee the state's recycling program and to study other ways to encourage waste reduction. DER is also responsible for researching and identifying recycled materials markets.

- All municipalities must recycle at least three materials from the following group: glass, colored glass, aluminum, steel "tin" and bimetal cans, newsprint, high-grade office paper, plastics, and corrugated cardboard. Disposal facilities must also provide drop-off containers for at least three of these materials.
- All state and local agencies must recycle office paper, corrugated cardboard, aluminum, and leaf waste. Additionally, they are required to implement comprehensive waste reduction programs.
- All educational institutions must source-separate and collect recyclable materials and institute source reduction programs as well.
- Lead-acid batteries must be recycled, and battery sellers cannot sell a new battery unless they receive the old one for recycling.
- Leaf waste is banned from landfills.
- Used oil is to be recycled.
- There is a procurement preference program for supplies and goods made from recycled materials. Of the total volume of paper purchased, at least 10 percent must be recycled paper in 1989, 25 percent in 1991, and 40 percent in 1993. Federal guidelines are to be followed with respect to recycled material content. Newsprint is considered recycled if it contains at least 40 percent postconsumer newspaper waste. Recycled paper must have a total weight consisting of not less than 20 percent secondary materials in 1989; not less than 30 percent secondary materials in 1991; not less than 40 percent secondary materials in 1993; and not less than 50 percent secondary materials in 1996 and thereafter, at least 10 percent of which must be postconsumer waste.
- All public agencies are expected to use composted materials as much as possible in maintaining public lands.

SOURCE: Purdon's Pennsylvania Statutes Annotated: Title 53, Part 1, Chapter 17A (The Municipal Waste Planning, Recycling, and Waste Reduction Act), Chapter 7 (Recycling Fee), s 4000.701, s 4000.702, s 4000.706, Chapter 9 (Grants), s 4000.902 through 4000.904, Chapter 15 (Recycling and Waste Reduction), s 4000.1501 through 4000.1503, s 4000.1509, s 4000.1511; Title 58, Chapter 9 (Pennsylvania Used Oil Recycling Act), s 476.

Rhode Island

- This state's recycling goal is 15 percent by 1993.
- Rhode Island passed the first mandatory source separation law in the country in June 1986—the Rhode Island Recycling Act.
- A Plastic Recycling and Litter Commission was created and required to submit a plan to the governor and general assembly by 1 January 1991 that would provide for the maximum recycling

of plastic and foam food service items. For nonrecyclable products, the commission was to establish guidelines on photodegradability and biodegradability that would take effect on 1 January 1992.

- A Litter and Recycling Advisory Council was established to create recycling centers throughout the state and to encourage their use.
- By 1 January 1988, the state's central landfill was to construct and begin operating a recycling facility.
- Although the state recognizes that the definition of recyclable materials may change due to market conditions, it stipulates that the following materials must be separated and collected for recycling by all municipalities: food and beverage containers made of aluminum, glass, and other metals; newspapers; plastic soft drink bottles and milk jugs; and white goods.
- The Department of Environmental Management is directed to establish, maintain guidelines for, and enforce the proper use of a recycling logo.
- Only those beverage containers that have obtained a 50 percent recycling rate by 1992 and are free of any components that render them less recyclable or unrecyclable may be sold in Rhode Island.
- Telephone directories must be accepted for recycling by directory distributors, and the bindings must be such that they do not interfere with the recycling process.
- Commercial businesses have been required to separate and recycle office paper, corrugated cardboard, aluminum and steel "tin" cans, glass food and beverage containers, and newspapers since 1 January 1989. Businesses with more than 500 employees had to submit source reduction and recycling plans by 30 June 1989, those with more than 250 employees were required to do the same by 31 December 1989, and those with over 100 had to produce reports by 30 June 1990.
- By 30 June 1991, all state departments and agencies were to present recycling plans to the Department of Environmental Management.
- State officials are required to encourage the purchasing of recycled oil products.

SOURCE: General Laws of Rhode Island Annotated 1956, Reenactment of 1989: Title 21, Chapter 27.1 (Plastic Recycling and Litter Act), s 21-27.1-3; Title 23, Chapter 18.8 (Waste Recycling), s 23-18.8-3, s 23-18.8-5, Chapter 18.12 (Beverage Container Recyclability), s 23-18.12-3, Chapter 19 (Solid Waste Management Corporation), s 23-19-31, Chapter 19.6, s 23-19.6-8 and 6-9, Chapter 60, s 23-60-7, Chapter 63, s 23-63-4; Title 37, Chapter 15 (Litter Control and Recycling), s 37-15-4; Title 42, Chapter 20, s 42-20-16.

South Carolina

- The only mention of recycling in this state's laws at this time appears in Title 56, which refers to the recycling of motor vehicles.

SOURCE: Code of Laws of South Carolina 1976 Annotated.

South Dakota

- Counties are directed to establish solid waste management policies.
- South Dakota subscribes to the following priorities of integrated waste management: (1) source reduction, (2) recycling and reuse, (3) incineration, and (4) landfill disposal.
- State agencies are to purchase recycled paper if the price and quality are competitive. Agencies using recycled paper may print the notation "printed on recycled paper" on any product that has been certified as such by the state.
- Procurement goals for recycled paper are set as percentages of the total volume of paper and paper products purchased in a given fiscal year: at least 10 percent in 1992, at least 20 percent in 1993, at least 30 percent in 1994, at least 40 percent in 1995, and at least 50 percent for 1996 and subsequent years.
- Elementary and secondary schools are to attempt to recycle any used textbooks before disposing of them as solid waste.
- After 1 July 1978, all beverage containers offered for sale must be reusable, recyclable, or biodegradable.
- After 1 January 1991, no beverage containers may be offered for sale if they are connected to other beverage containers by a material that is neither biodegradable nor photodegradable.
- After 1 January 1992, no plastic garbage bag or garbage can liner may be offered for sale unless it is recyclable, biodegradable, photodegradable, or "otherwise degradable."

SOURCE: South Dakota Codified Laws: Title 5, Chapter 5-23 (State Purchases and Printing), s 5-23-22.4 through 5-23-22.6; Title 7, Chapter 7-33 (Solid Wastes Management Systems), s 7-33-6; Title 13, Chapter 13-34, s 13-34-26; Title 34A (Environmental Protection), Chapter 34A-6, s 34A-6-1.2, s 34A-6-1.5, s 34A-6-1.6, Chapter 34A-7 (Litter Disposal and Control), s 34A-7-5, s 34A-7-5.1.

Tennessee

- This state's recycling goal is a 25 percent reduction of solid waste by 31 December 1995.

- The Division of Energy (DOE) is directed to promote research and development into a number of fields, including resource recycling. The DOE is also responsible for promoting the development of material recycling, handling, and management systems.
- All university establishments must develop annual source reduction, recycling, and waste management plans. Additionally, their curriculum sequences must assure adequate treatment of issues pertaining to recycling, source reduction, and waste management for undergraduate courses, continuing education programs, and training courses for local officials.
- A property tax exemption is offered on property owned by nonprofit organizations that recycle or dispose of waste products in a manner other than landfill disposal.
- The Department of Health is directed to develop a grant program for research and development in the field of solid waste disposal technologies, which include source separation and recycling.
- The general assembly has declared that source reduction and recycling should be practiced to the greatest extent possible to lessen the state's dependence on landfills. As of 1 January 1991, the State Planning Office was to establish a comprehensive solid waste management plan for the state. The integrated solid waste management hierarchy is defined as (1) source reduction; (2) recycling, mulching, and composting; (3) incineration; and (4) landfill disposal.
- The state hopes to educate all waste producers and handlers about reducing the amount of solid waste destined for landfill disposal as much as possible and to promote markets for recyclable materials.
- The state plan had to include educational programs and encourage governmental entities to recycle and buy recycled materials. The state planning office was also directed to assist in preparing and adopting regional solid waste management plans by the nine development districts within the state. Each of those districts must also produce a recycling plan that, among other things, provides for the disposal of household hazardous wastes and for citizen education programs. The state plan was also expected to establish goals for the reduction of solid wastes disposed of in landfills. Beginning 1 March 1994, each region must submit an annual report to the state, including information on its recycling programs.
- Within each municipal solid waste planning district, a Municipal Solid Waste Planning Advisory Committee was to be established.
- The State Planning Office has also been required to establish guidelines for source reduction, source separation, and collection of recyclable materials in all state agencies, including the school

system. It must also establish and maintain a statewide solid waste management database.

- The following goals are established for the purchase of recycled paper and paper products as percentages of the total volume of paper purchased by the state: at least 10 percent in 1990, at least 25 percent in 1992, and at least 40 percent in 1994.
- The state requires that at least 40 percent of the recycled fiber in newsprint and newsprint products come from postconsumer newspaper waste.
- With the funds available from the state's Solid Waste Management Fund, an Office of Cooperative Marketing for Recyclables is expected to be established by 1 July 1992. This office is charged with preparing and maintaining recycling directories for both buyers and sellers of recycled materials, creating a database to assist marketing efforts, and maintaining all information necessary to promote recycled materials markets within the state. Additionally, a Recycling Market Advisory Council will also be created to further assist in marketing efforts.
- The State Planning Office must establish an information clearinghouse on source reduction and recycling and conduct statewide and regional conferences and workshops on these subjects and on solid waste management.
- The Department of Transportation was directed to study the feasibility of using recycled plastic materials in guardrail posts or right-of-way fence posts. The results of that study were to be submitted to the state by 1 January 1991.
- Grant programs are available to fund the purchase of recycling equipment by nonprofit organizations.
- All educational institutions must provide and encourage education on solid waste, source reduction, and recycling. The State Planning Office has established an awards program to recognize outstanding accomplishments in this area.
- By 1 January 1996, all counties are required to provide at least one site for the collection of recyclables, and such facilities must file annual reports to the state regarding details of their recycling efforts. The University of Tennessee has been directed to provide technical assistance for the design and management of these recycling programs.
- All state agencies have to recycle paper, aluminum cans, glass bottles, newsprint, plastic bottles, mixed paper, and steel "tin" cans to the maximum extent possible. Additionally, these agencies must purchase recycled products or products made from recycled materials whenever possible.

- As of 1 January 1995, the following items are banned from landfills and incinerators and are required to be recycled: whole waste tires, lead-acid batteries, and used oil and automotive fluids.

  SOURCE: Tennessee Code Annotated: Title 4, Chapter 3, Part 7, s 4-3-709 and 710; Title 7, Chapter 21, Part 3, s 7-21-301, Chapter 54, s 7-54-101, s 7-54-103, Chapter 58 (Resource Recovery and Solid Waste Disposal), s 7-58-101, s 7-58-110; Title 12, Chapter 3 (Public Purchases), Part 5, s 12-3-531; Title 49 (Education), Chapter 7, Part 1, s 49-7-121, Part 2, s 49-7-202, Chapter 9, Part 4, s 49-9-406; Title 67, Chapter 5 (Property Taxes), Part 2, s 67-5-208, Part 6, s 67-5-604; Title 68 (Safety and Health), Chapter 1, Part 1, s 68-1-104, Chapter 31 (Solid Waste Disposal), Part 1 (Solid Waste Disposal Act), s 68-31-103, Part 4, s 68-31-401, s 68-31-405, Part 5, s 68-31-501 through 503, Part 6, s 68-31-602 through 607, Part 8, s 68-31-802, s 68-31-803, s 68-31-812, s 68-31-815, s 68-31-825 through 827, s 68-31-841 through 846, s 68-31-848, s 68-31-854, s 68-31-861, s 68-31-863 through 866, s 68-31-871 and 872, Part 9 (Solid Waste Authority Act of 1991), s 68-31-902.

Texas

- Texas funds its recycling programs through a Solid Waste Fee Revenue of $.50 per ton of solid waste disposed.
- The Department of Health has been directed to establish and administer a Recycling and Waste Minimization Office to provide technical assistance to local governments on recycling and waste minimization. The department must also work with the Department of Commerce to develop recycled materials and compost markets.
- An Interagency Coordination Council is charged with responsibilities that include considering "the use of incentives to encourage waste minimization and reusing and recycling of waste, and the use of resource recovery facilities."
- The state's integrated solid waste management hierarchy is prioritized as follows: (1) waste minimization, (2) reuse/recycling, (3) waste-to-energy or safe incineration, and (4) land disposal.
- Local governments are entrusted with the control of solid waste collection and disposal. Regional or local solid waste management plans must include efforts to recycle or reuse waste as well as identify other opportunities for waste minimization, reuse, or recycling. Each plan must also include recommendations for improving the regional or local programs.
- Funding for recycling projects is available from the Technical Assistance Fund.
- Sludge recyclers are exempt from a franchise tax.

- The state requires that all products purchased by its agencies contain the highest amounts of recycled materials possible. A price preference of 15 percent is allowed in the purchase of highway paving materials made of recycled tires. Furthermore, all state agencies are expected to collect and recycle their wastepaper and to participate in waste minimization programs.
- Plastic bottles and other rigid plastic containers sold in the state must carry a code identifying the resin they are made of (per Society of the Plastics Industry specifications). Violators of this law are subject to a civil penalty.
- The use of recycled paper in the court system is "strongly encouraged."

SOURCES: Vernon's Texas Statutes and Codes Annotated: Health and Safety Code, Title 5 (Sanitation and Environmental Quality), Subtitle B, Chapter 361, Subchapter A, Subchapter B, s 361.014, s 361.0151, s 361.021 through 023, Subchapter C, s 361.0861, Chapter 363 (Municipal Solid Waste), Subchapter A, s 363.003, s 363.006, Subchapter D, s 363.064, Subchapter E, s 363.095, Chapter 368, Subchapter B, s 368.013; Tax Code, Title 2, Subtitle F (Franchise Tax), Chapter 171, Subchapter B, s 171.085; Civil Statutes, Title 20, Article 1, s 3.21, s 3.211, Title 70, Chapter 8, Article 4413(33b), s 2 and 3, Title 71, Chapter 4A, Article 4477-7G (Coding of Plastic Containers). Texas Rules of Civil Procedure, Part II, Section 4A, Rule 45. Texas Rules of Appellate Procedure, Section 2, Rule 4.

Utah

- The Solid and Hazardous Waste Control Board has been directed to establish a comprehensive statewide solid waste management plan by 1 July 1993. The plan must include an assessment of the state's ability to minimize and recycle wastes.
- The state's chief procurement officer was to provide, on or before 1 June 1990, guidelines and requirements on the purchase of recycled paper and paper products for state agencies. Recycled paper is defined as any paper containing no less than 50 percent secondary waste paper fibers (by weight). State agencies are given a 5 percent pricing preference for the purchase of recycled paper and paper products. Goals for purchasing specific percentages of the total amount of paper bought by the state per year begin with a 5 percent minimum requirement in fiscal year 1990–1991. The goal rises by 5 percent each year thereafter until the minimum purchase requirement is 50 percent.
- State agencies were also required to evaluate their potential for recycling paper by 1 October 1990. Subsequently, they were to implement recycling programs if they could be run in a cost-effective manner.

- The legislature encourages waste tire recycling and the development of the recycling industry. As of 1 July 1990, a recycling fee was imposed on each new tire purchased from a retailer. The fee varies according to the size of the tire: 14 inches or less is $1, and greater than 14 inches is $1.50. The proceeds from this fee are deposited into the Waste Tire Recycling Expendable Trust Fund, which may be used to partially reimburse persons for the costs of using waste tires, waste chips, or similar products to create energy or a new product (on or after 1 January 1991). This Waste Tire Recycling Act will be automatically repealed on 1 July 1995.
- As of 1 January 1992, lead-acid batteries could no longer be disposed of and had to be recycled. Battery sellers must post this law, act as collection centers, and accept up to two old batteries when a new one is purchased.
- The legislature encourages the recycling of used oil and the use of recycled oil.

SOURCE: Utah Code: Title 19 (Environmental Quality Code), Chapter 6, Part 1 (Solid and Hazardous Waste Act), s 19-6-102, s 19-6-104, Part 5 (Solid Waste Management Act), s 19-6-502 and 503, Part 6 (Lead Acid Battery Disposal), s 19-6-602 through 605; Title 26 (Health Code), Chapter 32a (Waste Tire Recycling Act), s 26-32a-101 through 113; Title 40, Chapter 9 (Oil Rerefinement Act), s 40-9-2 through 3.5; Title 63, Chapter 55, Part 2 (Repeal Dates), s 63-55-226, Chapter 56, Part B, s 63-56-9, Part D, 63-56-20.7.

Vermont

- This state has a recycling goal of 40 percent by the year 2000.
- The governor created a state recycling program to promote source reduction and the recovery of recyclable and reusable materials by state agencies in 1987. Documentation of compliance was required by 15 January 1987 and must be submitted each odd-numbered year after that. At the same time, the director of purchasing was directed to review and modify all procurement specifications to encourage the purchase of products made from recycled materials. Recycled paper is defined as that containing not less than 50 percent postconsumer waste. Other recycled products include retreaded automobile tires, compost materials, and rerefined oils.
- The state's Solid Waste Management Plan must include goals that emphasize the greatest possible amount of source reduction, reuse, and recycling. Additionally, the state encourages educational programs, investment and employment opportunities, and industries and businesses that promote recycling and source reduction.

- The state must provide technical and financial leadership to municipalities regarding solid waste plans. Such plans must give priority to reducing the waste stream through recycling and to the reduction of nonbiodegradable and hazardous ingredients.
- A Solid Waste Management Advisory Committee was created in 1986 to assist the state in managing its solid waste.
- As of 1 July 1991, an integrated solid waste management plan was to be published, using the following hierarchy: (1) source reduction, (2) reuse/recycling, (3) waste processing to reduce the volume of waste, and (4) landfill disposal of residuals. This plan is to be revised at least once every five years.
- Vermont has a mandatory deposit-redemption law for all beverage containers.
- Funding for recycling and other solid waste disposal alternatives is available through the state secretary's office and through the Waste Management Assistance Fund, which is administered by the secretary of the Agency of Natural Resources.
- Any solid waste district that wishes to be eligible for grant monies must include a source separation plan in its solid waste management plan. A recycling awareness component for public education is also required. Additional incentives for source separation include the stipulation that unless ordinances mandating source separation are effective prior to 1 July 1993, the district or municipality is no longer eligible for grant funding. The sooner the ordinances are in effect, the more money the agency is eligible to receive.
- The secretary of natural resources has been informed that on 15 January 1991 and every year thereafter, a report must be submitted advising the legislature on the status of the newsprint industry's purchase of recycled newsprint. The Vermont Newspapers Users' Task Force has set goals for the annual postconsumer fiber consumption of recycled newsprint: 11 percent by 1992 and 23 percent by 1995.
- Towns and cities are responsible for operating and maintaining their own solid waste facilities, including recycling centers. If a private recycling center existed prior to the municipality's, the government center may not adversely affect it.
- State purchasing agents are advised to purchase items made from recycled materials whenever possible. A 5 percent purchasing incentive is provided, and this may be exceeded if permission is obtained from the commissioner of general services. The goal for the state purchase of recycled materials is 40 percent by the end of 1993.
- Recycled materials accepted for recycling are exempt from the state's franchise tax on waste facilities.

SOURCE: Vermont Statutes Annotated: Title 3, Chapter 7, Executive Order No. 17 and 24; Title 10, Part 2, Chapter 53 (Beverage Containers; Deposit-Redemption System), Part 5, Chapter 159 (Waste Management), Subchapter 1, s 6601, s 6602, s 6603b, s 6603e, s 6603f, s 6604, s 6605, s 6618, s 6619, s 6622, s 6622a; Title 24, Part 2, Chapter 61, Subchapter 8 (Rubbish and Garbage), s 2203a and b, s 2206; Title 29, Part 2, Chapter 49, s 903; Title 32 (Taxation and Finance), Part 3, Chapter 151, Subchapter 13, s 5953.

Virginia

- This state's recycling goal is 25 percent by 1995.
- Solid waste regions have been delineated, and each region is responsible for developing and implementing its own comprehensive solid waste management plan. The plans must include waste reduction, recycling, and reuse of solid wastes.
- The state's Litter Control and Recycling Program is to encourage recycling to the "maximum practical extent."
- As of 1 July 1992, every plastic bottle and rigid plastic container must carry a symbol identifying the resin it is made from (per the Society of the Plastics Industry specifications).
- On and after 1 January 1993, beverage containers that are connected with any plastic rings or devices that are not recyclable or degradable may not be sold.
- The Department of Litter Control and Recycling has been directed to develop and implement a plan to deal with waste tires.
- Lead-acid batteries may not be disposed of and must be recycled. Battery sellers must post signs that advise customers of this law and of the fact that their establishments are required to accept used motor vehicle batteries.
- All state agencies and universities had to establish recycling programs by 1 July 1991. The programs were to include the collection of used motor oil, glass, aluminum, office paper, and corrugated cardboard.
- All state agencies must buy recycled paper and paper products whenever possible. (Recycled paper is defined by EPA standards.) A 10 percent price preference is permitted for state and local agencies alike.
- By 1 July 1992, the Department of Education must develop guidelines for source reduction and recycling programs in public schools, including the use of recycled materials.
- The Department of Economic Development has been directed to encourage and promote the recycling industry within the state.
- The Department of Transportation is encouraged to purchase re-refined or recycled motor oil. The recycling of used oil is promoted but not required.

- Counties, cities, and towns are permitted to require source separation and the collection of recyclables in both the residential and commercial sections of their jurisdictions.
- A 10 percent income tax credit is available for both businesses and individuals for the purchase of recycling equipment between 1 January 1991 and 1 January 1993. Qualified recycling equipment may also be exempt from property taxes.
- The Virginia Resources Authority was created in part to encourage the investment of both public and private funds in recycling and resource recovery projects.

SOURCE: Code of Virginia: Title 2.1, Chapter 32, Article 3 (Purchases and Supplies), s 2.1-457; Title 10.1 (Conservation), Subtitle II, Chapter 14 (Virginia Waste Management Act), Article 1, Article 2, s 10.1-1408.1, s 10.1-1411, Article 3 (Litter Control and Recycling), s 10.1-1414 through 1425; Title 11 (Contracts), Chapter 7, Article 2, s 11-47.2; Title 15.1 (Cities, Counties, and Towns), Chapter 1, Article 2, s 15.1-11.5, s 15.1-11.5:01, s 15.1-11.5:2 and 3, s 15.1-28.01; Title 33.1, Chapter 1, Article 15, s 33.1-189.1; Title 45.1, Chapter 26, s 45.1-390.1; Title 58.1 (Taxation), Subtitle I, Chapter 3, Article 3, s 58.1-338, Article 14, s 58.1-445.1, Subtitle III, Chapter 36, Article 5, s 58.1-3661; Title 62.1, Chapter 21 (Virginia Resources Authority).

Washington

- This state's recycling goal is 50 percent by 1995.
- According to state policy, used oil must be collected and recycled and public education programs to promote such recycling must be developed.
- Cities and towns are empowered to enact ordinances that deal with solid waste or collection of recyclable materials.
- All state and local agencies are encouraged to give preference to goods made from recycled materials in their purchasing activities.
- The Department of Trade and Economic Development is to assist in establishing and improving recyclable materials markets both inside and outside the state. The Washington Committee for Recycling Markets was created within this department in 1989.
- Washington's Model Litter Control and Recycling Act was passed in 1971 to promote litter control and to stimulate private recycling programs throughout the state. The act gives the Department of Ecology the authority to fulfill these goals. The state must also create a competitive awards program for source reduction and recycling programs in the public schools.
- Local governments are responsible for solid waste handling, but a comprehensive statewide plan, which includes recycling, is mandated as well. The state takes responsibility for providing

technical and financial assistance to local governments for solid waste projects.

- Each county is responsible for preparing its own comprehensive solid waste management plan, and all cities within each county are directed to cooperate with such plans. Guidelines specifically dealing with waste reduction and recycling had to be submitted to the state by 15 March 1990 for approval. Within these plans, each county could decide what materials should be recycled. In addition, recycling and trash collectors must set rates that encourage recycling and discourage waste disposal (e.g., volume-based rates), and drop-off or buy-back recycling centers must be provided in rural areas.

- The recycling of waste tires is encouraged. A $1 fee is levied on the sale of new tires, to be collected by retailers and ultimately deposited in the Vehicle Tire Recycling Account. Grants from this fund may be allotted to projects dealing with tire recycling.

- The Department of Ecology has been directed to provide educational materials that promote the reduction and recycling of household hazardous waste.

- Lead-acid batteries may not be disposed of or incinerated and must be recycled. Written notices to this effect must be posted at all battery-selling locations, and old batteries are to be accepted when new ones are bought on a one-to-one exchange basis. Additionally, if a person does not surrender a used battery when buying a new one, retailers are required to charge an extra $5 (core charge).

- Grant monies have been appropriated to study the composting of food and yard wastes. Yard waste collection programs must be provided where composting markets are available.

- A 1 percent state tax on garbage bills is exacted until June 1993. Funds derived from this tax are to be spent on technical assistance and grants to local governments to fund research on hard-to-recycle materials and market development.

SOURCE: West's Revised Code of Washington Annotated: Title 19, Chapter 19.114 (Used Automotive Oil Recycling); Title 35 (Cities and Towns), Chapter 35.21, s 35.21.130, s 35.21.158, Chapter 35.22, s 35.22.620, Chapter 35.23, s 35.23.352; Title 36 (Counties), Chapter 36.32, s 36.32.250, Chapter 36.58 (Solid Waste Disposal), s 36.58.010, s 36.58.040, s 36.58.160; Title 39, Chapter 39.30, s 39.30.040; Title 43, Chapter 43.19, s 43.19.1911, Chapter 43.31, s 43.31.545, s 43.31.552, Chapter 43.160, s 43.160.077; Title 70 (Public Health and Safety), Chapter 70.93 (Model Litter Control and Recycling Act), Chapter 70.95 (Solid Waste Management—Recovery and Recycling), Chapter 70.95C

(Waste Reduction), s 70.95C.110, s 70.95C.120; Title 81 (Transportation), Chapter 81.77 (Garbage and Refuse Collection Companies).

West Virginia

- This state has a recycling goal of 30 percent by the year 2000.
- West Virginia's public policy includes provisions to establish comprehensive solid waste management plans with recycling as a component. To further these plans, a West Virginia Solid Waste Management Board was established in 1989.
- The responsibility for developing and implementing the solid waste management plan is assigned to the Division of Natural Resources (DNR). The DNR is also responsible for the West Virginia Litter Control Program, which encourages recycling. The legislature adds that "resource recovery and recycling reduces the need for landfills and extends their life and proper disposal, resource recovery, or recycling of solid waste is for the general welfare of the citizens of this state." The state's integrated solid waste management hierarchy is as follows: (1) source reduction; (2) recycling, reuse, and resource recovery; (3) environmentally acceptable incineration; and (4) landfill disposal.
- Each county and regional solid waste authority was responsible for developing and submitting to the state its own litter and solid waste control plan by 1 July 1991. Such plans had to include public education programs, timetables, and innovative incentives to encourage recycling efforts.
- Additionally, the West Virginia Recycling Act of 1989 requires each county to adopt a comprehensive recycling program for solid waste if the citizens vote to do so by petition and referendum. Such programs must encourage source separation, increase the purchasing of recycled products by local agencies, and educate the public about the benefits of recycling. Counties may decide which materials to recycle.
- A solid waste fee of $1.25 per ton funds solid waste and recycling programs. Any waste that is being reused or recycled is exempt from this fee.
- All state agencies must establish recycling programs for aluminum containers, glass, and paper, and any other recyclable materials that can be practicably collected and sold should be included in these programs. Such agencies are also required to encourage and promote recycling within all public facilities.
- State agencies are encouraged to purchase recycled products to the maximum extent possible.

SOURCE: West Virginia Code 1966: Chapter 16 (Public Health), Article 26 (West Virginia Solid Waste Management Board), Chapter

20 (Natural Resources), Article 5F (Solid Waste Management Act), Article 9 (County and Regional Solid Waste Authorities), Article 11 (West Virginia Recycling Program/Act).

Wisconsin

- This state has a recycling goal of 60 percent by 2000.
- Counties and municipalities are required to work together on solid waste management plans and advise the state by January 1993 as to how they will comply with the various landfill disposal bans and recycling requirements.
- Wisconsin expects to attain its solid waste disposal goals by banning numerous wastes from landfill disposal, including: lead-acid batteries, white goods, and waste oil by 1991; yard waste by 1993; and corrugated paper and other paperboards used for containers, aluminum and glass containers, polystyrene foam, magazines and other coated papers, newsprint, office paper, plastic and steel containers, and waste tires by 1995.
- State and local agencies must write their procurement specifications to promote the purchase of recyclable and recycled products. Additionally, single-use, disposable products are to be discouraged. Recycled content bid preferences of 1 percent for each 10 percent of recycled content in a product are permitted. By 1995, all recycled paper that is purchased must contain 40 percent recycled fiber.
- Newspaper publishers must use newsprint with at least 10 percent recycled content in 1991, progressing to 45 percent in 2001.
- Plastic containers must contain at least 10 percent recycled materials by 1993 and 25 percent by 31 January 1995.
- Cloth diapers and charges for diaper services are exempt from sales and use taxes.
- Beginning in the 1991–1992 fiscal year, a gross receipts tax was levied on businesses to fund recycling programs through a recycling fund.
- The Division of Natural Resources is to establish the state's priorities for developing markets for postconsumer waste materials.

SOURCE: Wisconsin Statutes Annotated: Chapter 159 (Solid Waste), Subchapter II (Solid Waste Reduction, Recovery, and Recycling).

Wyoming

- At this time, the only recycling legislation in this state prohibits the disposal of lead-acid batteries and requires that they be recycled. Battery sellers must accept old batteries when new ones are purchased, and signage must be posted to this effect.

SOURCE: Wyoming Statutes 1977: Title 35 (Public Health and Safety), Chapter 11 (Environmental Quality), Article 5 (Solid Waste Management).

6

Directory of State, Federal, and Private Recycling Organizations

State Recycling Associations and State Government Agencies

Alabama

Alabama Department of Environmental Management (ADEM)
Solid Waste Branch
1751 Congressman W. L. Dickinson Drive
Montgomery, AL 36130
(205) 271-7726
(205) 271-7950 (FAX)
Michael W. Forster and Walter Nichols, State Recycling Coordinators

The Solid Waste Branch of ADEM offers a number of recycling services and programs to the public. These include educational presentations to both the general population and school students, recycling market assistance, and information on recycled product procurement. ADEM also runs a grant program for local government agencies and nonprofit organizations that are starting or expanding recycling programs. Printed materials and fact sheets on recycling, most originating from the EPA and Scriptographic Books, are also available through ADEM.

Alaska

Alaska Department of Environmental Conservation (ADEC)
Recycling Division
P.O. Box O
Juneau, AK 99811-1800
(907) 465-5275
(907) 465-5274 (FAX)
In-state hotline: 1-800-478-2864 (in Anchorage: 276-2964)
David Wigglesworth, Manager of Pollution Prevention

Alaska embarked on a formal pollution prevention campaign in 1990, by legislative initiative. At that time, ADEC was directed to "actively promote the waste management practices of source reduction and recycling."

In response, ADEC created a Pollution Prevention Program that subsequently researched recycling and solid waste management in Alaska. The program's intent is to provide nonregulatory technical assistance.

PUBLICATIONS: In 1991, the program published *Pollution Prevention Resource Guide* in response to public interest and requests for information on environmental issues. The *Resource Guide* defines the program and lists a variety of other state agencies involved in recycling projects, as well as recycling equipment manufacturers and scrap dealers. Additionally, there are lists of recycling centers throughout the state and suppliers of recycled products.

Alaska Center for the Environment (ACE)
519 W. 8th Avenue, Suite 201
Anchorage, AK 99501
(907) 274-3621
Susan Libenson, Executive Director

The nonprofit ACE promotes "sound environmental policy, conservation of the state's natural resources, and education of the public and youth for wise decision-making." Encouragement of recycling and waste reduction is a part of these goals.

PUBLICATIONS: ACE's newsletter, *Center News,* is published bimonthly.

Arizona

Arizona Department of Environmental Quality (ADEQ)
Waste Planning Section, 4th Floor
2005 North Central Avenue
Phoenix, AZ 85004
(602) 257-6816
Eileen Miller, Recycling Unit Manager

ADEQ was created in 1990 by the Arizona Solid Waste Recycling Act. Because 1991 was its first year of allotting funds, all ADEQ programs are still in the beginning stages and publications have yet to be produced.

Arizona Department of Commerce
Phoenix City Square
3800 N. Central, Suite 1400
Phoenix, AZ 85012
(602) 280-1402
(602) 280-1305 (FAX)
Statewide toll-free hotline: 1-800-352-5499
Amanda S. Ormond, Recycling Markets Development

This department deals primarily with the markets development side of recycling. In 1991, it created an advisory committee that is currently studying recommendations to establish and promote recycled materials markets, as well as ways to match markets with sources.

Arkansas

Arkansas Department of Pollution Control and Ecology (PEC)
Solid Waste Management Division
8001 National Drive
P.O. Box 8913
Little Rock, AR 72219-8913
(501) 562-6533
(501) 562-2541 (FAX)
Donna H. Etchieson, Recycling Coordinator

Three divisions of PEC have programs relating to recycling and solid waste management. The Solid Waste Division regulates landfills and manages the solid waste planning and recycling grant program. The Recycling Division is charged with facilitating the development of a cooperative regional infrastructure for the collection, processing, quality control, and transportation of recyclables. As this book goes to press, PEC is hiring a person to oversee the development of a comprehensive recycling and solid waste education program.

The Marketing Division was recently established with a mission to develop markets within the state for postconsumer recyclables and to maintain an extensive data base of markets and specifications.

PUBLICATIONS: The *PCE Newsletter* is published quarterly, and locally pertinent educational material is distributed throughout the state. PCE has also published a booklet entitled *Recycling and Source Reduction,* as well as the *Recycling Reference Guide, A Manual for Planning and Implementing Community Recycling in Arkansas,* and a report of the Arkansas Solid Waste Fact Finding Task Force entitled *Solid Waste Strategies.*

California

Californians Against Waste Foundation (CAWF)
909 12th Street, Suite 201
Sacramento, CA 95814
(916) 443-8317
Sandra E. Jerabek, Executive Director

CAWF is a nonprofit, tax-exempt organization that is "working to create a renewable, sustainable economy by promoting the reuse, recycling, and renewal of our natural resources." The foundation's goal is for California to reach a 50 percent recycling and waste reduction by the year 2000. It is working on every aspect of promoting and implementing recycling and source reduction programs that other states will use as models.

CAWF's sister organization, Californians Against Waste (CAW), is a public interest citizens' lobby working to create "a recycling economy through the passage of state and local legislation." CAW led the successful fight to establish the state's bottle bill.

PUBLICATIONS: CAWF's publications include: *How-To Guide for Establishing Curbside Recycling Programs, Guide to Recycled Printing and Office Paper, Shopper's Guide to Recycled Products,* and *Buy Recycled: Keep a Good Thing Going.*

California Department of Conservation
Division of Recycling
1025 P Street
Sacramento, CA 95814
(916) 327-1869
(916) 327-8805 (FAX)
Randall M. Ward, Director

The Division of Recycling oversees the state's recycling programs in both the public and private sectors and publishes resource papers on various aspects of recycling, as well as an annual report on the California Beverage Container Recycling and Litter Reduction Act.

Two hotline phone numbers are also run by the division: For the nearest in-state recycling center, call 1-800-322-SAVE; for other beverage container recycling questions, call 1-800-642-KNOW.

California Integrated Waste Management Board (CIWMB)
1020 Ninth Street, Suite 300
Sacramento, CA 95814
(916) 322-3330
In-state recycling hotline: 1-800-553-2962
John E. Gallagher, Chairman

The CIWMB is responsible for overseeing California's waste management efforts, the highest priorities of which are "source reduction, recycling, and composting." The board also implements solid waste legislation.

PUBLICATIONS: The board publishes a monthly newsletter, the *CIWMB Update,* and both publishes and distributes educational literature on solid waste solutions.

Colorado

Colorado Office of Energy Conservation (COEC)
112 East 14th Avenue
Denver, CO 80203
(303) 894-2144
In-state hotline: 1-800-632-6662
Kelly Roberts, Recycling Coordinator

COEC coordinates and tries to facilitate the state's efforts in all areas of conservation, with a special division devoted solely to solid waste. COEC provides grants for a variety of educational projects and sponsors conferences on recycling on a regular basis (e.g., the "Colorado Buy Recycled Conference" and the "Paper Grades Workshop").

PUBLICATIONS: *Colorado Energy Talk* is a bimonthly newsletter published by COEC. The agency also publishes and/or provides funding for additional literature on recycling, including: *Buy Recycled: The Businessperson's Guide, Recycling Office Waste Paper—A Step-by-Step Guide,* and *Decision Maker's Guide: Waste Reduction and Recycling.*

Colorado Recycles (CR)
8745 W. 14th Avenue, #216
Lakewood, CO 80215
(303) 231-9972
In-state hotline: 1-800-438-8800
Nancy Larson, Executive Director

A nonprofit educational organization that promotes statewide recycling efforts, CR provides educational material for schools and runs a hotline to provide recycling information to Colorado residents.

PUBLICATIONS: CR produces a quarterly publication called *News to Re-Use* and publishes and distributes a recycling poster/guide to Colorado recyclers on an annual basis.

Rocky Mountain Recyclers Association (RMRA)
P.O. Box 224
Denver, CO 80214-1896
(303) 441-9445
Bill Schroer, Executive Director

The RMRA is a nonprofit group dedicated to improving economic conditions for the Colorado recycling industry. The association also assists citizens and businesses with their recycling/solid waste management concerns and facilitates public involvement in community events.

Connecticut

Connecticut Department of Environmental Protection (CDEP)
Bureau of Waste Management
165 Capitol Avenue
Hartford, CT 06106
(203)566-8722

(203) 566-4924 (FAX)
Lois Hager, State Recycling Coordinator

CDEP has a staff of seven, committed to recycling assistance efforts. They are available to answer questions on: state recycling policy, regionalization, interstate initiatives, grants administration, office paper recycling, recycling markets, commercial recycling, composting, collection systems and equipment, processing systems, enforcement, and public education. Printed fact sheets, posters, children's activities, a traveling exhibit, and school assembly programs, all of which deal with recycling, are available from this staff.

Connecticut Recyclers Coalition (CRC)
P.O. Box 445
Stonington, CT 06378
(203) 887-6368
Toby Goodrich, Chairman

CRC, a nonprofit organization composed of professional and volunteer recyclers, was created to initiate and engage in educational, scientific, and literary pursuits, specifically with regard to recycling. CRC promotes waste reduction and recycling programs, including composting, and helps to coordinate the cooperation of the public and private sectors. It also encourages the exchange of information and technical assistance among recyclers.

PUBLICATIONS: CRC publishes a quarterly newsletter, *Discard Discourse.*

Delaware

Delaware Department of Natural Resources and Environmental Control (DNREC)
Pollution Prevention Program
89 Kings Highway
P.O. Box 1401
Dover, DE 19903
(302) 739-3822
Andrea Farrell, Director

DNREC works to encourage recycling through a pollution prevention/waste minimization program entitled "Three Rs for the 90s," which "defines a statewide comprehensive pollution prevention program designed not only to maximize the reuse and recycling of wastes, but to reduce the actual production of waste products in the first place."

DNREC also administers the RECYCLE DELAWARE program, which establishes recycling centers in key locations throughout the state that accept glass, paper, aluminum, metals, plastics, motor oil, and button batteries (from watches, cameras, and hearing aids). RECYCLE DELAWARE's hotline number is 1-800-339-DSWA.

District of Columbia

District of Columbia Office of Recycling
Department of Public Works (DPW)
2000 14th Street, NW
Washington, DC 20009
(202) 727-5856
(202) 727-5872 (FAX)
Evelyn Shields, Recycling Project Manager

DPW is the agency responsible for running the district's solid waste hauling programs, including the collection of recyclables.

PUBLICATIONS: DPW publishes several informational brochures to assist the public in understanding the recycling program and in complying with the state's Solid Waste Management and Multi-material Recycling Act of 1988 (which took effect on 1 October 1989).

Florida

RecycleFlorida Today, Inc. (RFT)
P.O. Box 32906
Palm Beach Gardens, FL 33420
(813) 878-1144
Teresa Ilan, Chairperson

RFT is a nonprofit organization originally formed in 1991 as a state chapter of the National Recycling Coalition (NCR). RecycleFlorida acts as a liaison between government, industry, and others involved in recycling. It is both a professional and educational organization and will assist individual members in improving skills and techniques in recycling.

PUBLICATIONS: RecycleFlorida publishes a "periodic" newsletter, the *Renewable News*.

Georgia

Georgia Department of Natural Resources (GDNR)
Environmental Protection Division
Floyd Towers East
205 Butler Street, SE
Atlanta, GA 30334
(404) 362-2692
(404) 362-2654 (FAX)
Pam Thomas, Environmental Specialist in Charge of Recycling

The issue of recycling is just beginning to be addressed by the state of Georgia.

PUBLICATIONS: At this time, the only literature and public education programs being produced are concerned with the collection and recycling of used motor oil.

Hawaii

Hawaii Department of Health
Office of Solid Waste Management (OSWM)
5 Waterfront Plaza, Suite 250
500 Ala-Moana Boulevard
Honolulu, HI 96813
(808) 586-4226
(808) 586-4370 (FAX)
John Harder, Solid Waste Coordinator

OSWM is the state's regulatory agency and is also responsible for evaluating the integrated waste management plans of each county, which are to be filed by 1 January 1993. The office is working with local officials to create plans that emphasize source reduction, recycling, and composting. Public education programs are also being developed.

Copies of the state's legislative acts regarding solid waste are available through OSWM, as is a list of recycling coordinators from each of the islands that compose the state.

Recycling Association of Hawaii (RAH)
162-B North King Street
Honolulu, HI 96817
(808) 599-1976
(808) 531-5243 (FAX)
Janie Deuser, Director

RAH is committed to "educating the people of our state to reduce, reuse, and recycle through a variety of projects and events." RAH provides resource recovery curricula to schools and has a speakers bureau and public-access library. It also runs a state recycling hotline, 808-RECYCLE (808-732-9253).

PUBLICATIONS: RAH publishes a monthly newsletter called *RECYCLE.*

Idaho

Idaho Division of Environmental Quality (IDEQ)
IWRAP Bureau
1410 N. Hilton
Boise, ID 83720-9000
(208) 334-5882
(208) 334-0417 (FAX)
Jerome Jankowski, Solid Waste Specialist

The Idaho Waste Reduction Assistance Program (IWRAP) is a public education and technical assistance program devoted to promoting the 3Rs of reduce, reuse, and recycle. IWRAP also provides program development guidance for both businesses and communities. In addition, IDEQ administers an industrial waste reduction and recycling program.

PUBLICATIONS: Through a grant from the EPA, IWRAP published several materials, including *Recycling Awareness Program: An In-House Waste Reduction Handbook,* which guides readers through setting up waste reduction and recycling habits in their workplaces. Its directory, *Industrial Waste Reduction and Recycling in Idaho,* provides information about recycling resources and buyers for products such as copier toner cartridges, antifreeze, and paint wastes.

Illinois

Illinois Department of Energy and Natural Resources (ENR)
Office of Recycling and Waste Reduction (ORWR)
325 W. Adams Street, Room 300
Springfield, IL 62704-1892
(217) 524-5454
(217) 524-4177 (FAX)
Tim Warren, Director ORWR

ENR promotes recycling and recycling education throughout the state in businesses, schools, and communities. It produces reports on solid waste issues and a planning guide for residential recycling programs, and it sponsors conferences for the public and educators.

School education programs on solid waste alternatives are currently being developed by ENR, and many materials are already available, including coloring books, teachers' handbooks on waste reduction, classroom activity packets, and videotapes.

PUBLICATIONS: A collection of waste reduction/recycling "clip art" graphics is found in a novel and useful booklet available from ENR, which also maintains an information clearinghouse that publishes an extensive list of print and video resources on recycling, composting, and solid waste management. Publications are free, and videos are loaned to businesses and local governments only. However, individuals may borrow the videos through local libraries. The clearinghouse hotline, for in-state use, is 1-800-252-8955. ENR also publishes two quarterly newsletters: *Recycling Update* and *The Three R's* (for elementary teachers).

Illinois Recycling Association (IRA)
407 Dearborn Street, Suite 1775
Chicago, IL 60605
(312) 939-2985
(312) 939-2536
Dale Alekel-Carlson, President

IRA is a statewide coalition of individuals and organizations that provides for the exchange of information and ideas on resource conservation through recycling and waste reduction. As a state affiliate of the National Recycling Coalition, IRA sponsors workshops and conferences on recycling.

PUBLICATIONS: Each month, IRA publishes the *Illinois Recycling Association Newsletter,* which includes a section on regional markets.

Indiana

Indiana Department of Environmental Management (IDEM)
Office of Solid and Hazardous Waste Management (OSHWM)
105 S. Meridian Street
Indianapolis, IN 46225
(317) 232-8603
In-state toll-free hotline: 1-800-451-6027
Kathy Prosser, Commissioner

IDEM was established 1 April 1986 to protect the environment. OSHWM's responsibilities include enforcing the Resource Conservation and Recovery Act, and its goals include "working with local solid waste management districts to reach the state goal of reducing solid waste 35 percent by 1996, and 50 percent by the year 2001."

PUBLICATIONS: IDEM's Offfice of External Affairs produces numerous pamphlets for the public, including: *Recycle Indiana, Cool Things Kids Can Do to Help Save the Earth, Simple Substitutes for Household Hazardous Products,* and *Composting Is Nature's Recycling System.*

Indiana Recycling Coalition
P.O. Box 20444
Indianapolis, IN 46220-0444
(317) 283-6226
Tom Neltner, President

IRC, a not-for-profit corporation that represents concerned citizens, local officials, business, industry, and environmental groups, is working to "expand waste reduction, reuse, and recycling efforts throughout the state of Indiana." In addition to organizing in-state recycling conferences, the coalition "plans to serve as an information clearinghouse and coordinate efforts of those involved in the recycling cycle. IRC will also promote the use of recyclable and recycled materials, with a special emphasis on community education."

PUBLICATIONS: IRC publishes a monthly newsletter and *The Indiana Recycling Handbook* (everything you've always wanted to know about recycling in Indiana), which is updated every spring.

Iowa

Iowa Department of Natural Resources (DNR)
Waste Management Authority Division (WMAD)
Wallace Building
900 E. Grand Avenue
Des Moines, IA 50319-0034
(515) 281-8941
(515) 281-8895 (FAX)
In-state recycling hotline: 1-800-532-1114
Tom Blewett, Bureau Chief, Waste Reduction Bureau

WMAD was created in 1987 to assist Iowa in dealing with its waste management problems and to offer solutions. Its primary functions are to: plan the state's long-term waste management needs; research and demonstrate waste management options and markets for recycling; implement new waste management programs; and provide public education, outreach, and technical assistance. WMAD works in a nonregulatory capacity with businesses, governments, and individuals to help them cope with waste-related problems, protect the environment, and prepare for the future.

The division has extensive programs dealing with household hazardous waste, hazardous waste reduction, and solid waste recycling and reduction. (The state subscribes to the EPA hierarchy of integrated waste management.)

PUBLICATIONS: WMAD publishes a number of pamphlets on recycling, composting, waste reduction, and household hazardous waste. It also produces videos on solid waste alternatives and pollution prevention and a state recycling directory. More videos specifically on recycling are currently in production, and a curriculum package for kindergarten through twelfth grade classes, prepared in cooperation with the Department of Education, is also available through WMAD.

The division works with the Iowa Waste Reduction Center (IWRC) at the University of Northern Iowa, which has an in-state hotline as well to provide waste reduction information to businesses and industry: 1-800-422-3109.

Iowa Recycling Association (IRA)
P.O. Box 3184
Des Moines, IA 50316
(515) 265-0889
(515) 265-6690 (FAX)
Mick Barry, President

This nonprofit organization, self-described as "newly evolving," is composed of members from both the public and private sectors. The state chapter of the National Recycling Coalition, IRA sponsors statewide conferences and bimonthly forums on recycling, in addition to monthly membership meetings. It has also cosponsored workshops and public education campaigns dealing with recycling.

PUBLICATIONS: IRA publishes a quarterly newsletter, the *Iowa Recycling Association Newsletter.*

Kansas

Kansas Department of Health and Environment
Division of Environment
Forbes Field, Building 740
Topeka, KS 66620-0002
(913) 296-1535
(913) 296-6247 (FAX)
James Power, Director

The Division of Environment provides information on recycling programs throughout the state, marketing/information contacts, a package of six worksheets for studying the feasibility of setting up a local recycling program, and general educational materials on recycling.

Kentucky

Kentucky Department for Environmental Protection (KDEP)
Division of Waste Management
Resource Conservation and Local Assistance Branch
Frankfort Office Park
18 Reilly Road
Frankfort, KY 40601
(502) 564-6716
Vicki M. Pettus, Manager

The Division of Waste Management wrote and submitted to the legislature the State Solid Waste Reduction and Management Plan in March 1992. The division's work for the next few years "will focus on enforcing and enhancing the regulations and statutes [on solid waste management] already in place, educating and training regulators and regulated, and cooperating with other state agencies who are pursuing similar goals."

Currently, the division provides technical and informational assistance on recycling, and it networks with other state agencies. It also runs both a Clean Community Program (a Keep America Beautiful project) and a used oil recovery program. In addition, it is revising a solid waste currriculum guide for high schools and has a mobile "Eco-Home" that travels around the state for use by civic groups and schools.

PUBLICATIONS: A periodic bulletin, *Waste Action,* is published by the Division to provide information on the 3Rs. Another bulletin, *The Planning Edge,* deals with solid waste planning issues.

Kentucky Recycling Association (KRA)
P.O. Box 249
Frankfort, KY 40602
(606) 258-3470
Steve Feese, Director

KRA is a nonprofit organization dedicated to promoting recycling throughout the state. It is composed of members from industry, private business, state and local government, and public service groups as well as interested citizens who seek to improve recycling and waste management practices within Kentucky. KRA itself is a member of the National Recycling Coalition.

PUBLICATIONS: *Recycling in State Government* is available from KRA, which also provides information on recycling and composting programs as well as a market directory and a county recycling directory. A newsletter, *The KRA Connection,* is published on a quarterly basis.

Louisiana

Louisiana Department of Environmental Quality
Solid Waste Division
P.O. Box 44096
Baton Rouge, LA 70804-4096
(504) 342-9103

Maine

Maine Waste Management Agency
Office of Waste Reduction and Recycling
State House Station #154
Augusta, ME 04333-0154
(207) 289-5300
In-state toll-free hotline: 1-800-662-4545
Sherry F. Huber, Executive Director

MWMA was created by the state legislature to implement an integrated approach to waste management. The agency's responsibilities include: providing technical assistance on solid waste management and recycling to municipalities and businesses; promoting and emphasizing recycling and waste reduction in the state; initiating, conducting, and supporting research and demonstration projects; and coordinating all state agency research programs pertaining to waste management and recycling.

PUBLICATIONS: MWMA publishes a newsletter, *The Waste Watcher*, on a quarterly basis.

Maine Solid Waste Management and Recovery Association
c/o Maine Municipal Association
Community Drive
Augusta, ME 04330
(207) 775-5401
Cathy Callahan, Director

Maryland

Maryland Department of the Environment (MDE)
Office of Waste Minimization and Recycling (OWMR)
2500 Broening Highway
Building 40, 2nd Floor
Baltimore, MD 21224
(301) 631-3315
In-state recycling hotline: 1-800-I RECYCLE
Lori Scozzafava, Chief OWMR

OWMR's main focus is on the recycling goals of the 24 state jurisdictions. (The Maryland Recycling Act of 1988 mandated the minimum goals by population size.) OWMR also is responsible for: writing and overseeing the state's recycling plan, which requires the state to reduce waste by at least 10 percent; regulating the 1991 Used Tire Recycling Act; reviewing the County 10-Year Solid Waste Management Plans; and developing the State Solid Waste Management Plan. Other OWMR duties include planning of recycling programs, transfer of technical information, market analysis and development, and public education.

PUBLICATIONS: OWMR publishes two pamphlets: *Reduce, Reuse, Recycle* and *Starting at Home—Recycling to Protect Our Environment*.

Maryland Recyclers Coalition (MRC)
P.O. Box 6097
Annapolis, MD 21401
(410) 553-2082
Amy D. Burdick, President

MRC is a nonprofit association of members from the public, private, and nonprofit sectors. The coalition is deeply involved in promoting source reduction as well as recycling, and it is working to further the buy-recycled concept. Priorities for 1992 include focusing on legislative issues, aiding commercial recycling programs, and providing outreach to recycling coordinators throughout the state.

PUBLICATIONS: The *MRC Newsletter* is published on a quarterly basis.

Massachusetts

Massachusetts Department of Environmental Protection
Division of Solid Waste Management
1 Winter Street
4th Floor
Boston, MA 02108
(617) 292-5980
(617) 556-1049 (FAX)
Robin Ingenthron, Recycling Programs Director

Massachusetts's Department of Environmental Protection (DEP) is the Commonwealth's lead agency for solid waste management. Working with other offices within the Executive Office of Environmental Affairs and through the Division of Solid Waste Management, DEP's broad mission is to ensure that the state's solid waste system integrates source reduction, recycling, combustion with energy recovery, and environmentally safe operation of landfills.

The department offers technical assistance and outreach from staff on recycling and composting issues, and it acts as an information resource.

Massachusetts Recycling Coalition/MassRecycle
P.O. Box 3111
Worcester, MA 01613
(508) 345-5385
William Stanwood, Education Chair

MassRecycle is the only statewide recycling coalition in Massachusetts. It is a nonprofit and member-operated organization "dedicated to bringing together individuals, local and state governments, industry, and environmental groups—a broad base of business and community interests—for the purpose of promoting and facilitating waste reduction, reuse, and recycling."

MassRecycle also organizes conferences, provides educational information, and loans a variety of resource materials, including videotapes (send for a current list).

PUBLICATIONS: MassRecycle publishes a quarterly newsletter, *The MASSRECYCLER.*

Michigan

Michigan Department of Natural Resources
Office of Waste Reduction Services
P.O. Box 30004
Lansing, MI 48909
(517) 335-1178

PUBLICATIONS: Michigan's DNR publishes a list of recycling publications that are free to the public. A listing of solid waste/recycling studies is available for a nominal charge.

Michigan Recycling Coalition
P.O. Box 10240
Lansing, MI 48901
(313) 849-2864
Terry Guerin, Chair

MRC is a nonprofit organization dedicated to promoting sound solid waste management through recycling of waste material. It also promotes cooperation between the public and private sectors, encourages information exchange and technical assistance among recyclers, and works on public education, legislation, and marketing with respect to recycling. MRC also sponsors an annual recycling conference.

PUBLICATIONS: MRC publishes a quarterly newsletter.

Minnesota

Minnesota Office of Waste Management
1350 Energy Lane
St. Paul, MN 55108
(612) 649-5482
(612) 649-5749 (FAX)
In-state hotline: 1-800-877-6300
Michael Robertson, Director

OWM's goal is to achieve sound waste management in Minnesota. The agency "stresses the national and state priorities in managing both solid and hazardous waste: Reduce, reuse, recycle." OWM works with government, the private sector, and the public and is responsible for overseeing the state's solid waste management programs. It also administers three grant and loan programs dealing specifically with recycling market development.

PUBLICATIONS: The agency has published a recycling technical manual, the *Minnesota Recycling Directory,* and a community waste education manual, and it is preparing curricula on waste education. It also has an extensive list of printed resource materials that are available to the public at no charge, as well as videotapes available for two-week loans.

Minnesota Pollution Control Agency
520 Lafayette Road
St. Paul, MN 55155
(612) 296-6300
Toll-free hotline: 1-800-652-9747
Gerald Willett, Commissioner

MPCA is a state-run agency designed to help the public and private sectors comply with state and federally mandated environmental laws. The agency also is responsible for enforcing the majority of these laws.

PUBLICATIONS: MPCA publishes a series of fact sheets on solid waste subjects, as well as a bimonthly newsletter entitled *Minnesota Environment.*

The Minnesota Project
1885 University Avenue W., Suite 315
St. Paul, MN 55104
(612) 645-6159
(612) 645-6044 (FAX)
Beth Waterhouse, Executive Director

This is a private, nonprofit organization. According to its mission statement, "the Minnesota Project is committed to working with rural communities as they build their capacity to solve their own development and resource management problems." One of its major programs is known as Alternative Solid Waste Management, and the project works to "empower grassroots leadership, small-scale and sustainable solutions."

The project has organized a regional cooperative marketing network for recycled materials in 9 counties in southeastern Minnesota (and it is working with 14 northern Minnesota counties to do the same). It is also helping select counties develop waste reduction projects and creating a training program with the Minnesota Pollution Control Agency for personnel involved with the operation and management of recycling programs and centers within the state.

PUBLICATIONS: A newsletter is planned for future publication.

Mississippi

Mississippi Department of Environmental Quality
Office of Pollution Control
P.O. Box 10385
Jackson, MS 39289-0385
(601) 961-5171
(601) 354-6612 (FAX)
Thomas E. Whitten, Director

MDEQ/OPC organizes conferences and workshops on solid waste management, including recycling issues, and works with both the public and private sectors by providing educational information and a speakers bureau.

The agency also funds the Mississippi Solid Waste Reduction Assistance Program (MSSWRAP) through Mississippi State University, offering technical assistance to citizens in the areas of waste minimization and reduction [telephone: (612) 325-8454].

PUBLICATIONS: MSSWRAP publishes a state recycling list and a monthly newsletter, the *MISSTAP NEWS*; it also runs a solid waste clearinghouse/library.

Missouri

Missouri Department of Natural Resources
Environmental Improvement and Energy Resources Authority
512 E. Capitol Avenue
P.O. Box 1293
Jefferson City, MO 65102
(314) 635-3265
In-state toll-free hotline: 1-800-334-6946
Stephen Mahfood, Director

The Environmental Improvement and Energy Resources Authority is an independent agency created by the Missouri legislature "to provide low- or no-cost financing for projects that would reduce, control, and prevent environmental pollution, and to encourage research and development of energy alternatives while promoting economic development."

PUBLICATIONS: The Department of Natural Resources publishes a quarterly magazine entitled *Missouri Resource Review.*

Missouri State Recycling Association (MSRA)
P.O. Box 331
St. Charles, MO 63301
(314) 947-9766
Jane Bishop, Director

This association is in the process of reorganizing due to changes and difficulties with solid waste legislation in the state, according to its director. Presently, MSRA is "on hold," waiting to see what happens with Senate Bill 530, which established several controversial solid waste regions within the state. Numerous state and local agencies in these regions have filed lawsuits against the state to protest some of the boundaries.

Affiliated with the Missouri Waste Control Coalition, the association is designed to serve as a networking organization between the various state recycling interests.

PUBLICATIONS: MSRA does not publish a newsletter at this time.

Montana

Montana Department of Health and Environmental Sciences (MDHES)
Cogswell Building
Helena, MT 59620
(406) 444-1430
(406) 444-1499 (FAX)
Christine Kaufmann, Waste Reduction and Recycling Coordinator

The recycling plan of the Solid Waste Program of the MDHES is currently being drafted. The main goal of the coordinator, whose position was created and filled in 1992, is to write the state's recycling plan, which is expected to be completed in February 1993.

Associated Recyclers of Montana (ARM)
458 Charles
Billings, MT 59101
(406) 252-5721
Mark Richlen, President

ARM is a nonprofit organization that works through the Keep Montana Clean and Beautiful program. It is composed primarily of recyclers in the beverage and solid waste industries.

PUBLICATIONS: ARM publishes a directory to the state's recycling centers.

Montana Environmental Information Center (MEIC)
P.O. Box 1184
Helena, MT 59624
(406) 443-2520
(406) 442-1316 (FAX)
In-state recycling hotline: 1-800-823-MEIC
Bryan McNit, Director

MEIC is a nonprofit, statewide organization dedicated to protecting and enhancing Montana's environment. As such, it runs a recycling hotline to provide information on community recycling activities, locations of recycling centers, retailers that sell recycled products, and any other questions specifically related to recycling. The hotline is designed to provide free information and increase public awareness about source reduction and recycling.

PUBLICATIONS: MEIC also publishes and distributes several fact sheets on a variety of subjects, such as backyard composting, setting up an office recycling program, and cutting down on household hazardous waste.

Nebraska

Nebraska Department of Environmental Control
Litter Reduction and Recycling Program
P.O. Box 98922
Lincoln, NE 68509-8922
(402) 471-4210
Dannie E. Dearing, Environmental Program Specialist

This agency oversees the state's activities with regard to the Litter Reduction and Recycling Act. It administers grants to programs dealing with the education and promotion of proper solid waste management techniques in three main areas: public education, cleanup, and recycling.

PUBLICATIONS: The agency publishes an annual report to the governor and teams up with the Nebraska State Recycling Association to produce the *Nebraska Recycling Directory*.

Nebraska State Recycling Association (NSRA)
P.O. Box 80729
Lincoln, NE 68501
(402) 475-3637
In-state toll-free hotline: 1-800-248-7328
Monte McKillip, Director

NSRA is a private, nonprofit membership organization devoted to increasing the recycling of resources. The association offers a toll-free hotline, runs a state recycling conference each fall, provides educational materials for youth groups and schools, and presents and distributes a variety of informative articles and papers.

PUBLICATIONS: NSRA publishes a directory of the state's recyclers and a monthly newsletter, the *Recycling Sentinel.*

Nevada

Nevada Office of Community Services
400 W. King Street, Suite 400
Capitol Complex
Carson City, NV 89710
(702) 687-4603
(702) 687-4914 (FAX)

This office serves as a state point of contact on recycling and is involved with the issue from an educational perspective.

PUBLICATIONS: The office publishes a pamphlet called *Recycle Nevada,* which is a guide to recycling facilities and other resource centers within the state. It also provides several other informational pamphlets.

New Hampshire

New Hampshire Department of Environmental Services (NHDES)
Waste Management Division
6 Hazen Drive
Concord, NH 03301-6509
(603) 271-2901
(603) 271-2456 (FAX)
Sharon A. Yergeau, Administrator

NHDES is a regulatory agency whose permitting authority applies to recycling activities. It is also involved in recycling to the extent that it oversees each of the state's solid waste districts, which are required to make recycling a component of their programs. As resources allow, NHDES also participates in market development and other related activities.

New Hampshire Resource Recovery Association (NHRRA)
P.O. Box 721
Concord, NH 03302-0721
(603) 224-6996
Ray Pierce, Executive Director

NHRRA is a tax-exempt, nonprofit organization that provides marketing, educational, and technical services in waste reduction, recycling, composting, and other issues dealing with solid waste management. Its mission, in part, is "to provide leadership and support in promoting environmentally sound and economically viable waste reduction and recycling solutions."

The association manages a cooperative marketing program, organizes regional workshops, and presents an annual conference and exposition.

PUBLICATIONS: NHRRA publications include: *Recycling in NH: An Implementation Guide, "Waste Plan"—A Solid Waste Planning Model,* and a pamphlet entitled *Recycling in New Hampshire: A Beginner's Guide,* which includes a directory to the state's recycling centers. The NHRRA also produces a quarterly newsletter, *ReSource.*

New Jersey

New Jersey Department of Environmental Protection (NJDEP)
Office of Recycling
840 Bear Tavern Road
CN414
Trenton, NJ 08625-0414
(609) 530-8208
(609) 530-8899 (FAX)
Steven Gamble, Director

NJDEP's goals include implementing the state's solid waste policy guidelines, which were written in response to Governor James Florio's Emergency Solid Waste Task Force's final report/recommendations. NJDEP is thus directed by executive order to "develop a program maximizing source reduction and recycling and fashion a sound statewide planning process for managing our waste residues."

NJDEP is expected to work cooperatively with other state agencies and districts to achieve a variety of goals, among them: the design of strategies to attain at least a 60 percent recycling rate by 1995, implementing aggressive source reduction programs, and creative planning and intergovernmental dialogue to achieve greater regionalization of recycling and waste disposal facilities.

PUBLICATIONS: A list of over 40 publications dealing with recycling, composting, and source reduction is available from NJDEP, along with a variety of promotional materials such as magnets, stickers, and rulers. The department intends to begin publishing a quarterly newsletter, *The ComPost*, some time in 1992.

Association of New Jersey Recyclers (ANJR)
120 Finderne Avenue
Bridgewater, NJ 08807
(908) 722-7575
(908) 722-8344 (FAX)
Marie Kruzan, Director

ANJR is a nonprofit network, composed of members from both the private and public sectors, whose mission is "to serve as the voice of recycling in New Jersey through education and advocacy and the promotion of professional standards." This association promotes an integrated solid waste management plan through recycling, source reduction, composting, and reduction of household hazardous waste.

The association coordinates roundtable discussions, equipment shows, and symposiums on solid waste issues, and recently it received a grant to design an online resource board providing information on recycling and marketing.

PUBLICATIONS: Several publications are available from the ANJR, including *Small Business Guide to Cost-Effective Recycling* and a quarterly newsletter, *Beyond the Curb*.

New Mexico

New Mexico Health and Environment Department
Solid Waste Bureau
Harold Runnels Building
1190 St. Francis Drive
Santa Fe, NM 87503
(505) 827-2892
Marilyn G. Brown, State Recycling Coordinator

NMHED oversees state compliance with New Mexico's Solid Waste Act of 1990. The Community Assistance division of NMHED deals specifically with recycling and education on solid waste issues.

PUBLICATIONS: The Community Assistance division publishes a quarterly newsletter entitled *Focus on Solid Waste,* which is distributed "as a service for those who have an interest in solid waste. We will keep you in touch with issues, innovative technologies, and new regulations that relate to solid waste practices."

Recycle New Mexico
P.O. Box 27682
Albuquerque, NM 87125
(505) 761-8176
Gene Crabtree, Director

Recycle New Mexico is a nonprofit organization devoted to promoting recycling throughout the state.

PUBLICATIONS: The organization publishes a *State Directory of Recyclers* each year, which is distributed to recyclers and government agencies "to help keep lines of communication, regarding recycling, open between citizens, business, and lawmakers in New Mexico."

New York

New York State Department of Environmental Conservation (NYSDEC)
Waste Reduction and Recycling
50 Wolf Road
Albany, NY 12233-4015
(518) 457-7337
(518) 457-1283 (FAX)
Norman H. Nosenchuck, Director, Division of Solid Waste

NYSDEC is the state regulatory agency that deals with recycling and other solid waste issues. As such, it was responsible for writing the State Solid Waste Management Plan, which was first issued in 1987. One goal outlined in this plan called for reducing the waste stream by 50 percent by 1997 through the 3Rs of reduce, reuse, and recycle.

PUBLICATIONS: Copies of the plan and more than 20 other publications are available at no cost through NYSDEC, as is a list of educational curricula and videos.

New York State Association for Recycling
1152 County Road #8
Farmington, NY 14425

North Carolina

North Carolina Department of Environment, Health, and Natural Resources
Solid Waste Section
P.O. Box 27687
Raleigh, NC 27611-7687
(919) 733-0692

North Carolina Recycling Association
P.O. Box 25368
Raleigh, NC 27611-5368
(919) 782-8933
Bobbi Tousey, Executive Director

NCRA is a membership organization composed of government and private industry representatives and individuals involved with recycling. Their goal is to facilitate the development of the recycling industry and to assist recyclers by offering practical advice and solutions to help them achieve their solid waste management goals.

PUBLICATIONS: NCRA publishes a newsletter, *The R-Word*, on a quarterly basis.

North Dakota

North Dakota Department of Health and Consolidated Laboratories (NDDHCL)
Solid Waste Management Program
1200 Missouri Avenue
P.O. Box 5520
Bismarck, ND 58502-5520
(701) 221-5166
(701) 221-5200 (FAX)
Catherine A. Berg, Recycling Coordinator

The Solid Waste Management Program of NDDHCL regulates the storage, collection, transportation, and disposal of municipal solid wastes to preserve and enhance water and land resources and to protect public health and property. In 1991, legislation was passed declaring goals for the reduction of landfilled solid waste. This bill also directed the department to provide public education in the areas of waste reduction, source separation, reuse, recycling, and appropriate management of solid waste. Such programs are being developed and implemented.

PUBLICATIONS: Pamphlets on composting, grass clippings, and recycling, as well as a state recycling directory, are available from the NDDHCL, as is a copy of *Guidelines for Solid Waste Management Planning in North Dakota,* published in January 1992.

North Dakota Waste Handlers Association (NDWHA)
c/o Sam McQuade
P.O. Box 1196
Bismarck, ND 58502-1196
(701) 223-6850
(701) 223-6624 (FAX)
Sam McQuade, Jr., Recycling Contact

After the passage of 1991 legislation that gave the state direction in the field of solid waste management, this association decided to reorganize. In the future, it intends to play an active role in the further evolution of recycling and waste handling in North Dakota.

PUBLICATIONS: At this time, NDWHA has no newsletter or publications available; literature should, however, be available by the end of 1992.

Ohio

Ohio Department of Natural Resources (ODNR)
Division of Litter Prevention and Recycling (DLPR)
1889 Fountain Square, Building F-2
Columbus, OH 43224
(614) 265-7069
(614) 262-9387
Tom Davis, Recycling Unit Manager

DLPR is responsible for administering grants for recycling projects, promoting recycling through educational and public awareness programs, and providing advisory and technical assistance to recycling programs around the state. From 1985 to 1990, over 143,000 tons of recyclable materials were processed through grant-assisted programs of DLPR.

Educational programs run by DLPR include: Super Saver Investigators, Ohio Recycle Month, a recycling exhibit at the Ohio Center of Science and Industry, a Governor's Award for student research, a science workbook on litter prevention and recycling, a Girl Scout merit patch, and "Recycle with Ohio Zoos."

DLPR also runs an office paper recycling program called PAPERCYCLE and has worked to encourage the state's procurement of products made from recycled materials.

PUBLICATIONS: Published materials include: *Super Saver Investigators,* a 400-page elementary guide about solid waste and recycling; *Ohio Science Workbook: Litter Prevention and Recycling; Recycling Basics; Directory of Ohio Recyclers; PAPERCYCLE: A Guide to Office Paper Recycling;* and *Recycled Products Guide,* as well as various studies on recycling and solid waste.

Association of Ohio Recyclers
200 S. Green Street
Georgetown, OH 45121
(419) 281-6874
Willie Geiser, Director

Oklahoma

Oklahoma Department of Health
Solid Waste Services
P.O. Box 53551
Oklahoma City, OK 73152
(405) 271-7169

Oregon

Oregon Department of Environmental Quality (ODEQ)
811 SW Sixth Avenue
Portland, OR 97204
(503) 229-6046
(503) 229-6124
In-state toll-free hotline: 1-800-452-4011
Pat Vernon, Manager of Solid Waste Reduction and Recycling Section

ODEQ oversees the state's 18 separate recycling programs, dealing with the public, communities, and other large generators and manufacturers of solid waste. It is primarily concerned with legislation, education, and economics and with promoting the effectiveness of its programs. The department has also developed a recycling curriculum (known as Re:Thinking Recycling) that has been widely distributed and utilized in state schools.

Association of Oregon Recyclers (AOR)
P.O. Box 15279
Portland, OR 97215
(503) 233-7770
Bruce Walker and Charlotte Becker, Directors

AOR is "a non-profit organization of recycling professionals and activists committed to reducing waste and improving recycling in Oregon." AOR has "furthered recycling in Oregon through networking assistance and information exchange among recyclers; advocating improved market conditions and prices; promotions and education about recycling; and promoting legislation for recycling." The association also holds a yearly conference.

PUBLICATIONS: AOR publishes a membership directory and a monthly newsletter.

Pennsylvania

Commonwealth of Pennsylvania Department of Environmental Resources (DER)
Bureau of Waste Management
Division of Waste Minimization and Planning
P.O. Box 2063
Harrisburg, PA 17105-2063
(717) 787-7382
Recycling hotline: 1-800-346-4242

DER oversees compliance with the state's Municipal Waste Planning, Recycling, and Waste Reduction Act (Act 101), and it administers grants in conjunction with this legislation. Additionally, the department has developed a school curriculum on waste reduction and recycling, and it provides speakers, sponsors conferences, and offers technical assistance.

PUBLICATIONS: DER publishes a series of fact sheets on solid waste, including one on recycling information and technical services. The department also provides a list of free publications.

Pennsylvania Resources Council (PRC)
P.O. Box 88
Media, PA 19063-0088
(215) 565-9131
(215) 892-0504 (FAX)
In-state toll-free hotline: 1-800-GO-TO-PRC
Ruth Becker, Director

PRC was founded in 1939 and was originally called the Pennsylvania Roadside Council. It is the oldest environmental organization in the state and currently works with a wide range of groups that implement recycling programs.

PRC provides recycling and waste reduction expertise, community education publications and programs, conferences, seminars, videos, and materials for educators. Additionally, it runs an Environmental Shopping Campaign. Technical information and assistance are also available through PRC on such subjects as waste reduction, recycling, litter control, and beautification.

PenCycle, a statewide computer information network, is another program currently run by PRC. A second network, strictly a bulletin board system, is presently being created.

PUBLICATIONS: An extensive list of publications, games, and promotional materials on subjects ranging from litter control to recycling and composting is available from PRC. Three newsletters are published on a quarterly basis: *PRC Newsletter, All about Recycling,* and *Environmental Shopping Update.*

Rhode Island

Rhode Island Department of Environmental Management
OSCAR
83 Park Street
5th Floor
Providence, RI 02903
(401) 277-3434
(401) 277-2591 (FAX)
In-state toll-free recycling hotline: 1-800-CLEANRI
Robert L. Bendick, Director

OSCAR works in partnership with the Solid Waste Management Corporation, the Rhode Island Department of Administration, municipalities, and businesses to reduce the amount of waste placed in state landfills. Rhode Island's mandatory recycling program is coordinated by the state and applies to both homeowners and big business.

PUBLICATIONS: This organization's literature includes *Recycling in Rhode Island: A Blueprint for Success, Hazardous Wastes from Homes,* and *We Recycle: Getting Started with Recycling. OSCAR's CALL* is a newsletter that is "published on a regular basis."

South Carolina

South Carolina Department of Health and Environmental Control (SCDHEC)
Office of Waste Reduction and Recycling (OWRR)
J. Marion Sims Building
2600 Bull Street
Columbia, SC 29201
(803) 734-5200   (803) 734-5199 (FAX)
Bill Culler, Director of Solid Waste Management

SCDHEC was directed by the governor and general assembly to develop a state solid waste plan by 27 November 1992 that would "reflect serious deliberation not given to energy and environmental issues before in this State." OWRR is a relatively new agency.

PUBLICATIONS: At this time, OWRR has produced the *Layman's Guide to the Solid Waste Management and Recycling Act* and *Waste Tire Management and Disposal in South Carolina.*

South Carolina Recycling Association
c/o South Carolina Clean and Beautiful
1205 Pendleton Street, Room 203
Columbia, SC 29201
(803) 642-7610
Stanley Quarles, Director

South Dakota

South Dakota Department of Water and Natural Resources
Waste Management Program
523 E. Capitol Street
Pierre, SD 57501
(605) 773-3153

South Dakota Solid Waste Management Association (SDSWMA)
Recycling Branch
P.O. Box 3471
Rapid City, SD 57709
(605) 394-6747
Debby Barton, Executive Director

SDSWMA was incorporated as a nonprofit organization in September 1991. It is composed of three branches: collection, disposal, and recycling. Membership is open to anyone interested in recycling, including persons or groups from the public, private, and nonprofit sectors.

The organization promotes "environmentally sound solid waste management practices" and provides an information network for its membership. Solid waste management training and seminars, technical information and assistance, and research support are other services offered to members.

PUBLICATIONS: The SDSWMA newsletter, *UPDATE,* is currently published on a monthly basis.

Tennessee

Tennessee Department of Environment and Conservation (TDEC)
Bureau of Resources Management
701 Broadway
Nashville, TN 37243
(615) 742-6781
(615) 742-6594 (FAX)
Paul Davis, Director of Solid Waste Assistance

TDEC started the state government's recycling program in 1989, and presently, waste is being sorted into two categories: wet and dry. Plans for the future include developing public education programs on recycling.

PUBLICATIONS: Two pamphlets are published by TDEC for state offices: *The Whys and Hows of Recycling at the Office* and *It's Getting Easier!*

Tennessee Recycling Coalition (TRC)
P.O. Box 23796
Nashville, TN 37203
(615) 862-8620
DeAnna Moore, President

TRC is a nonprofit association consisting of a membership consensus from public, private, and nonprofit environmental organizations. It presents a conference on recycling within the state each year.

PUBLICATIONS: TRC produces the *Tennessee Recycling Report* on a quarterly basis. An educational brochure on recycling is being developed by the membership at this time.

Texas

Texas Bureau of Solid Waste Management
Recycling and Waste Minimization Branch
1100 West 49th Street
Austin, TX 78756-3199
(512) 458-7271
Hector H. Mendieta, Director

The Recycling Branch provides technical assistance to local governments and the public, and the bureau is in the process of enhancing its solid waste resource center and video library.

PUBLICATIONS: The resource center (1-800-45-TXSWM) produces publications and will maintain databases on recycling markets, programs, and information sources.

Recycling Coalition of Texas (RCT)
P.O. Box 2359
Austin, TX 78768
(512) 328-4486
Bill Carter, President

RCT, a nonprofit alliance of recyclers from around the state, cosponsors recycling conferences and seminars with Texas A&M University and promotes recycling and sound solid waste practices throughout the state.

PUBLICATIONS: A newsletter, the *Resource Manager,* is published on a quarterly basis by RCT.

Utah

Utah Department of Environmental Quality (UDEQ)
Division of Solid and Hazardous Waste
288 North 1460 West
Salt Lake City, UT 84114-4880
(801) 538-6170   (801) 538-6715 (FAX)
Sonja F. Wallace, State Recycling Coordinator

Utah's Recycling Task Force was established by H.B. 334 (Waste Recycling Task Force) in 1991. This task force issued a report to the legislature in December of that year, recommending more state action with regard to recycling, source reduction, and use of recycled materials. The UDEQ is currently in the process of designing a plan to address these goals.

Salt Lake Valley Solid Waste Management Council (SLVSWMC)
Recycling Information Office
2250 South Redwood Road, #7
West Valley City, UT 84119
(801) 974-6902
Joyce Y. Leach, Recycling Coordinator

SLVSWMC is associated with the Salt Lake Valley Landfill. It promotes alternatives to the landfill disposal of solid waste and provides a list of pamphlets on recycling, composting, household hazardous waste, and source reduction. Other materials, such as videotapes, books, and periodicals, are available for loan. The council also distributes a recycling guide/directory.

Vermont

Vermont Agency of Natural Resources (VANR)
Solid Waste Division/Recycling & Resource Recovery Section
103 S. Main Street
Laundry Building
Waterbury, VT 05671-0407
(802) 244-7831
(802) 244-5141 (FAX)
Paul Markowitz, Chief

The Recycling & Resource Recovery Section is the part of the VANR that deals specifically with recycling. Its 1992 work plan identified six goals: (1) to reduce the amount of unregulated hazardous waste being disposed of; (2) to educate the public about recycling, reduction, and hazardous waste; (3) to increase local markets for recyclables; (4) to provide technical assistance to Vermont municipalities, solid waste districts, and businesses; (5) to increase composting of high-quality organic wastes; and (6) to reduce the amount of state government waste requiring disposal and increase the purchase of materials with recycled content.

PUBLICATIONS: This section has published numerous reports, brochures, and guidance documents on recycling, environmental shopping habits, and composting that are available to state residents for free; a small fee is charged for out-of-state orders.

The Association of Vermont Recyclers
P.O. Box 1244
Montpelier, VT 05601
(802) 229-1833
Glenn McRae, Executive Director

AVR is "a coalition of businesses, institutions, schools, environmental groups, municipalities, and citizens working to reduce, reuse, and recycle." It sponsors an annual conference, offers recycling seminars, provides technical services, and promotes public education.

PUBLICATIONS: AVR publishes three newsletters: *Out of the Dumps,* for the general public (quarterly); *Re-Act,* for state schools (quarterly); and *The Recycling Planner,* for businesses (bimonthly). The association also publishes a variety of materials on recycling and solid waste issues that are free to the public.

Virginia

Virginia Department of Waste Management
101 N. 14th Street
James Monroe Building
11th Floor
Richmond, VA 23219
(804) 225-2667
In-state toll-free hotline: 1-800-552-2075

Washington

Washington State Department of Ecology (WDE)
Office of Waste Reduction, Recycling, and Litter Control
Mail Stop PV-11
Olympia, WA 98504-8711
(206) 438-7541
In-state toll-free hotline: 1-800-RECYCLE (1-800-732-9253)
Chuck Clarke, Director

WDE was created in 1970 to promote educational programs and enforce the State Environmental Policy Act. Since then, it has created recycling and waste reduction programs for offices and businesses, conducted studies on solid waste management alternatives, and established public education programs throughout the state.

The department sponsors an Ecology Youth Corps for 14- to 17-year-olds to teach the importance of waste reduction, recycling, and litter control.

PUBLICATIONS: WDE publishes many brochures and fact sheets on recycling and litter control, composting, and recycled paper products. It also publishes materials on household hazardous wastes and a waste management curriculum for kindergarten through twelfth grade. Educational videos, brochures, and posters can be ordered through the statewide hotline.

Washington State Recycling Association
203 East Fourth Avenue, Suite 307
Olympia, WA 98501
(206) 352-8737
Gregory D. Wright, Executive Director

WSRA is the professional trade organization for the recycling industry in Washington State. The association "has been active in providing recycling information to the general public, establishing and maintaining standards for the recycling industry, and providing a forum for its members to exchange information." It also holds an annual conference/trade show.

PUBLICATIONS: WSRA publishes a monthly newsletter.

West Virginia

West Virginia Department of Commerce, Labor, and Environmental Resources
Division of Natural Resources (DNR)
Office of Conservation, Education, and Litter Control
1900 Kanawha Boulevard, East
Room 732
Charleston, WV 25305
(304) 348-3370
(304) 348-2768 (FAX)
Ollie M. Harvey, Recycling Coordinator

DNR has developed and distributed a curriculum on solid waste management for kindergarten through twelfth grade classes. The division intends to assist individuals, communities, businesses, and industry in meeting the legislated goal of a 30 percent reduction in the state's waste stream by the year 2000 through source reduction, recycling, reuse, and resource recovery.

PUBLICATIONS: DNR publishes several pamphlets on recycling.

Wisconsin

Wisconsin Department of Natural Resources
Recycling Customer Service-IE/4
Box 7921
101 S. Webster
Madison, WI 53707-7921
(608) 267-0873
Shelley Williams

The Recycling Customer Service Office, in the Bureau of Information and Education, acts as "a resource clearinghouse for responsible units, Department of Natural Resource's employees, communities, businesses, associations, interest groups, and any individuals that need non-technical assistance or have questions about recycling in Wisconsin."

PUBLICATIONS: The department has a list of approximately 100 free publications on recycling/solid waste, including educational materials for kindergarten through twelfth grade, that are available to the public; DNR can also provide a bibliography of technical assistance publications on recycling and resource recovery.

Associated Recyclers of Wisconsin
16940 W. Shadow Drive
New Berlin, WI 53151
(414) 679-2132
Bill Tarman-Ramcheck, President

AROW is an organization composed of people involved in or with an interest in the recycling and solid waste industries. In 1991, AROW received grant monies to provide support to municipalities, regional planning commissions, or other interested entities for forming regional recyclables marketing cooperatives through the creation of a statewide Cooperative Marketing Council. The association also presents various regional workshops, as well as an annual conference.

PUBLICATIONS: AROW publishes a newsletter six times a year.

Wyoming

Wyoming Department of Environmental Quality
Solid Waste Management
122 W. 25th Street
Herschler Building
4th Floor, West
Cheyenne, WY 82002
(307) 777-7752
(307) 777-5973 (FAX)
Diana Hogle, Recycling Coordinator

In January 1992, the Wyoming Governor's Committee on Recycling presented its recommendations to the governor. Shortly thereafter, the state created the position of recycling coordinator, responsible for providing communities with "direct, functional technical assistance regarding market and transportation information." The coordinator is also directed to gather information on cooperative marketing between communities and nonconventional market sources with regard to recycling.

PUBLICATIONS: A copy of the committee's report, a *Wyoming Recycling Directory,* and a pamphlet entitled *Do It!* are available through WDEQ. Other literature is being planned, as are educational programs for the public.

National Organizations and Federal Government Agencies

Aluminum Association, Inc. (AA)
900 19th Street, NW
Washington, DC 20006
(202) 862-5100
(202) 862-5164 (FAX)
David N. Parker, President

AA is composed of aluminum can sheet manufacturers (e.g., Alcoa and Reynolds) throughout the country.

PUBLICATIONS: AA publishes a list of these manufacturers as well as a booklet entitled *Aluminum Recycling—America's Environmental Success Story,* which contains information on aluminum recycling and solid waste in the United States.

American Paper Institute, Inc. (API)
260 Madison Avenue
New York, NY 10016-2499
(212) 340-0626
(212) 689-2628 (FAX)
Tom Kraner, Director of Public Relations

API is the national trade association serving the U.S. pulp, paper, and paperboard industries. API's Paper Recycling Committee, which specifically deals with the recycling side of the paper industries, has been involved in recycling programs since World War II. It is also active in developing methods to improve the quality of wastepaper through education about contamination, as well as creating improved techniques for collecting, processing, transporting, and storing wastepaper.

PUBLICATIONS: The committee publishes several pamphlets on paper recycling and its role in solid waste management.

Center for Plastics Recycling Research (CPRR)
Rutgers, The State University of New Jersey
Busch Campus, Building 3529
Piscataway, NJ 08855
(908) 932-4402
Darrell R. Morrow, Director

The center was founded and funded by the Plastics Recycling Foundation (PRF) in order to quantify facts about recycling plastics. CPRR has three divisions—research, process development, and information services—that "work on covering the scientific, technological, economic, environmental, and practical sides of recycling plastics."

PUBLICATIONS: CPRR staff members have produced a VHS videotape on their research; it is available for a $20 handling fee (see Chapter 7).

Council for Solid Waste Solutions (CSWS)
1275 K Street, NW, Suite 400
Washington, DC 20005
(202) 371-5319

(202) 371-5679 (FAX)
Donald Shea, Executive Director

CSWS is a program of the Society of the Plastics Industry, Inc., that was founded in 1988 for the purpose of "developing comprehensive, realistic programs for the environmentally sound disposal and recycling of plastics." CSWS has technical, government affairs, and communications programs to promote the plastics recycling industry, and it runs an information hotline on solid waste issues (1-800-2-HELP-90).

PUBLICATIONS: The council publishes a variety of materials on plastics and solid waste management issues, including a videotape, a slide show, a series of fact sheets, and various reprints. In addition, CSWS produces a quarterly newsletter, *Handlers News*. (Also see Society of the Plastics Industry, Inc., p. 188.)

Council on Plastics and Packaging in the Environment (COPPE)
1001 Connecticut Avenue, NW
Suite 401
Washington, DC 20036
(202) 331-0099
(202) 466-5447 (FAX)
Edward J. Stana, Executive Director

COPPE is a coalition of plastic resin producers, packaging manufacturers and users, recyclers, retailers, and other related trade associations. The membership's primary directive is to establish and maintain open communications on issues surrounding the use of plastics and packaging, especially with regard to their impact on the environment.

COPPE also sponsors a series of "dialogue" forums for roundtable discussions about solid waste and related environmental issues. These forums encourage COPPE's members and organizations, such as the Audubon Society and the Environmental Action Foundation, to keep communication channels open.

PUBLICATIONS: COPPE publishes a variety of brochures, backgrounders, and issue papers about plastics, packaging, and solid waste disposal options; these materials are distributed to COPPE members, the media, and the public.

Environmental Action Foundation (EAF)
1525 New Hampshire Avenue, NW
Washington, DC 20036

(202) 745-4879
Ruth Caplan, Executive Director

EAF is part of Environmental Action, Inc., a national membership-based organization that works for strong state and federal environmental laws. Part of EAF is a Solid Waste Alternatives Project (SWAP), which promotes source reduction, recycling, and composting.

PUBLICATIONS: SWAP publishes a quarterly newsletter, *Wastelines*, and EAF publishes the bimonthly *Environmental Action Magazine*. EAF also has a list of 21 other publications available for purchase, many of which deal specifically with solid waste/recycling issues.

Environmental Defense Fund (EDF)
257 Park Avenue South
New York, NY 10010
(212) 505-2100
Fred Krupp, Executive Director

EDF created the slogan, "If you're not recycling, you're throwing it all away." A large, nonprofit, national environmental organization, EDF is devoted to protecting the environment, mainly through legislative lobbying and lawsuits against major corporate offenders. It was EDF's work with McDonald's Corporation that led that company to discontinue its use of polystyrene and establish its national incentive program to "buy recycled." EDF has six regional offices in addition to its New York location.

PUBLICATIONS: EDF publishes the *EDF Letter* on a monthly basis. For a free copy of the organization's recycling brochure, dial 1-800-CALL-EDF.

Flexible Packaging Association (FPA)
1090 Vermont Avenue, NW
Washington, DC 20005
(202) 842-3880
(202) 842-3841 (FAX)
Glenn E. Braswell, President

FPA is a trade association for converters and suppliers of flexible packaging materials and allied products. The goals of the association include communicating with state and federal governments regarding the packaging industry, promoting the use of flexible packaging, and conducting research.

PUBLICATIONS: Numerous publications, mostly technical, are available from FPA, as are several videotapes, including one entitled *Flexible Packaging Creates Solid Waste Solutions* that discusses life-cycle analysis and source reduction. A newsletter, *FPA Update,* is published on a monthly basis.

Foodservice & Packaging Institute, Inc. (FPI)
1901 North Moore Street
Suite 1111
Arlington, VA 22209
(703) 527-7505
(703) 527-7512 (FAX)
Joseph Bow, President

FPI, also known as the Association for the Single-Use Foodservice Products Industry, is a trade association largely dedicated to the promotion of disposable items in the foodservice industry on the basis of "sanitation, convenience, and versatility." This is accomplished through both public education campaigns and legislative lobbying against the banning of disposables, or single-use foodservice and packaging products. FPI also enthusiastically encourages the recycling of its products, as opposed to disposal.

PUBLICATIONS: Several informational pamphlets, a litter control checklist, and sanitation studies on disposables are available through the FPI office. FPI also distributes an information package and videotape entitled *Foodservice Disposables: Should I Feel Guilty?*

Glass Packaging Institute (GPI)
1801 K Street, NW
Suite 1105L
Washington, DC 20006
(202) 887-4850
(202) 785-5377 (FAX)
Lewis Andrews, President

GPI is a trade association that represents over 90 percent of the glass container manufacturers in America. The association supports glass recycling efforts across the United States through consumer education, technical assistance to municipalities, and industry education and promotion.

PUBLICATIONS: GPI publishes several pamphlets and fact sheets (*Issue Alerts*) about glass recycling. Included in their pamphlet entitled

Glass Recycling: Why? How? is a directory of all domestic glass container manufacturing plants (a total of 79). This association does not publish a newsletter.

INFORM, Inc.
381 Park Avenue South, Suite 1201
New York, NY 10016
(212) 689-4040
Joanna D. Underwood, President

INFORM is a nonprofit environmental research and education organization. Its main goal is to identify "practical ways to protect our natural resources and public health." The research, reports, and communications prepared by INFORM are focused on four areas: solid waste management, chemical hazards prevention, urban air quality, and land and water conservation. INFORM neither lobbies nor litigates.

PUBLICATIONS: The organization has published a number of books and reports on solid waste management, all of which are available directly through INFORM. Their newsletter, *INFORM Reports,* is published quarterly.

Institute for Local Self-Reliance (ILSR)
2425 18th Street, NW
Washington, DC 20009
(202) 232-4108
(202) 332-0463 (FAX)
Neil Seldman, Codirector

ILSR is a nonprofit educational and research organization. It works in urban areas to join "technical ingenuity with a sense of community to establish sustainable, environmentally sound forms of consumption and production." It promotes self-reliance in communities by "investigating examples of closed-loop manufacturing, materials policy, materials recovery, energy efficiency, and small scale production."

PUBLICATIONS: The institute publishes comprehensive studies based on applied research and policy analysis; a pamphlet listing the various publications is available through the ILSR office.

Institute of Scrap Recycling Industries, Inc. (ISRI)
1627 K Street, NW, Suite 700
Washington, DC 20006

(202) 466-4050
(202) 775-9109 (FAX)
Richard E. Abrams, President

ISRI is a trade association representing approximately 1,800 companies that process, broker, and consume scrap commodities. Such commodities include ferrous and nonferrous metals, paper, glass, textiles, and plastic. The membership also includes suppliers of equipment and services that serve the scrap industry.

In 1989, ISRI members handled over 90 million tons of recyclables, and they consider themselves to be experts in the field of recycling and resource recovery. They offer this expertise to communities and organizations in planning, establishing, and implementing recycling activities.

PUBLICATIONS: ISRI publishes a quarterly newsletter, *Phoenix,* and offers subscriptions to *SCRAP Processing and Recycling* magazine. The organization also offers several free pamphlets and fact sheets on recycling (a self-addressed stamped envelope must be provided).

Keep America Beautiful, Inc. (KAB)
Mill River Plaza
9 West Broad Street
Stamford, CT 06902
(203) 323-8987
(203) 325-9199 (FAX)
Roger W. Powers, President

KAB was founded in 1953 specifically to confront the issue of litter, and it developed a network of community-based programs to handle this problem. Today, KAB affiliates are adapting their programs to "encourage recycling and educate the public about solid waste disposal."

PUBLICATIONS: KAB publishes several informational pamphlets as well as the yearly *Award Winning Newsletter.* KAB's Solid Waste Task Force publishes a bimonthly newsletter called *FOCUS: Facts on Municipal Solid Waste.* In addition, KAB publishes a catalog containing educational and promotional materials (e.g., videotapes, posters, and buttons).

National Association for Plastic Container Recovery (NAPCOR)
5024 Parkway Plaza Boulevard, Suite 200
Charlotte, NC 28217
(704) 357-3250

Toll-free hotline for PET plastic information: 1-800-7NAPCOR
Luke Schmidt, Executive Director

NAPCOR is a nonprofit trade association set up to promote and facilitate plastic container recycling, specifically for polyethylene terephthalate bottles. Its members include the major manufacturers of PET resin as well as companies that manufacture bottles made from PET.

With a mission to "facilitate the economical recovery of plastic containers," NAPCOR would like to increase the current recycling rate for soft drink bottles from 20 percent to 50 percent by 1993.

NAPCOR works "with communities to develop effective programs for comprehensive recycling including PET bottles, or to incorporate PET collection into existing recycling systems."

PUBLICATIONS: Publications produced by NAPCOR include the booklet *Recycling PET: A Guidebook for Community Programs* and a quarterly newsletter entitled *PET Projects*.

National Association of Towns and Townships (NATaT)
1522 K Street, NW, Suite 730
Washington, DC 20005
(202) 737-5200
(202) 289-7996 (FAX)
Jeffrey Schiff, Director

NATaT is a nonprofit membership organization that offers technical assistance, public policy support, and educational services to local government officials in over 13,000 towns, townships, and small communities throughout the United States. The association conducts research and develops public policy recommendations aimed at improving the quality of life for people living in rural areas.

PUBLICATIONS: NATaT has developed a comprehensive information package about starting recycling programs, specifically geared toward small towns and rural communities. This package, *Why Waste a Second Chance?*, includes a guidebook, a VHS video, and a video user's guide. The videotape may be rented or bought; guidebooks may be ordered in quantity.

National Consumers League (NCL)
815 15th Street, NW
Suite 516
Washington, DC 20005

(202) 639-8140
Linda F. Golodner, Executive Director

NCL is a nonprofit, membership organization representing consumers and workers on the federal level. NCL provides consumers with useful information on issues surrounding recycling and educates the public on topics ranging from energy conservation to child labor.

PUBLICATIONS: NCL publishes a bimonthly newsletter, the *NCL BULLETIN*, and two brochures specifically dealing with solid waste and recycling: *The Garbage Problem: Effective Solutions for Consumers* and *The Earth's Future Is in Your Grocery Cart.*

National Polystyrene Recycling Company (NPRC)
25 Tri-State International
Lincolnshire, IL 60069
(708) 945-1991
(708) 945-2147 (FAX)
Jim Schneiders, President

Established in 1989, NPRC is funded by eight leading manufacturers of polystyrene plastics. It promotes "a program through which the polystyrene industry will continue to manufacture needed environmentally friendly consumer products, help collect those products after they are used, and re-make them into new products to be used over and over again." NPRC plans to reach its objectives "through a combination of owning and operating recycling centers and/or financing independent operators."

It is affiliated with the Council for Solid Waste Solutions, the Polystyrene Packaging Council, Inc., and the Society of the Plastics Industry, Inc.

PUBLICATIONS: NPRC publishes an information packet full of brochures and booklets and sells two videotapes: *Do the Right Thing: Recycle* and *Recycling Riddles.*

National Recycling Coalition (NRC)
1101 30th Street, NW, Suite 305
Washington, DC 20007
(202) 625-6406
(202) 625-6409 (FAX)
David Loveland, Executive Director

NRC is the largest organization in the country that deals exclusively with recycling issues. Its board of directors and committee chairpersons include many leaders from other environmental organizations, as well as corporate executives, municipal administrators, and other professionals in the field of recycling.

PUBLICATIONS: NRC publishes a quarterly newsletter, *The NRC Connection,* and its members may receive discounts on subscriptions to the following recycling periodicals: *Resource Recycling, BioCycle, GARBAGE,* and *Recycling Times.*

National Soft Drink Association (NSDA)
1101 Sixteenth Street, NW
Washington, DC 20036
(202) 463-6732
(202) 463-6700 (Solid Waste Programs Division)
(202) 463-6731 (FAX)
Gifford Stack, Vice President of NSDA and Solid Waste Programs Director

NSDA is a national trade association representing the entire American soft drink industry, which encompasses approximately 560 soft drink bottling firms in the United States. The association's members include companies that manufacture and market soft drinks, suppliers to the industry, and franchise companies.

In April 1989, NSDA created the Solid Waste Programs Division in order to better articulate the industry's proactive commitment to recycling and comprehensive solid waste management. This division considers its mission "to recycle more of our containers." To this end, it provides hands-on assistance to bottler members, works closely with state soft drink associations, elected officials, and administrators, and it consults with professional recyclers, opinion leaders, and other trade associations in the recycling field.

PUBLICATIONS: The Solid Waste Programs Division publishes a quarterly newsletter entitled *The Soft Drink RECYCLER.*

National Solid Wastes Management Association (NSWMA)
1730 Rhode Island Avenue, NW, Suite 1000
Washington, DC 20036
(202) 659-4613
Toll-free hotline: 1-800-424-2869
Eugene J. Wingerter, Director

NSWMA is a national trade association representing 2,500 member companies that are involved in private waste collection and disposal, recycling, landfill and waste-to-energy facility design and operation, and medical and hazardous waste treatment and disposal.

The association also has two nonactive membership categories for individuals or groups with an interest in receiving information from NSWMA. Associate memberships are offered to individuals who are not in the waste business, and affiliate memberships are available to public officials, nonprofit organizations, and government agencies.

Several professional institutes and councils are managed by NSWMA, including the Waste Recyclers Council (WRC), which works to "promote recycling efforts within and beyond the industry, and focus greater attention on recyclable materials markets."

PUBLICATIONS: NSWMA produces an extensive list of periodicals, brochures, indexes, fact sheets, and special reports, many of which specifically deal with recycling (see Chapter 7). One special report, entitled *Recycling in the States,* is updated twice a year and reviews recycling legislation throughout the United States.

Polystyrene Packaging Council (PSPC)
1025 Connecticut Avenue, NW, Suite 508
Washington, DC 20036
(202) 822-6424
(202) 331-0538 (FAX)
Betsy de Campos, Operations Manager

PSPC is a nonprofit organization dedicated to promoting polystyrene recycling and providing "accurate, reliable information about environmentally sound waste disposal practices."

PSPC also tracks and monitors state and local legislation throughout the country in order to keep the polystyrene industry, along with distributors and end users, informed of all relevant activity.

PUBLICATIONS: Several fact sheets on polystyrene recycling and the environment are published by PSPC for free distribution to the public. In addition, a video entitled *Solid Waste Solutions* is also available for educational efforts.

Renew America
1400 16th Street, NW, Suite 710
Washington, DC 20036
(202) 232-2252
(202) 232-2617
Tina Hobson, Executive Director

Renew America is a nonprofit, membership-funded organization that works to "provide others with examples of environmental programs that work." Its mission is "to spread the word about working solutions to today's environmental problems so that people can more easily improve their communities."

PUBLICATIONS: The organization publishes the *Environmental Success Index,* which is a clearinghouse of verified, working programs that protect, restore, and enhance the environment. The index is also part of the group's Searching for Success Program, which attempts to identify, promote, and reward successful environmental programs across the nation. One of the 20 issues highlighted in this program is solid waste reduction and recycling.

Society of the Plastics Industry, Inc. (SPI)
1275 K Street, NW, Suite 400
Washington, DC 20005
(202) 371-5200
(202) 371-1022 (FAX)
Larry L. Thomas, President

SPI is a trade association serving as "the voice of the plastics industry." Founded in 1937, it is a well-established organization including dozens of divisions, market councils, and special purpose groups devoted to every aspect of plastics use and manufacture. The Council for Solid Waste Solutions (CSWS) is one of SPI's special purpose groups.

SPI sponsors conferences throughout the United States and maintains regional offices in Washington, DC; Des Plaines, Illinois; Weymouth, Massachusetts; and Long Beach, California.

PUBLICATIONS: SPI's literature catalog includes several hundred publications on plastics, ranging from public information brochures to technical research papers.

Solid Waste Association of North America (SWANA)
P.O. Box 7219
Silver Spring, MD 20910
(301) 585-2898
(301) 589-7068 (FAX)
H. Lanier Hickman, Executive Director

Formerly known as GRCDA, SWANA is a nonprofit educational organization that serves individuals and communities responsible for the management and operation of municipal solid waste management systems. Its membership includes professionals from both the public and private sectors. "Dedicated to the advancement of professionalism in the field," SWANA offers several certified training courses, technical assistance, and other educational opportunities. It has chapters throughout the United States.

PUBLICATIONS: SWANA publishes a monthly newsletter, *Municipal Solid Waste News*. It also cosponsors, along with the Environmental Protection Agency, the Solid Waste Information Clearinghouse (SWICH). SWICH is an electronic computer-based information and assistance service that is available by subscription.

Southwest Public Recycling Association (SPRA)
P.O. Box 27210
Tucson, AZ 85726
(602) 791-4069
(602) 791-5417 (FAX)
Gary Olson, Executive Director

SPRA is a regional effort of over 20 municipalities in five states. Its goal is to improve existing markets for recycled goods, attract new recycling industry to the Southwest, and increase the power of the slogan, "Buy Recycled." The association was founded in January 1991 by mayors and staff from municipalities in Arizona, Colorado, Nevada, New Mexico, and Utah.

Solid Waste Composting Council (SWCC)
601 Pennsylvania Avenue, NW, Suite 900
Washington, DC 20004
(202) 638-0182
(202) 639-8238 (FAX)
Toll-free hotline: 1-800-457-4474
John T. Dunlop, President

SWCC was created by a variety of professionals in the composting and solid waste industry to "promote composting as an important contributor in solving the solid waste problem in the United States." The council's primary objectives are to encourage the production of high-quality, waste-derived compost that will meet the demands of an emerging market and to seek the support of government officials for municipal solid waste composting.

PUBLICATIONS: The council has a brief publications list composed of technical papers, conference proceedings, studies, and informative brochures. A short educational video about composting, *Sights and Sounds of Composting,* is also available through the council.

Steel Can Recycling Institute (SCRI)
680 Andersen Drive
Foster Plaza 10
Pittsburgh, PA 15220
(412) 922-2772
Toll-free: 1-800-876-SCRI
William H. Heenan, Director

"SCRI is a nonprofit industry-sponsored association with the mission of promoting and sustaining steel can recycling throughout the United States." It is available to help community leaders, recyclers, businesspeople, and educators develop steel can recycling programs and promote them to the public. It is in the process of establishing regional offices and maintains its national toll-free number to answer questions and provide technical assistance to recycling programs.

PUBLICATIONS: SCRI publishes a quarterly newsletter, *The Recycling Magnet,* that is devoted to publishing interesting stories about steel can recycling. Copies of several videotapes are available through SCRI for previewing by government officials, recycling coordinators, and educators.

U.S. Environmental Protection Agency (EPA)
Office of Solid Waste
401 M Street, SW
Washington, DC 20460
(202) 475-9872
Hotline for recycling brochures: 1-800-424-9346
Sylvia K. Lowrance, Director, Office of Solid Waste

EPA is the federal agency that deals with solid waste and recycling, as well as all other environmental issues. It is also responsible for administering the Resource Conservation and Recovery Act (RCRA).

PUBLICATIONS: The Environmental Protection Agency has an extensive list of educational publications on solid waste and recycling, which can be ordered by calling the EPA hotline. In addition, the Office of Solid Waste publishes a quarterly newsletter on recycling entitled *Reusable News,* which is available to the public at no cost. (See Chapter 7 for more information.)

EPA also has ten regional offices throughout the United States, each of which coordinates its own recycling education programs and produces additional recycling information specific to the area it administers. The names and phone numbers listed below refer to primary contacts in each regional division's Office of Solid Waste:

U.S. EPA Region 1
HER-CAN6
JFK Federal Building
Boston, MA 02203-2211
(617) 573-9670
John Hackler

Region 1: Connecticut, Massachusetts, Maine, New Hampshire, Rhode Island, and Vermont.

U.S. EPA Region 2
II-AWM
26 Federal Plaza
New York, NY 10278
(212) 264-0002
Mike DeBonis

Region 2: New York, New Jersey, Puerto Rico, and the Virgin Islands.

U.S. EPA Region 3
3HW53
841 Chestnut Street
Philadelphia, PA 19107
(215) 597-7936
Andrew Uricheck

Region 3: Delaware, Washington, DC, Maryland, Pennsylvania, Virginia, and West Virginia.

U.S. EPA Region 4
4WD-RCRAFF
345 Courtland Street, NE
Atlanta, GA 30365
(404) 347-0077
Jim Scarbrough

Region 4: Alabama, Florida, Georgia, Kentucky, Mississippi, North Carolina, South Carolina, and Tennessee.

U.S. EPA Region 5
HRP-8J

230 South Dearborn Street
Chicago, IL 60604
(312) 886-0976
Andy Tschampa

Region 5: Illinois, Indiana, Michigan, Minnesota, Ohio, and Wisconsin.

U.S. EPA Region 6
68-HH
First Interstate Bank Tower
1445 Ross Avenue
Dallas, TX 75202-2733
(214) 655-6655
Guanita Reiter

Region 6: Arkansas, Louisiana, New Mexico, Oklahoma, and Texas.

U.S. EPA Region 7
RCRA-SPG
726 Minnesota Avenue
Kansas City, KS 66101
(913) 551-7666
Chet McLaughlin

Region 7: Iowa, Kansas, Missouri, and Nebraska.

U.S. EPA Region 8
8HWM-RI
999 18th Street
Denver, CO 80202-2405
(303) 293-1667
Judy Wong

Region 8: Colorado, Montana, North Dakota, South Dakota, Utah, and Wyoming.

U.S. EPA Region 9
H-3-1
75 Hawthorne Street
San Francisco, CA 94105
(415) 744-2091
Jeff Scott

Region 9: California, Hawaii, Guam, and American Samoa.

U.S. EPA Region 10
HW-072
1200 Sixth Avenue
Seattle, WA 98101
(206) 553-2857
Mike Bussell

Region 10: Alaska, Idaho, Oregon, and Washington.

Worldwatch Institute
1776 Massachusetts Avenue, NW
Washington, DC 20036
(202) 452-1999
(202) 296-7365 (FAX)
Lester R. Brown, Director

"The Worldwatch Institute is an independent, nonprofit research organization created to analyze and to focus on global problems." The group considers that solid waste is one of those problems and believes recycling and reuse are among the solutions.

PUBLICATIONS: The institute publishes a series of *Worldwatch Papers,* several of which deal specifically with recycling and solid waste issues. The bimonthly magazine *World Watch,* an annual *State of the World* report, and the *Worldwatch Environmental Alert* book series are also published by the institute.

7

Reference Materials

IN A SEARCH THROUGH AVAILABLE LITERATURE, the subject of recycling can be found by itself, within texts that discuss environmental issues and in studies on solid waste management. This selected bibliography provides a wide perspective of books, periodicals, curriculum guides, government documents, and popular articles as well as videocassettes, databases, and computer networks that deal with recycling in whole or in part.

Books, Brochures, Reports, and Directories

Recycling, Solid Waste, and General Environmental Issues

Baldwin, J., ed. **Whole Earth Ecolog.** New York: Harmony Books, 1990. 129p. $15.95. ISBN 0-517-57658-9.

A catalog containing "the best of environmental tools and ideas." This collection of products and resources is arranged by subjects such as recycling, urban ore, and composting. Information on other publications and environmental essays is also included.

BioCycle, The Staff, eds. **The BioCycle Guide to Collecting, Processing and Marketing Recyclables.** Emmaus, PA: BioCycle, 1991. 229p. $49.95 pb. ISBN 0932-424-112.

An all-in-one reference on successful recycling for community and industry, published by *BioCycle, Journal of Waste Recycling*. This volume contains comprehensive data on developing curbside collection programs; systems and equipment analysis, together with advice on marketing materials; and a special report on MRFs. It is a valuable guide for all involved in waste reduction, recycling, resource conservation, and general environmental improvement.

BioCycle, The Staff, eds. **The BioCycle Guide to Yard Waste Composting.** Emmaus, PA: BioCycle, 1991. 197p. $49.95 pb. ISBN 0932-424-104.

A very complete reference guide to starting and operating a community yard waste composting program efficiently. From the editors of *BioCycle* magazine, which has been reporting on scientific studies of composting since 1960, this book includes sections on planning, collection, site selection and regulations, methods and operations, and composting principles. A directory of equipment suppliers, a section on marketing and utilization, and cost and economic comparisons are also included.

Blumberg, Louis, and Gottlieb, Robert. **War on Waste: Can America Win Its Battle with Garbage?** Washington, DC: Island Press, 1989. 325p. $34.95. ISBN 0-933280-92-0.

This book, written for the average person who is not an expert in the field of solid waste, provides an in-depth analysis of the fundamental causes of our current garbage crisis. It offers suggestions and proposals for public officials, community organizations, and concerned citizens who must find solutions to solid waste problems in their locales.

Branson, Gary D. **The Complete Guide to Recycling at Home.** Charlottesville, VA: Betterway Publications, 1991. 150p. Appendixes. $14.95. ISBN 1-55870-189-3.

Emphasizes source reduction before recycling, with suggestions for changes in the home. This volume also includes information on energy conservation, and an appendix lists sources of products for use in recycling programs as well as those made from recycled materials.

Chandler, William U. **Worldwatch Paper 56, Materials Recycling: The Virtue of Necessity.** Washington, DC: Worldwatch Institute, 1983. 52p. $4. ISBN 0-916468-55-0.

Gives a good, concise overview to the solid waste problems facing the world. Although the statistics are outdated, the basic principles and statements presented here are still current. The author also addresses the economic requirements that societies must establish to make recycling work—that consumers must pay the true environmental costs of the products they use, that world markets for scrap must be built and developed, and that collection of recyclable wastes must increase.

Denison, Richard A., and Ruston, John. **Recycling and Incineration: Evaluating the Choices.** Covelo, CA: Island Press, 1990. 322p. $34.95. ISBN 1-55963-055-8.

Examines the technology, economics, environmental concerns, and legal intricacies behind recycling and incineration as two high-priced approaches to tackling a community's solid waste problems. Rather than looking at two parts of an integrated solid waste system, the authors treat the issues in an "either/or" fashion.

A good overview of the basics of waste reduction, recycling, and incineration, this book offers cost comparisons of the two approaches, an evaluation of the perceived health and environmental impacts, and a roadmap through the tangle of regulations. This is a book for policymakers, waste management officials, municipal employees, and concerned citizens who are analyzing different solutions to solid waste problems.

Earthworks Group, The, eds. **50 Simple Things You Can Do to Save the Earth.** Berkeley, CA.: Earth Works Press, 1989. 96p. $4.95. ISBN 0-929-634-06-3.

A concise list of practical suggestions that any individual or family can use to tackle the environmental problems we all face. Many of the ideas relate to various aspects of recycling, and further resources are given.

Earthworks Group, The, eds. **The Next Step: 50 More Things You Can Do to Save the Earth.** Kansas City, MO: Andrews and McMeel, 1991. 120p. $5.95. ISBN 0-8362-2302-0.

An overview of various successful environmental projects throughout the United States and Canada. This is essentially a reference book on how to organize and educate one person or an entire community on specific environmental issues. Several of the projects deal with recycling and issues surrounding solid waste.

Earthworks Group, The, eds. **50 Simple Things Your Business Can Do to Save the Earth.** Kansas City, MO: Andrews and McMeel, 1991. 120p. $6.95. ISBN 1-879682-02-8.

More projects and ideas from Earthworks, specifically geared toward businesses. Office recycling programs, source reduction, and waste exchanges between industries are among the solid waste solutions addressed in this book.

Earthworks Group, The, eds. **The Recycler's Handbook.** Berkeley, CA: Earth Works Press, 1990. 132p. $4.95. ISBN 0-929634-08-X.

Another well-composed how-to book by the Earthworks Group. This volume deals specifically with all aspects of recycling in the home, school, or office, and includes tips for starting community recycling programs.

Hassol, Susan, and Richman, Beth. **Recycling: 101 Practical Tips for Home and Work.** Snowmass, CO: Windstar Foundation, 1989. 91p. $3.95. ISBN 0-9622492-3-8.

A handbook in the Windstar EarthPulse series providing practical tips on how to reduce, reuse, and recycle in the home and at work. Background information on the 3Rs, landfills, and other waste management measures, interesting statistics on solid waste recycling, and resources for recycled products and products to be used in recycling programs are also included. One section offers recycling suggestions and projects for paper, glass, aluminum, scrap, plastic, organic material, and household hazardous waste.

Hershkowitz, Dr. Allen, and Salerni, Dr. Eugene. **Garbage Management in Japan—Leading the Way.** New York: INFORM, 1987. 152p. $15. ISBN 0-918780-43-8.

A comprehensive report on Japan's sophisticated solid waste management techniques, including recycling. Documenting Japan's evolution in the garbage business, this report offers American planners and investors a lesson plan to help them avoid economic pain and environmental degradation. Japan has one of the highest recycling rates in the world, primarily because the country has so many people and so little space for landfills.

Hollender, Jeffrey. **How to Make the World a Better Place.** New York: William Morrow, 1990. 303p. $9.95. ISBN 0-688-08479-6.

A general book about global environmental issues, with an informative chapter on waste and recycling. Littering and source reduction are also addressed.

INFORM. **Business Recycling Manual.** Washington, DC: INFORM, 1991. 196p. $92 (binder format). ISBN 0-918780-57-8.

A complete guide to business recycling systems for recycling managers. This manual begins with the program development phase, explaining how to gather data and conduct a waste audit, and includes information on monitoring and evaluating different recycling programs and marketing recyclables. Worksheets are included.

Institute for Local Self-Reliance. **Beyond 40 Percent: Record-Setting Recycling and Composting Programs.** Covelo, CA: Island Press, 1990. 270p. $39.95. ISBN 1-55963-074-4.

A practical guide for communities seeking solutions to solid waste problems. This book is based on case studies of 17 cities in the United States and includes information on collection and processing methods, equipment, and costs. A local contact is given for each featured community to help the reader communicate with officials who have established successful recycling programs.

Jones, Teresa, Calabrese, Edward J., Gilbert, Charles E., and Winder, Alvin E. **Solid Waste Education Recycling Directory.** Chelsea, MN: Lewis Publishers, 1990. 109p. $57. ISBN 0-87371-359-1.

A state-by-state guide to recycling education curricula for kindergarten through twelfth grade. This directory provides information on ordering these programs and itemizes the costs of materials.

Lamb, Marjorie. **2 Minutes a Day for a Greener Planet.** San Francisco, CA: Harper & Row, 1990. 243p. $7.95. ISBN 0-06-250507-6.

Informative, easy-to-read suggestions for improving the environment one step at a time. Although several chapters address solid waste issues with regard to saving paper, excess packaging, reuse, and recycling, this is basically another broad look at multiple issues, with little in-depth treatment.

National Solid Wastes Management Association. **Resource Recovery in the United States.** Washington, DC: NSWMA, 1989. 8p. $7.50. Order number 906446.

A statistical analysis, with charts and tables, of recycling and waste-to-energy programs and how they integrate into comprehensive solid waste planning. This work addresses the problems associated with waste-to-energy plants in an easy-to-read fashion.

National Solid Wastes Management Association. **Waste Recycler's Council Directory.** Washington, DC: NSWMA, 1989. 36p. $5. Order number: 908624.

A comprehensive list of members of the Waste Recycler's Council. In 1989, council members handled nine million tons of recyclable materials and spent over $385 million for facilities and equipment to collect and process those recyclables.

National Solid Wastes Management Association. **Waste Recycler's Council Policy Positions.** Washington, DC: NSWMA, 1989. 8p. $7.50. Order number: 910803. (A newer version of this work will be published in September 1992.)

A listing of the policy positions of NSWMA's Waste Recycler's Council on key issues facing recycling today, such as market development, disposal bans, mandatory recycling, deposit laws, the role of state governments, and grants and subsidies.

National Solid Wastes Management Association. **The Future of Newspaper Recycling.** Washington, DC: NSWMA, 1990. 12p. $7.50. Order number: 001175.

An authoritative report, based on NSWMA-sponsored research, describing today's newspaper glut and prospects for de-inking plants in the future. The report addresses the nation's growing stock of old newsprint and presents possible solutions. American market projections, mill locations, and cost comparisons are also provided.

National Solid Wastes Management Association. **Garbage Then and Now.** Washington, DC: NSWMA, 1990. 8p. $1.50. Order number: 003118.

A garbage timeline from 500 B.C. to the 1990s. Fun and informative, this is a good educational tool for children and adults alike and can be ordered in packages of 50 for $18.75.

National Solid Wastes Management Association. **Public Attitudes toward Garbage Disposal.** Washington, DC: NSWMA, 1990. 11p. $7.50. Order number: 910783

Examines public attitudes about recycling, incineration, and landfilling. This volume also surveys state recycling goals across America.

National Solid Wastes Management Association. **Recycling in the States 1991.** Washington, DC: NSWMA, 1991. 20p. $7.50. Order number: 107138.

A mini-encyclopedia of state legislative recycling activity. This work identifies the goals states have set, discusses their plans to reach these goals, and analyzes their progress. State laws through 1990 are covered, and maps, charts, and tables are used to organize the large amount of data presented.

National Solid Wastes Management Association. **Recycling Solid Waste at-a-Glance.** Washington, DC: NSWMA, 1991. 4p. $1.50. Order number: 906419.

A quick-reference fact sheet on recycling, including product-by-product rates and information on what is involved in recycling, what makes it work, and what impedes its progress.

Pollock, Cynthia. **Worldwatch Paper 76, Mining Urban Wastes: The Potential for Recycling.** Washington, DC: Worldwatch Institute, 1987. 58p. $4. ISBN 0-916468-77-1.

A Worldwatch Paper focusing on urban solid waste that could potentially be recycled. Pollock promotes the environmental benefits of using secondary, or recycled, materials instead of virgin resources and addresses the issues of household hazardous wastes entering landfills, as well as food and yard waste composting. Although the statistics are not current, the basic precepts and conclusions presented in this report still hold true for today's urban areas.

Rifkin, Jeremy, ed. **The Green Lifestyle Handbook—1001 Ways You Can Heal the Earth.** New York: Henry Holt, 1990. 198p. $10.95. ISBN 0-8050-1369-5.

A book about global environmental problems, with solutions that individuals and communities can implement. One chapter deals specifically with recycling and solid waste.

Steel Can Recycling Institute. **Recyclable Steel Cans: An Integral Part of Your Curbside Recycling Program.** Pittsburgh, PA: Steel Can Recycling Institute, 1990. 24p. Free.

A "comprehensive guide to steel can recycling through curbside collection." This booklet explains the basics of recycling steel cans, with chapters ranging from "What Is a Steel Can?" to the "Economic Impact of Steel Can Recycling in Curbside Programs." It can be obtained by writing or calling the Steel Can Recycling Institute. (See Chapter 6, Steel Can Recycling Institute, p. 189.)

Thompson, Claudia G. **Recycled Papers: The Essential Guide.** Cambridge, MA: MIT Press, 1992. 162p. $24.95 pb. ISBN 0-262-70046-8.

A clear and concise layman's guide to recycled printing and writing papers. Thompson is a graphic designer who has researched recycled papers since 1988. The dimensions of the solid waste problem, a history of papermaking, and an examination of the varieties and characteristics of available papers are included in this text, which is printed on four different types of recycled paper.

Underwood, Joanna D., Hershkowitz, Dr. Allen, and de Kadt, Dr. Maarten. **Garbage: Practices, Problems & Remedies.** New York: IN-FORM, 1988. 32p. $3.50. ISBN 0-918780-47-0.

A source of concise, accurate data on solid waste management practices in the United States. Presenting useful facts about the garbage Americans create and how they manage it, this booklet also identifies waste management alternatives such as source reduction, recycling, improved incineration, and better planned and monitored landfills.

U.S. Environmental Protection Agency. **Recycle.** Washington, DC: USEPA, 1988. 4p. Free. EPA/530-SW-88-050.

A brochure featuring basic information on recycling and solid waste management. It succinctly explains the problem of solid waste and identifies the solutions, encouraging both source reduction and recycling.

U.S. Environmental Protection Agency. **How to Set Up a Local Program to Recycle Used Oil.** Washington, DC: USEPA, 1989. 41p. Free. EPA/SW-89-039a.

U.S. Environmental Protection Agency. **Recycling Used Oil: For Service Stations and Other Vehicle-Service Facilities.** Washington, DC: USEPA, 1989. Free. EPA/530-SW-89-03d.

U.S. Environmental Protection Agency. **Recycling Used Oil: What Can You Do?** Washington, DC: USEPA, 1989. 4p. Free. EPA/530-SW-89-039b.

U.S. Environmental Protection Agency. **Recycling Used Oil: 10 Steps to Change Your Oil.** Washington, DC: USEPA, 1989. Free. EPA/SW-89-039c.

The four booklets listed above provide most of the information necessary to recycle used oil or set up a program to do so. These booklets are all available through the RCRA/Superfund hotline: 1-800-424-9346.

U.S. Environmental Protection Agency. **Recycling Works! State and Local Success Stories.** Washington, DC: USEPA, 1989. 52p. Free. EPA/530-SW-89-014.

Examines 14 city and state recycling programs across America, each recycling different products. The type of program, a community overview, background facts, a program description, unique characteristics, and obstacles overcome are detailed for each locale.

U.S. Environmental Protection Agency. **The Solid Waste Dilemma: An Agenda for Action.** Washington, DC: USEPA, 1989. 70p. Free. EPA/530-SW-89-019.

The final report of the EPA's Municipal Solid Waste Task Force, which was to "fashion a strategy for improving the nation's management of municipal solid waste." This agenda offers specific suggestions for actions industry, citizens, and all levels of government can take to deal with solid waste problems. The systems approach of integrated solid waste management, rather than a focus on any one or two partial solutions, is emphasized.

U.S. Environmental Protection Agency. **Yard Waste Composting: A Study of Eight Programs.** Washington, DC: USEPA, 1989. 49p. Free. EPA/530-SW-89-038.

An informative introduction to yard waste composting, with case studies of eight communities from coast to coast. Additional contacts, references, and resources are listed as well.

U.S. Environmental Protection Agency. **Characterization of Municipal Solid Waste in the United States: 1990 Update** (Executive Summary). Washington, DC: USEPA, 1990. 15p. Free. EPA/530-SW-90-042A.

A report identifying the various components of our municipal solid waste. Weight and volume percentages on the contents of U.S. landfills are presented in pie chart form. An even more condensed fact sheet is also available as EPA/530-SW-90-042B.

U.S Environmental Protection Agency. **Recycling in Federal Agencies.** Washington, DC: USEPA, 1990. Free. EPA/530-SW-90-082.

U.S. Environmental Protection Agency. **School Recycling Programs—A Handbook for Educators.** Washington, DC: USEPA, 1990. 24p. Free. EPA/530-SW-90-023.

A brochure describing several options for setting up a school recycling program. It spotlights a number of successful efforts in this area and encourages the implementation of such programs to teach the concepts of source reduction and recycling.

U.S. Environmental Protection Agency. **A Catalogue of Hazardous and Solid Waste Publications.** 5th ed. Washington, DC: USEPA, 1991. 61p. Free. EPA/530-SW-91-013.

A catalog listing the most-requested documents of the Office of Solid Waste. Many of the documents are highly technical, but a few on recycling are geared to the general public (and therefore are included in this reference section). A number of documents about the Resource Conservation and Recovery Act (RCRA) are also included.

Wolf, Nancy, and Feldman, Ellen. **Plastics: America's Packaging Dilemma.** Covelo, CA: Island Press, 1991. 128p. $19.95. ISBN 1-55963-063-9.

An extensive treatment of the subject of plastics, including information on packaging, building materials, electrical products, adhesives, and related legislative and regulatory issues. This book also deals with controversies over the recyclability, degradability, and incineration of plastics.

Children's Books

The works listed in this section are specifically geared toward juvenile readers. Each can be read alone by a child or with a parent or scout leader as a group project.

Earthworks Group, The, eds. **50 Simple Things Kids Can Do to Save the Earth.** Kansas City, MO: Andrews and McMeel, 1990. 156p. $6.95. ISBN 0-8362-2301-2.

For 8- through 12-year-old children, but most of the ideas in this book can also be used by adults for family or class projects. Beginning with an explanation of environmental problems, this book offers information, experiments, and projects that teach children that they, too, can make a difference to the environment.

Elkington, John, Hailes, Julia, Hill, Douglas, and Makower, Joel. **Going Green: A Kid's Handbook to Saving the Planet.** New York: Puffin Books, 1990. 111p. $8.95. ISBN 0-14-034597-3.

An excellent guide to "going green," from the editors of *The Green Consumer Letter* and the authors of *The Green Consumer.* Simple explanations and projects are included, along with a guide to the 3Rs, many pertinent facts, and a children's version of how to conduct a "green audit" at home, in school, and in the community. Color illustrations by British illustrator Tony Ross add to the well-organized and entertaining text.

Goodman, Billy. **A Kid's Guide to How to Save the Planet.** New York: Avon Books, 1990. 137p. $2.95. ISBN 0-380-76041-X.

For reading level 7.8. This is another good book for children that provides an introduction to environmental problems and solutions. Filled with black-and-white photographs and illustrations, each chapter is divided into facts and simple explanations, followed by a "What You Can Do" section. One chapter is devoted to solid waste issues.

McQueen, Kelly, and Fassler, David. **Let's Talk Trash: The Kid's Book about Recycling.** New York: Waterfront Books, 1991. 159p. $14.95. ISBN 0-914525-10-0.

A good introduction to the subject of trash and recycling for younger children (kindergarten through third grade). This book incorporates the thoughts, ideas, and drawings of children in this age group in a broad discussion of trash, with an emphasis on recycling. The Environmental Law Foundation supported the writing of this paperback.

Savage, Candace. **Trash Attack.** Buffalo, NY: Firefly Books, 1990. 56p. $9.95. ISBN 0-920668-73-9.

Part of the Earth Care Books series for children, geared toward readers in the fourth through sixth grades. The contents of this simple but thorough treatment of solid waste are divided into two sections— "The Problem" and "The Solutions"—with excellent color illustrations by Steve Beinicke.

Journals

BioCycle
JG Press, Inc.
419 State Avenue
Emmaus, PA 18049
Monthly. $55.

Also known as the *Journal of Waste Recycling*, this magazine reports on new solutions to sludge and trash problems, focusing on composting, land application, materials recycling, and anaerobic digestion. Monthly information is provided on research findings, new equipment, financing options, health issues, government policies, innovative technologies, and marketing of treated residuals.

GARBAGE
Old House Journal Corp.
435 Ninth Street
Brooklyn, NY 11215
Bimonthly. $21.

This magazine strives for balanced reporting on people-based, as opposed to wildlife-based, environmental issues. Much of its contents are devoted to articles and advertisements on recycling, and the solid waste dilemma is covered extensively. A regular department, "In the Dumpster," describes products that purport to be "environmental" but are actually adding to solid waste problems. This is a down-to-earth periodical, geared toward thoroughly educating the concerned public on key environmental issues.

P3, The Earth-based Magazine for Kids
P3 Foundation
P.O. Box 52
Montgomery, VT 05470
5 issues per year. $18 (two-year subscription, or 10 issues).

P3 is an environmental magazine for 7- to 10-year-old children. Filled with colored pictures, short stories, and environmental news, it is a wealth of information for the younger set. The magazine also offers ideas for projects and activities that kids can accomplish without parental help. Subscription discounts are available to elementary schools and their libraries, nonprofit organizations, public libraries, and universities.

Resource Recycling: North America's Recycling Journal
Resource Recycling, Inc.
P.O. Box 10540
Portland, OR 97210-9893
Monthly. $42.

This periodical is a trade journal for those in the business of recycling. It highlights various solid waste management programs around the country and delves into specific issues each month (e.g., citywide composting, office paper recycling, or aluminum foil recycling programs). Regular segments include: "Association Watch," "State/Province Watch," "Federal Watch," "Programs in Action," "Equipment & Product News," and "Paper Recycling Markets." Although geared to the industry, *Resource Recycling* also contains a wealth of information useful to the budding recyclist interested in forming or running a recycling program outside the household. Resource Recycling, Inc., also publishes two monthly newsletters: *Plastics Recycling Update* ($85 per year) and *Bottle/Can Recycling Update* ($75 per year). Subscription information can be obtained by calling 1-800-227-1424.

Recycling Today
GIE, Inc.
4012 Bridge Avenue
Cleveland, OH 44113-3320
Toll-free subscription information number: 1-800-456-0707
Monthly. $32.

Three periodicals are produced by GIE, Inc., for *Recycling Today*. The *Scrap Market Edition*, published monthly, is geared toward the scrap recycling industry. The *Municipal Market Edition,* also published on a monthly basis, focuses on topics of interest to government and private recycling professionals. Regular departments in the *Municipal Market Edition* include: "Washington," "State," "Municipal," "Metal," "Paper," "Plastic," "Glass," and "Market Trends." The *Fibre Market News* is published weekly and covers all facets of the paper recycling market.

World Wastes
Communications Channels, Inc.
6255 Barfield Road
Atlanta, GA 30328
Monthly. $45.

This periodical, written for the wastes industry in general, includes monthly information on the ever-evolving world of recycling. It deals with all the different technologies available to handle every type of waste produced in the world. Regular departments include: "Financing," "Recycling," "Waste/Energy," "Landfills," "Transportation," "Hazwastes," and "Incineration."

Solid Waste/Recycling Bibliographies

National Soft Drink Association. **Solid Waste & Recycling Bibliography**. Washington, DC: NSDA, 1990. 31p. Free.

A pamphlet listing numerous state publications, waste exchanges, EPA documents, and scientific studies and research reports on specific commodities.

U.S. Environmental Protection Agency. **Bibliography of Municipal Solid Waste Management Alternatives**. Washington, DC: USEPA, 1989. 10p. Free. EPA/530-SW-89-055.

A listing of approximately 200 publications available from government, industry, and environmental groups.

Newsletters

Information on most of the state recycling newsletters may be found in Chapter 6 under individual state listings. The resources given here are national in scope.

The Franklin Report
Franklin Associates, Ltd.
4121 West 83rd Street, Suite 108
Prairie Village, KS 66208
Biweekly. $795.

This 2-to-8-page newsletter, along with supplemental materials, is designed to keep readers abreast of current and expected environmental policies and how they are being formulated. Franklin Associates is well known for its extensive research studies in the environmental field, especially with respect to solid waste and recycling. This is the key company devoted to life-cycle analysis of products to determine their true environmental costs.

The Green Business Letter
Tilden Press, Inc.
1526 Connecticut Avenue, NW
Washington, DC 20036

Toll-free subscription information number: 1-800-955-GREEN
Monthly. $97.

This independently produced newsletter is aimed at helping companies make sound environmental ("green") choices that save money in the process. Discussion of recycling programs, products, and technologies is often included.

The Green Consumer Letter
Tilden Press, Inc.
1526 Connecticut Avenue, NW
Washington, DC 20036
Monthly. $27.

This independently produced newsletter advises individuals on how to maintain a "green" lifestyle, with extensive information on shopping for environmentally sound products.

Reusable News
Office of Program Management and Support (OPMS) OS-305
U.S. Environmental Protection Agency
401 M Street, SW
Washington, DC 20460
Quarterly. Free.

This newsletter, produced by EPA's Office of Solid Waste, reports on the efforts of EPA and other public and private groups at federal, state, or local levels to address the solid waste dilemma. The publication provides useful information about key issues and concerns in municipal solid waste management, including developments in recycling, source reduction, composting, landfilling, and procurement of recycled products. Additional information resources are listed in each issue.

Waste Age's Recycling Times
Waste Age Publications
National Solid Wastes Management Association
1730 Rhode Island Avenue, NW, Suite 1000
Washington, DC 20036-3196
Toll-free subscription information number: 1-800-424-2869
Biweekly. $95.

This newspaper provides up-to-the-minute coverage of recycling markets and keeps subscribers informed on trends, legislation, and regulations affecting the recycling industry. It features in-depth reporting for the recycling professional.

Curriculum Guides and Educational Materials

Most curriculum guides on solid waste and recycling can be obtained through state agencies and regional offices of the EPA, which are listed in Chapter 6. These offices often have environmental curriculum guides that are specific to their individual areas.

Keep America Beautiful, Inc.
Mill River Plaza
9 West Broad Street
Stamford, CT 06902
Attn: KAB Materials
(203) 323-8987

Waste in Place, a sequential curriculum supplement for teachers of grades kindergarten through six, deals with proper waste handling. It is interdisciplinary in approach, with activities relating to math, language arts, science, civics, and social studies. $40.

Waste: A Hidden Resource is written for teachers of students in grades seven through twelve and is designed to help teenagers develop responsible behaviors and attitudes toward the environment. The interdisciplinary course deals with the various waste disposal solutions. $50.

National Solid Wastes Management Association
Publications Department
Attn: Brian Medley
1730 Rhode Island Avenue, NW Suite 1000
Washington, DC 20036
(202) 659-4613
Toll-free order line: 1-800-424-2869

NSWMA produces a number of publications geared specifically toward educating children about solid waste:

Garbage Then and Now, a timeline approach to the history of solid waste in the world, is a colorful and informative brochure. $1.50 (may be

ordered in packages of 25 for $18.75, 50 for $29.50, and 100 for $45).
#003118.

In the *Walt Wastenot Activity Book,* a waste-watching squirrel named
Walt teaches children about recyling, hazardous wastes, and the
collection and transfer of solid waste. Puzzles, mazes, and other fun
games to enhance learning are included. $4.50. #001039.

The *Mini-Page on Trash,* a Sunday newspaper comics supplement, was
first published across the country on the 1989–1990 New Year's weekend.
Using fun facts and illustrations, it examines issues such as what we throw
away, what and why we recycle, and how landfills work. $1. #90001.

The RCRA Information Center
OS-305
U.S. Environmental Protection Agency
401 M Street, SW
Washington, DC 20460
Hotline number: 1-800-424-9346

The center produces *Recycle Today!,* a curriculum about recycling and
other solid waste issues for grades kindergarten through twelve. This
program, developed by the EPA's Office of Solid Waste with advice
from several national educational organizations, teaches language,
science, math, art, and social studies skills as it educates about recycling. It consists of four publications, each of which may be ordered
individually by its reference number: *Recycle Today! Curriculum—*
EPA/530-SW-90-005; *How-to Handbook—*EPA/530-SW-90-023; *Comic
Book—*EPA/530-SW-90-024; *Poster—*EPA/530-SW-90-010.

Refuse Industry Productions, Inc.
P.O. Box 1011
Grass Valley, CA 95945
(916) 272-7289
(916) 272-8539 (FAX)
Toll-free outside of California: 1-800-535-9547

This organization produces educational videos and curricula on the
3Rs for kindergarten through twelfth grade classes, as well as numerous promotional items (e.g., coloring books, pencils, erasers, stickers,
and wallcharts with "reduce, reuse, recycle" themes). Each grade pack
may be ordered separately and includes flexible lesson plans and
reproducible loose-leaf worksheets for students. Some samples are
available on request.

Articles

Ackerman, Frank. "Solid Waste: The Hidden Utility." *BioCycle* 31 (August 1990): 84–85.

Andress, Carol. "Innovative Funding for Recycling Programs." *BioCycle* 31 (August 1990): 50–53.

Apotheker, Steve. "Glass Containers: How Recyclable Will They Be in the 1990s?" *Resource Recycling* 10 (June 1991): 25–32.

———. "Office Paper Recycling: Collection Trends." *Resource Recycling* 10 (November 1991): 44–52.

Bloyd-Peshkin, Sharon. "Taming the Waste Stream in Your Office." *Vegetarian Times* 155 (July 1990): 54–61.

Breen, Bill. "Selling It! The Making of Markets for Recyclables." *GARBAGE* 2 (November/December 1990): 44–49.

Brewer, Gretchen. "Plastic Bottles Close the Loop." *Resource Recycling* 10 (May 1991): 88–95.

———. "Buried Alive: The Garbage Glut." *Newsweek* 114 (November 27, 1989): 66–76.

Christrup, Judy. "Duped by Plastics." *Greenpeace* 14 (September/October 1989): 18.

Daniel, Joseph E. "The Glossy Truth of Recycled Paper." *Buzzworm* 2 (July/August 1990): 20–21.

Davis, Alan, and Kinsella, Susan. "Recycled Paper: Exploding the Myths." *GARBAGE* 2 (May/June 1990): 48–54.

DeYoung, R. "Recycling as Appropriate Behavior: A Review of Survey Data from Selected Recycling Education Programs in Michigan." *Resources, Conservation, and Recycling* 3 (1990): 253–266.

Easterbrook, Gregg. "Cleaning Up Our Mess." *Newsweek* (July 24, 1989): 26–42.

Environmental Action, eds. "Recycling Plastics: A Forum." *Environmental Action* (July/August 1988): 21–25.

Erkenswick, Jane L. "Office Paper Recycling: A Look at the Ledger Grades." *Resource Recycling* 10 (November, 1991): 64–68.

Farmanfarmaian, Roxane. "Saving the Environment." *McCall's* 118 (January 1991): 65–69, 139.

Frosch, Robert A., and Gallopoulos, Nicholas E. "Strategies for Manufacturing." *Scientific American* 261 (September 1989): 144–152.

Gibson, Susan. "Manufacturers Eye Design for Recycling Options." *Recycling Today* 28 (October 15, 1990): 121–124.

Glenn, Jim. "After the Crisis." *BioCycle* 31 (July 1990).

———. "The State of Garbage in America." *BioCycle* 31 (March 1990): 48–53.

Grassy, John. "Bottle Bills: Headed for a Collision at Curbside?" *GARBAGE* 4 (January/February 1992): 45–47.

Grogan, Peter L. "Beyond Recycled Fiber Content." *BioCycle* 31 (June 1990): 85.

———. "Grassroots Grass Clippings." *BioCycle* 31 (July 1990): 80.

Harler, Curt. "Keeping It All in the Family." *Recycling Today* 2 (March 1991): 50–53.

Hasek, Glenn. "Hotels Keeping Watch on Waste." *Resource Recycling* 10 (January 1991): 56–60.

Hong, Peter, and Yang, Dori Jones. "Cutting the Trash Heap Down to Size." *Business Week* (September 30, 1991): 100L.

Keene-Osborn, Sherry. "Recycling: Will the Cycle Be Unbroken?" *Colorado Business* 18 (April 1991): 34–42.

Kourik, Robert. "What's So Great about Seattle?" *GARBAGE* 2 (November/December 1990): 24–31.

Levetan, Steve. "Can Government Dictate Who Handles Recyclables?" *Recycling Today* 29 (January 1991): 8.

Logsdon, Gene. "Agony and Ecstasy of Tire Recycling." *BioCycle* 31 (July 1990): 44–85.

Long, Lynda. "Smart Budgeting to Promote Recycling." *BioCycle* 31 (March 1990): 54–55.

Luoma, Jon R. "Trash Can Realities." *Audubon* 92 (March 1990): 86–97.

Marshall, Jonathon, and Vasquez, Daniel. "Recycling Goals May Need Recycling." *San Francisco Chronicle* (December 17, 1991): 1.

Mayville, Gail. "Paper Recycling at the Office." *E Magazine* 2 (January/February 1991): 48.

Moll, Lucy. "The Plastics Rap." *Vegetarian Times* 138 (February 1989): 40–51.

Monk, Randall. "Municipal Composting Comes of Age." *World Wastes* 34 (October 1991): 34–40.

Montanari, Richard. "Getting Connected." *Recycling Today* 2 (April 1991): 74–77.

Newton, James W., and Rohwedder, W. J. "Environmental Computer Networking." *E Magazine* 1 (March/April 1990): 45–47.

Pardue, Leslie. "Plastics, Plastics Everywhere." *E Magazine* 2 (November/December 1991): 48–50.

Patterson, Gene E. "How Much Does Recycling Reduce the Waste Stream?" *BioCycle* 31 (July 1990): 46–49.

Porter, J. Winston. "Let's Go Easy on Recycling Plastics." *Philadelphia Inquirer* (August 6, 1991): 2.

Powell, Jerry. "All Types and Sizes Available: Recent Scrap Tire Recycling Legislation." *Resource Recycling* 9 (December 1990): 60–64.

Powell, Jerry, and McEntee, Ken. "Office Paper Recycling: Existing and Emerging Markets." *Resource Recycling* 10 (November 1991): 53–57.

Rathje, William L. "Rubbish." *The Atlantic Monthly* 265 (December 1989): 99–109.

———. "The History of Garbage." *GARBAGE* 2 (September/October 1990): 32–39.

———. "Recycled Phone Books Find Home in Brewery Sludge." *BioCycle* 32 (November 1991): 62.

Reutlinger, Nancy, and de Grassi, Dan. "Household Battery Recycling: Numerous Obstacles, Few Solutions." *Resource Recycling* 10 (April 1991): 24–29.

Rockland, Dr. David B. "Paper Recycling: Fact from Fiction." *Home Mechanix* 9 (October 1991): 15–16.

Schut, Jan H. "McDonald's Move Jolts PS Recycling but Won't Halt Numerous Ventures." *Plastics Technology* 37 (January 1991): 99–101.

Tedeschi, Bruno. "Recycling at GARBAGE." *GARBAGE* 2 (March/April 1990): 50–51.

Thayer, Ann M. "Solid Waste Concerns Spur Plastic Recycling Efforts." *Chemical & Engineering News* 67 (January 30, 1989): 7–15.

Trank, Andrea. "Green Paper." *In Business* 12 (November/December 1990): 36–38.

Watson, Tom. "Heading for the Hills: Rural Curbside Recycling." *Resource Recycling* 10 (November 1991): 23–26.

Westerman, Martin. "Restaurants Recycle." *Resource Recycling* 10 (January 1991): 78–83.

Wirka, Jeanne. "A Plastics Packaging Primer." *Environmental Action* (July/August 1988): 17–20.

Young, John E. "Tossing the Throwaway Habit." *World Watch* 4 (May/June 1991): 26–33.

Videocassette Tapes

There has been a paucity of audiovisual resources in the fields of solid waste and recycling, but this situation is changing. Although many trade associations produce their own videos to further their visions of the industry and to promote their products, purely educational productions can sometimes be difficult to find.

In many cases, state government agencies and regional offices of the Environmental Protection Agency produce videos specific to the areas they serve. It is best to consult such local offices (see Chapter 6) to see what is available because these resources may not be listed here. Also, organizations that publish solid waste management curricula often produce videotapes as well (mentioned earlier in this chapter), and many state agencies produce videos that are available for rental or sale.

Solid Waste/Recycling

Changing Skylines: The Garbage Crisis

Type: VHS videotape
Length: 29 minutes
Date: 1990
Cost: Free for public education
Source: EPA Region 8
8HWM-RI
999 18th Street
Denver, CO 80202-2405

Garbage: The Movie—An Environmental Crisis

Type: VHS videotape
Length: 25 minutes
Date: 1990
Cost: $350
Source: Churchill Films
12210 Nebraska Avenue
Los Angeles, CA 90025

This award-winning film takes a neatly organized look at solid waste problems in the United States. Using the "Garbage Barge" of Islip, New York, as a central theme, the producers explain the modern garbage dilemma and offer steps toward solutions. The 3Rs are demonstrated in this positive and informative film, and the viewer learns how recycling saves energy, how high school students can start their own recycling programs, and how individuals and communities are composting yard wastes.

In Partnership with Earth: Pollution Prevention for the 1990s
Type: VHS videotape
Length: 58 minutes
Date: 1990
Cost: $40
Source: Versar Inc.
           6850 Versar Center
           P.O. Box 1549
           Springfield, VA 22151

John Denver hosts and narrates this film, which reviews environmental achievements over the past 20 years. Nature's ways of preventing pollution through recycling are compared with those developed by men and women. With a positive look at the progress in recycling made by large corporations such as IBM and Eastman Kodak, this video is aimed at general audiences, age 12 and older.

Recycle It Yourself
Type: VHS videotape
Length: 37 minutes
Date: 1990
Cost: $29.95
Source: Aylmer Press
           P.O. Box 2735
           Madison, WI 53701

Designed for students in grades kindergarten through twelve, this video is more of an arts and crafts presentation than an environmental statement. Although it demonstrates how different items (e.g., coasters, necklaces, and paper) can be made at home with recycled materials, it offers no comments on an individual's need to recycle or to be concerned about the environment.

Reducing, Reusing, and Recycling: Environmental Concerns
Type: VHS videotape
Length: 20 minutes
Date: 1990
Cost: $89
Source: Rainbow Educational Video
           170 Keyland Court
           Bohemia, NY 11716

Recommended for six- to eight-year-old children, this film defines basic terms such as *solid waste, decompose,* and *nonrenewable resource* and intelligently discusses the 3Rs. An accompanying teacher's guide and worksheet can further the learning process.

The Rotten Truth

Type: VHS videotape
Length: 30 minutes
Date: 1990
Cost: $19.95 (including a 32-page teacher's guide)
Source: Wings for Learning
            1600 Green Hills Rd.
            P.O. Box 660002
            Scotts Valley, CA 95067
            Toll-free number for orders: 1-800-321-7511

This is an excellent tour through the world of trash with child actress Stephanie Yu from the PBS series *3-2-1 CONTACT*. The tape emphasizes the fact that "you can't make nothing from something" when it comes to trash. Landfills, incineration, composting, and recycling are covered, as well as source reduction (with a lively song on excessive packaging by "The Wrapper").

Save the Earth: A How-To Video

Type: VHS videotape
Length: 60 minutes
Date: 1990
Cost: $19.95
Source: Tri-Coast International
            1020 Pico Boulevard
            Santa Monica, CA 90405

Although it ignores economic policy, global politics, and sustainable development issues, this video does a good job of advocating the 3Rs. Few environmental activist tactics, such as sending excess packaging back to the manufacturer, are suggested. The video contains the warning, "Life as we know it cannot continue."

The Earth Day Special

Type: VHS videotape
Length: 99 minutes
Date: 1990
Cost: $9.95
Source: Warner Home Video
            4000 Warner Boulevard
            Burbank, CA 91522

A made-for-television special with major motion picture stars such as Bette Midler, Robin Williams, and Meryl Streep, this is an entertaining but lengthy look at conservation of resources and energy. Several community recycling projects are shown.

Tinka's Planet

Type: VHS videotape
Length: 12 minutes
Date: 1990
Cost: $24.94, home use; $55, public performance
Source: The Video Project
          5332 College Avenue, Suite 101
          Oakland, CA 94618

Geared toward children in the primary grades, this video features a child who talks to a garbage collector to find out how to help the planet. After learning about landfills, Tinka learns how to recycle cans, glass, plastic, and paper. A catchy rap music song summarizes the main tips.

What You Can Do to Save the Planet

Type: VHS videotape
Length: 45 minutes
Date: 1990
Cost: $29.95, public performance; $39.95, with guide
Source: Intellimation
          130 Cremona Drive
          Santa Barbara, CA 93117

This film is a practical guide to what individuals can do to make a difference to the environment and is written for general audiences. It defines the 3Rs and applies these concepts to garbage and household waste as well as four other conservation issues. The accompanying educational guide, by Valerie Thor, is a valuable booklet containing discussion topics and environmental activities for children in grades kindergarten through twelve.

Why Waste a Second Chance?

Type: VHS videotape
Length: 12 minutes
Date: 1990
Cost: $80 nonmembers; $50 members
          (two-week rental: $40 nonmembers, $20 members)
Source: National Association of Towns and Townships
          1522 K Street, NW, Suite 730
          Washington, DC 20005

This motivational video focuses on common solid waste disposal problems and highlights several recycling alternatives being used with success by small communities throughout the country. This video is designed to help community leaders and other concerned citizens generate interest and support for recycling. It is intended to be used with the accompanying guidebook; see Chapter 6, National Association of Towns and Townships, p. 184.

Plastics

Center for Plastics Recycling Research, The
Type: VHS videotape
Length: 8 minutes
Date: 1988
Cost: $20
Source: Center for Plastics Recycling Research
           Information Services Division Building 3529
           Busch Campus
           Piscataway, NJ 08855

Convenience Recycled
Type: VHS videotape
Length: 13minutes
Date: 1991
Cost: Free
Source: Polystyrene Packaging Council, Inc.
           1025 Connecticut Avenue, NW, Suite 515
           Washington, DC 20036

Examining the industry view of the paper versus plastic controversy, this video appears to be a response to efforts to limit or ban polystyrene products. It promotes the recycling of plastics, especially polystyrene, and shows what products can be manufactured from this process. Profiles of several local polystyrene recycling programs around the country are also included.

Everybody's Talking about the Environment
Type: VHS videotape
Length: 13 minutes
Date: 1990
Cost: Free
Source: Foodservice & Packaging Institute, Inc.
           1901 North Moore Street, Suite 1111
           Arlington, VA 22209

This film presents the National Polystyrene Recycling Company's views on recycling their products, as opposed to disposing of them. It also shows the variety of products that can be made from recycled polystyrene.

Foodservice Disposables: Should I Feel Guilty?
Type: VHS videotape
Length: 12 minutes
Date: 1991
Cost: Free
Source: Foodservice & Packaging Institute, Inc.
1901 North Moore Street, Suite 1111
Arlington, VA 22209

From an industry viewpoint on the controversy over reusables versus disposables, this film discusses issues such as environmental trade-offs, natural resource conservation, and litter. The focus is on the fast-food habits of Americans.

Polystyrene: Solid Waste Solutions
Type: VHS videotape
Length: 14 minutes
Date: 1990
Cost: Free
Source: Polystyrene Packaging Council, Inc.
1025 Connecticut Avenue, NW, Suite 508
Washington, DC 20036

This video provides more industry information on polystyrene recycling.

Plastics Recycling Today: A Growing Resource
Type: VHS videocassette
Length: 12 minutes
Date: 1990
Cost: Members: $25; nonmembers: $40
Source: The Council for Solid Waste Solutions
1275 K Street, NW, Suite 400
Washington, DC 20005

The current state of plastics recycling in the United States is reviewed in this film, which features visits to communities that recycle plastics, interviews with recyclers and community officials, and information on products being made from recycled plastics.

Databases and Computer Networks

CompuServe. CompuServe, 5000 Arlington Center Boulevard, P.O. Box 20212, Columbus, OH 43220. (614) 457-8600; 1-800-848-8990. Cost: variable.

This network, which provides over 14,000 services, has two special interest groups that deal with environmental issues, including recycling: Network Earth Forum and Goodearth Forum. The Network Earth Forum is a message and conference area for viewers of the Turner Broadcasting Systems show *Network Earth*, as well as an arena for other environmentally aware CompuServe users.

EcoNet. Institute for Global Communications, 18 De Boom Street, San Francisco, CA 94107. (415) 442-0220; (415) 546-1794 (FAX). Cost: variable.

This major, full-service, international environmental telecommunications network features e-mail, teleconferencing, database, FAX, and telex services. Several of the online conferences focus on recycling issues and information.

Kids Network. National Geographic Society, Educational Services, Department 1001, Washington, DC 20077. 1-800-368-2728; (301) 921-1575 (FAX). Cost: $325 for "Too Much Trash?" kit; $97 for tuition and telecommunications. (Discounts are available, based on the number of children participating and the amount of materials ordered.)

This telecommunications-based science and geography curriculum is currently being used by students in America. Units of study include waste, weather, acid rain, and energy. The unit "Too Much Trash?" examines the environmental impact of trash while teaching data analysis and math skills.

LEXIS–NEXIS. Mead Data Central, 9393 Springboro Pike, P.O. Box 933, Dayton, OH 45401. (513) 865-6800; 1-800-227-4908 (for sales and subscription information only). Cost: variable.

Both LEXIS and NEXIS are full-text, online legal, news, and business information services, with nearly 4,000 databases. LEXIS concentrates on legal research services and has a specialized library, ENVIRN, on environmental laws and legislation. NEXIS provides extensive news and business information services and includes the ECLIPSE feature, which functions as an electronic clipping service to search and save user-specific information. Mead Data Central also offers the NEXIS EX-PRESS service, which provides search and retrieval services on NEXIS for nonsubscribers (call 1-800-843-6476 for more information).

NewsNet. NewsNet, 945 Haverford Road, Bryn Mawr, PA 19010. (215) 527-8030; 1-800-345-1301. Cost: variable.

This online newsletter service compiles up-to-the-minute information from all electronic sources. Approximately 60 newsletters deal with environmental issues, and several are specific to waste issues, including the *Solid Waste Report, Plastic Waste Strategies,* and the *Waste Treatment Technology News.* Another service offered is NewsFlash, which will search hundreds of documents and serve as an electronic clipping service to provide select information specified by the user. For a current list of all services available in "Energy and Environment," call 1-800-952-0122.

Solid Waste Information Clearinghouse (SWICH). Solid Waste Information Clearinghouse, P.O. Box 7219, Silver Spring, MD 20910. 1-800-67-SWICH; (301) 585-0297 (FAX). Cost: variable.

SWICH is a computer network jointly sponsored by the Solid Waste Association of North America (SWANA) and the EPA's Office of Solid Waste. The system is designed primarily for online use and includes information on solid waste issues, current legislation and regulations, fact sheets and case studies, hotlines and information sources, a solid waste "experts" listing for basic assistance, a calendar, library publications listings, and training programs offered by SWANA.

Glossary

acid test: A test that uses the acid phloroglucinol to test for the presence of groundwood in a paper grade. The acid reacts with the lignin in the groundwood and will turn the paper red/pink or purple.

alloy: A substance composed of two or more metals.

baler: A machine in which recyclables are deposited, compacted, and compressed into wirebound bales to reduce their volume and facilitate their transport to a processing plant.

bimetal can: Any food or beverage can that has a steel body and an aluminum lid (considered 100 percent recyclable by the steel industry).

biodegradable: Able to be broken down, by bacteria or other living organisms, into basic biological components (such as carbon dioxide and water) that can be assimilated back into the natural environment without causing any hazards. Most organic wastes, such as paper and food leftovers, are biodegradable under conditions allowing for the circulation of water, oxygen, and microorganisms.

bottle bill: A law that requires a monetary deposit on beverage containers bought by consumers from retail establishments; the deposit may be refunded when the container is brought back to be recycled.

broker: A person or group of persons acting as an agent or middleman between the sellers and buyers of recyclable materials.

buy-back center: A place where people bring their recyclables and exchange them for payment.

buy-back program: A program that purchases recyclables from the public.

coated paper: Paper coated with a material that improves its printing surface. The coating most frequently used for this purpose is clay.

comingle: To mix recyclables with nonrecyclables. This trash will be collected and subsequently separated into its various recyclable components for further processing at a recycling center. Some curbside programs also allow comingling of recyclables only—e.g., aluminum and steel cans, glass and plastic containers, or any combination of these recyclables may all go in one container to be sorted at the recycling facility.

commercial waste: Waste that has originated in nonresidential places, e.g., offices, businesses, hotels, or warehouses.

compost: The stable end product of the decomposition of organic matter that results from the composting process (also called *humus*).

composting: An aerobic (oxygen-dependent) degradation process by which plant and other organic wastes decompose under controlled conditions. A mass of biodegradable waste, in the presence of sufficient moisture and oxygen, undergoes "self-heating," a process by which microorganisms metabolize organic matter (their food source) and release energy in the form of heat as a by-product. This process is nothing more than an accelerated version of the breakdown of organic matter that occurs under natural conditions, such as on the forest floor (EPA/530-SW-89-038, *Yard Waste Composting*).

container deposit legislation: Laws requiring that a monetary deposit be made when a certain type of container is bought. The theory behind these laws is that a required deposit will provide an incentive for consumers to return the containers to their place of purchase in order to collect the refund, thereby making recycling more probable.

contaminant: When used in the recycling industry, this word refers to any substance that might be found mixed in with the product targeted for recycling. Most processors set strict limits on the percentage of contaminants allowed in the materials they accept from sellers. Therefore, for example, glass would be a contaminant when mixed with aluminum cans that were to be recycled into more cans, and an aluminum can would be a contaminant in a container of glass that was to be processed into recycled glass.

CPO: Computer printout paper; fanfolded and usually with pastel-colored horizontal bars.

cullet: Cleaned, crushed glass that is used to make glass products.

curbside collection: Collection programs run by disposal/recycling companies that pick up recyclable materials, either source separated or comingled, from residential curbsides and deliver them to processing facilities.

decomposition: A process in which something breaks down into its basic components or elements.

de-inking: The mechanical and chemical process of removing ink from paper that has been printed on (especially newsprint).

depolymerization: The process of recycling plastic resins, specifically the breaking down of scrap plastics into their basic molecular parts, or polymers.

detinning: A process whereby the tin is separated from the steel in a "tin" can. Detinner companies buy steel cans and other tin mill products and, after detinning the recovered materials, sell the steel to steel mills and foundries and the tin to other markets.

diversion rate: A measurement of the amount of material being diverted from the waste stream for recycling, compared with the total amount of waste that was discarded.

drop-off center: A place where recyclable or compostable materials are brought and left for a recycling processor to collect. Typically, they are centrally located within a community to facilitate recycling.

end-users: Factories, mills, foundries, refineries, plants, and other businesses that use secondary or recyclable materials to manufacture new products.

ferrous: A term describing iron-based products, including steel. Iron (chemical symbol Fe) gives steel its magnetic attraction. (This word is derived from the Latin term for iron: *ferrum.*)

flotation de-inking: A process of removing ink from printed papers that uses a substance, such as clay, to bind with the ink and carry it off the paper fibers.

free sheet: Paper that has been chemically treated to remove all lignin; paper that does not contain groundwood.

groundwood: Paper manufactured from pulp that has been acquired through a relatively inexpensive mechanical process and without the use of chemicals. It refers to a low-grade paper, usually used in its uncoated form in newspapers and in its coated form in magazines. Papers with groundwood will contain the chemical lignin and will react to the acid test by turning reddish-purple.

head box: The part of a papermaking machine that holds the pulp and distributes the pulp fibers onto the wire screen in a paper mill.

heavy metals: Hazardous elements, such as cadmium, lead, and mercury, that can be found in the waste stream in such discarded items as light fixtures, batteries, coloring dyes, and inks.

HDPE: High-density polyethylene.

high-density polyethylene: A recyclable plastic often used for milk jugs, detergent bottles, and food containers, commonly known by its abbreviation, HDPE. Products made from this plastic are identified by the plastics identification code number 2.

high-grade papers: Papers with longer wood fibers, generally considered more valuable than other paper grades. They include white ledger and computer printout papers.

hydropulper: A machine, similar to a giant blender, used in the recycled paper industry to repulp used paper by churning it in hot water; the hydropulper reduces paper back to its fiber component.

incineration: The burning of waste materials.

incinerator ash: The material left as the combustion by-product of burned waste materials. This ash may also contain noncombustibles, such as metals.

inorganic waste: Waste made of materials that are neither plant nor animal and therefore contain no carbon.

integrated solid waste management: The practice of handling solid waste with several different prioritized approaches, in order to recover the highest amount of energy possible from that waste. Such approaches usually include composting, recycling, source reduction, and waste-to-energy incineration, with landfilling used as the final option.

landfill: A site where municipal solid waste is disposed of. Landfills are federally regulated by the Environmental Protection Agency under the authority of the Resource Conservation and Recovery Act (RCRA), specifically Subtitle D. Subtitle D ensures the environmental safety of a landfill from its inception to its closure and even provides for regulation for up to 30 years after closure. Leachate collection, groundwater monitoring, and the monitoring of methane gas are also required by Subtitle D. Landfills are becoming the last resort in an integrated solid waste management system, but they are considered the ultimate answer for wastes that cannot be recycled. Some landfills are specially engineered to recover the methane gas given off from decomposition. The gas is then burned to create steam, which in turn drives turbines. The turbines provide energy that is subsequently sold back to electric utility companies.

leachate: Liquid that has passed through solid waste and has pulled out various substances, including some that may be hazardous. The collection and treatment of leachate is a major concern at landfills, and Subtitle D (see *landfill*) mandates that all operating landfills must have leachate collection systems conforming to EPA specifications by 1993.

lead-acid battery: Generally known as an automobile battery; a type of battery where the main interior components consist of lead plates submerged in a sulphuric acid electrolyte solution.

lignin: A naturally occurring chemical found in wood; a substance present in groundwood paper that will react with light over time, causing the paper to yellow and turn brittle.

magnetic separation: A system in which a powerful magnet is used to separate ferrous metal objects from other materials in a mixed solid waste stream.

mandatory recycling: Programs that legally require consumers to separate their garbage and remove specific items that must be collected for recycling.

manual separation: The process of sorting and separating recyclables and/or compostable materials by hand from mixed solid waste.

materials recovery: The practice of removing useful materials from the waste stream for recycling or reuse.

materials recovery facility (MRF): Usually refers to a place that accepts a variety of mixed wastes and separates the useful, recyclable materials from the rest either by human labor or mechanical extraction. (MRF is pronounced "murf.")

mechanical separation: The process of sorting and separating recyclables and/or compostable materials from waste streams by mechanical means, such as magnets, screens, and blowers.

methane: An explosive gas, odorless and colorless in its pure state, that is produced by municipal solid waste or other organic matter that is decomposing. Municipal solid waste landfills emit methane gas, and some landfills recover the gas for use in energy production.

mill broke: Scrap paper produced from the paper manufacturing process; waste paper that has not been used by a consumer but has been produced, discarded, collected, and repulped within the papermaking facility in order to make new paper.

municipal solid waste (MSW): All nonhazardous waste produced in a city or town, including waste from households, businesses, and light industry.

MSW may also contain mining waste and sewage sludge; definitions vary in different locales.

NIMBY: An acronym for "not in my back yard," which refers to the general public's attitude toward the siting of solid waste facilities.

nonferrous: A term describing metals that do not contain iron and thus have no magnetic properties.

nonrenewable: Refers to natural resources that cannot be replaced in their original form.

organic waste: Waste matter that contains carbon, including wood, paper, yard wastes, and food wastes.

out-throws: Papers of a grade different from the one being collected; papers manufactured or treated in a way that makes them unsuitable for use as the grade specified.

participation rate: A measurement referring to the number of people participating in a given recycling program compared to the total number of possible participants.

PET: Polyethylene terephthalate.

phloroglucinol: An acid solution, mostly hydrochloric in content, that reacts with the lignin in groundwood paper, turning the paper reddish-purple. In the paper recycling industry, this solution is commonly called "groundwood tester."

plastics: Manmade materials created from polymers. Polymers are large molecules containing mainly carbon and hydrogen, with smaller amounts of oxygen or nitrogen.

polyethylene: A family of plastic resins created by the polymerization of ethylene gas, commonly grouped into two main categories: HDPE and PET.

Polyethylene terephthalate: A type of plastic resin often used to make soda pop bottles. Commonly known by the abbreviation PET, it is identified by the plastics identification code number 1.

postconsumer recycling: The reuse of materials that have been used by consumers, then collected from residential and commercial waste. This excludes materials that are the by-products of industrial manufacturing processes and have never reached the consumer (e.g., paper shreddings that have been cut off edges to make stationery).

preconsumer waste: Waste produced in the manufacturing process; such waste has not been used and discarded by consumers.

pulp: A solution of fibers and water used to manufacture paper.

recycling: Any and all processes by which materials that would have otherwise become part of the solid waste stream are collected, sorted, and/or processed and returned to the consumer in a usable form as either raw materials or finished products.

resource recovery: Refers to the beginning of the recycling process, when materials and energy are extracted from the waste stream (to be used in manufacturing new products), converted into another form of fuel, or used as an energy source.

scrap: Any item or items that are no longer considered useful, e.g., appliances, cars, construction materials, and postconsumer steel cans. The term can also refer to new materials that are by-products of metals processing and manufacturing procedures. Steel scrap is recycled in steel mills and made into new products.

secondary material: Another term for recyclable material; any material that has fulfilled its original use and can be collected and used again in another manner.

solid waste: Garbage, refuse, sludge, and any other discarded solid materials. The term can be used to describe any such waste that originates from municipal, industrial, commercial, and agricultural operations.

solid waste management: Those activities that concentrate on the systematic collection, source separation, storage, transportation, transfer, processing, treatment, or disposal of solid waste. (See *integrated solid waste management.*)

source reduction: The reduction of solid waste at its source, i.e., at the consumer level. For example, environmentalists are encouraging shoppers to bring their own reusable cloth bags to grocery stores, thereby eliminating the use of either plastic or brown paper bags at the source, or consumer, level.

source separation: The separation of recyclables (cans, glass, plastics, paper, etc.) at their source or point of origin, i.e., in the household, office, or school where the product is used and initially discarded.

steel: A malleable alloy made of iron and carbon that is wholly recyclable.

steel can: A rigid container made primarily or exclusively of steel; commonly known as the "tin" can, steel cans are often used to store food, beverages, and paint, and are 100 percent recyclable.

stickies: Any non-water-soluble adhesive that will clog pulp preparation cleaning equipment or dissolve in the pulping process and later solidify in the finished paper product, causing spots and tears (e.g., self-adhesive address labels, self-sticking notes, and peel-and-press labels).

tin: A metallic element that is often used as a coating on the inside of steel cans to stabilize the flavors of food contents.

tin can: A term commonly used to describe a steel food can. When steel cans were first used to preserve foods, the tin coating on the inside was quite thick, but modern technology has reduced the tin to less than one-third of 1 percent of the weight of a steel can.

tipping fee: The fee charged for unloading or dumping waste at a landfill, transfer station, or waste-to-energy facility, usually measured in dollars per ton.

transfer station: A place where waste materials are taken from smaller collection vehicles, such as garbage trucks, and put into larger transporting units, such as semitrailers, for movement to a final disposal area, such as a landfill.

uncoated paper: Paper that has not been coated with a substance to improve its printing surface.

virgin material: Material that has never been used in a manufacturing process (e.g., virgin paper pulp is made from trees; virgin aluminum is made from ore; virgin resins are chemically created to make plastics).

virgin pulp: Pulp made directly from plant fibers.

volume reduction: A reduction in the amount of space that materials occupy, usually accomplished by mechanical, thermal, or biological processes.

waste stream: An encompassing term referring to the waste material output of an area, location, or facility.

white goods: Large appliances such as refrigerators, washer, and dryers. The term originated when white was the standard color for such items.

wire screen: The part of a papermaking machine that picks the paper fibers up and out of the pulp and holds them in a thin, uniform layer while the excess moisture is removed.

Acronyms

CAWF	Californians Against Waste Foundation
CFC	chlorofluorocarbon
CONEG	Coalition of Northeast Governors
CPO	computer printout paper
DEC	Department of Energy Conservation
DER	Department of Environmental Resources
DNR	Department of Natural Resources or Division of Natural Resources
DOE	Division/Department of Energy
EAF	Environmental Action Foundation
ECLIPSE	(database)
ENVIRN	(database)
EPA	Environmental Protection Agency
GPI	Glass Packaging Institute
HDPE	high-density polyethylene
HHW	household hazardous waste
LDPE	low-density polyethylene
LEXIS	(database)
MEO	Maryland Energy Office
MRF	materials recovery facility
SWDA	Solid Waste Disposal Act
MSW	municipal solid waste
NCR	no carbon required (referring to type of paper)
NEA	Northeast Maryland Waste Disposal Authority
NEXIS	(database)
NEXIS EXPRESS	(database)
NIMBY	not in my back yard
NRC	National Recycling Coalition
NSWMA	National Solid Wastes Management Association

OWMR	Office of Waste Minimization and Recycling
PCB	polychlorinated biphenyl
PET	polyethylene terephthalate
PP	polypropylene
PVC	polyvinyl chloride
RCRA	Resource Conservation and Recovery Act
SCRI	Steel Can Recycling Institute
SWANA	Solid Waste Association of North America
SWICH	Solid Waste Information Clearinghouse
UCLA	University of California, Los Angeles
WESTLAW	(database)

Index